Palgrave Macmillan Studies in Banking and Financial Institutions

Series Editor: **Professor Philip Molyneux**

The Palgrave Macmillan Studies in Banking and Financial Institutions are international in orientation and include studies of banking within particular countries or regions, and studies of particular themes such as Corporate Banking, Risk Management, Mergers and Acquisitions, etc. The books' focus is on research and practice, and they include up-to-date and innovative studies on contemporary topics in banking that will have global impact and influence.

Titles include:

Steffen E. Andersen
THE EVOLUTION OF NORDIC FINANCE

Seth Apati
THE NIGERIAN BANKING SECTOR REFORMS
Power and Politics

Dimitris N. Chorafas
BASEL III, THE DEVIL AND GLOBAL BANKING

Dimitris N. Chorafas
SOVEREIGN DEBT CRISIS
The New Normal and the Newly Poor

Stefano Cosma and Elisabetta Gualandri (*editors*)
THE ITALIAN BANKING SYSTEM
Impact of the Crisis and Future Perspectives

Violaine Cousin
BANKING IN CHINA

Peter Falush and Robert L. Carter OBE
THE BRITISH INSURANCE INDUSTRY SINCE 1900
The Era of Transformation

Juan Fernández de Guevara Radoselovics and José Pastor Monsálvez (*editors*)
CRISIS, RISK AND STABILITY IN FINANCIAL MARKETS

Juan Fernández de Guevara Radoselovics and José Pastor Monsálvez (*editors*)
MODERN BANK BEHAVIOUR

Franco Fiordelisi and Ornella Ricci (*editors*)
BANCASSURANCE IN EUROPE
Past, Present and Future

Franco Fiordelisi, Philip Molyneux and Daniele Previati (*editors*)
NEW ISSUES IN FINANCIAL AND CREDIT MARKETS

Franco Fiordelisi, Philip Molyneux and Daniele Previati (*editors*)
NEW ISSUES IN FINANCIAL INSTITUTIONS MANAGEMENT

Kim Hawtrey
AFFORDABLE HOUSING FINANCE

Jill M. Hendrickson
REGULATION AND INSTABILITY IN U.S. COMMERCIAL BANKING
A History of Crises

Paola Leone and Gianfranco A. Vento (*editors*)
CREDIT GUARANTEE INSTITUTIONS AND SME FINANCE

Caterina Lucarelli and Gianni Brighetti (*editors*)
RISK TOLERANCE IN FINANCIAL DECISION MAKING

Roman Matousek (*editor*)
MONEY, BANKING AND FINANCIAL MARKETS IN CENTRAL AND EASTERN EUROPE
20 Years of Transition

Philip Molyneux (*editor*)
BANK PERFORMANCE, RISK AND FIRM FINANCING

Philip Molyneux (*editor*)
BANK STRATEGY, GOVERNANCE AND RATINGS

Imad A. Moosa
THE MYTH OF TOO BIG TO FAIL

Simon Mouatt and Carl Adams (*editors*)
CORPORATE AND SOCIAL TRANSFORMATION OF MONEY AND BANKING
Breaking the Serfdom

Victor Murinde (*editor*)
BANK REGULATORY REFORMS IN AFRICA

Anders Ögren (*editor*)
THE SWEDISH FINANCIAL REVOLUTION

Özlem Olgu
EUROPEAN BANKING
Enlargement, Structural Changes and Recent Developments

Fotios Pasiouras
GREEK BANKING
From the Pre-Euro Reforms to the Financial Crisis and Beyond

Daniela Pîrvu
CORPORATE INCOME TAX HARMONIZATION IN THE EUROPEAN UNION

Ramkishen S. Rajan
EMERGING ASIA
Essays on Crises, Capital Flows, FDI and Exchange Rate

Allesandro Roselli
FINANCIAL STRUCTURES AND REGULATION: A COMPARISON OF CRISES IN THE UK, USA AND ITALY

Yasushi Suzuki
JAPAN'S FINANCIAL SLUMP
Collapse of the Monitoring System under Institutional and Transition Failures

Ruth Wandhöfer
EU PAYMENTS INTEGRATION
The Tale of SEPA, PSD and Other Milestones Along the Road

The full list of titles available is on the website:
www.palgrave.com/finance/sbfi.asp

Palgrave Macmillan Studies in Banking and Financial Institutions
Series Standing Order ISBN 978-1-4039-4872-4

You can receive future titles in this series as they are published by placing a standing order. Please contact your bookseller or, in case of difficulty, write to us at the address below with your name and address, the title of the series and the ISBN quoted above.

Customer Services Department, Macmillan Distribution Ltd, Houndmills, Basingstoke, Hampshire RG21 6XS, England

---

The Italian Banking System

Impact of the Crisis and Future Perspectives

Edited by

Stefano Cosma
Department of Economics, University of Modena and Reggio Emilia

and

Elisabetta Gualandri
Department of Economics, University of Modena and Reggio Emilia

palgrave
macmillan

First published 2012 by
PALGRAVE MACMILLAN

Palgrave Macmillan in the UK is an imprint of Macmillan Publishers Limited, registered in England, company number 785998, of Houndmills, Basingstoke, Hampshire RG21 6XS.

Palgrave Macmillan in the US is a division of St Martin's Press LLC, 175 Fifth Avenue, New York, NY 10010.

Palgrave Macmillan is the global academic imprint of the above companies and has companies and representatives throughout the world.

Palgrave® and Macmillan® are registered trademarks in the United States, the United Kingdom, Europe and other countries

ISBN: 978–0–230–34314–6

This book is printed on paper suitable for recycling and made from fully managed and sustained forest sources. Logging, pulping and manufacturing processes are expected to conform to the environmental regulations of the country of origin.

A catalogue record for this book is available from the British Library.

Library of Congress Cataloging-in-Publication Data

The Italian banking system : impact of the crisis and future perspectives / edited by Stefano Cosma and Elisabetta Gualandri.
p. cm.
Includes bibliographical references.
ISBN 978–0–230–34314–6
1. Banks and banking – Italy. 2. Financial crises – Italy. 3. Finance – Italy. I. Cosma, Stefano. II. Gualandri, Elisabetta.

HG3078.I83 2013
332.10945—dc23 2012033385

10 9 8 7 6 5 4 3 2 1
21 20 19 18 17 16 15 14 13 12

Printed and bound in Great Britain by
CPI Antony Rowe, Chippenham and Eastbourne

To my father – S. C.

To Mary, Alessandra, Laura and Paola – E. G.

Contents

List of Illustrations x

Notes on Contributors xiv

List of Acronyms and Abbreviations xviii

1 Introduction 1
Stefano Cosma and Elisabetta Gualandri

2 The Impact of the Financial Crisis on Italian Banks 9
Elisabetta Gualandri
2.1 Introduction 9
2.2 A snapshot of the pre-crisis situation 10
2.3 From the subprime mortgage crisis to the Lehman Brothers crash 11
2.4 Towards the sovereign debt crisis 14
2.5 Anti-crisis measures and the role of the Italian government 15
2.6 The sovereign debt crisis, 2010–? 23
2.7 The role of supervision in combating the crisis 29
2.8 Conclusions 32

3 Main Features of the Italian Financial System 34
Valeria Venturelli
3.1 Introduction 34
3.2 The Italian financial system: structure and evolution in the international context 35
3.3 Evolution and composition of monetary financial institutions' balance sheets 43
3.4 Evolution of banking sectors: structural indicators 49
3.5 Conclusions 53

4 Consolidation and Governance of Italian Banks 55
Andrea Landi
4.1 Introduction 55
4.2 Consolidation in the banking system 56
4.3 The role of the foundations in banks' ownership structures 61

4.4 The cooperative and mutual banks 62
4.5 Conclusions 65

5 Performance and Efficiency of the Italian Banking System 67
Riccardo Ferretti, Marzia Torresetti, and Paola Vezzani
5.1 Introduction 67
5.2 Economic and financial performance 68
5.3 The stock market performance of Italian banks 82
5.4 A final comparison 93

6 Organisational and Business Models of Italian Banks 97
Stefano Cosma and Paola Vezzani
6.1 Introduction 97
6.2 Italian banks' organisational models 98
6.3 Empirical analysis 105
6.4 The mutual bank network organisational model 111

7 Retail Banking for Households in Italy 116
Stefano Cosma
7.1 Introduction 116
7.2 The role of Italian banks in lending to households 118
7.3 Credit to households in Italy 124
7.4 Italian banks and mortgage loans for house purchases 126
7.5 Banks and consumer credit 130
7.6 Retail funding and the role of the household sector 134

8 Corporate and Investment Banking in Italy 140
Cesare Bisoni, Andrea Ferrari, and Alessandro Giovanni Grasso
8.1 Introduction 140
8.2 Lending to companies 140
8.3 The practice of multibanking 143
8.4 The process of change within the banking system 148
8.5 From the Consolidated Law on Banking to Basel II: implications for the bank–company relationship 150
8.6 Towards a new bank–firm relationship 153
8.7 The development of the corporate and investment banking business 156
8.8 The structure of the supply of corporate and investment banking services 159
8.9 Corporate and investment banking business areas 162

9 Private Banking and Asset Management in Italy 170
Valeria Venturelli
9.1 Introduction 170
9.2 Asset management and private banking definitions 171
9.3 Asset management 174
9.4 Private banking 183

10 Italian Banks between Scylla and Charybdis? 192
Stefano Cosma and Elisabetta Gualandri
10.1 Introduction 192
10.2 The economic and financial scenario 193
10.3 The financial stability of Italian banks 194
10.4 Effect on traditional intermediation model of Italian banks: The microeconomic equilibrium 197

References 201

Index 209

Illustrations

Figures

4.1	Public intervention in support of banks, 2008–10	61
5.1	Total assets in billions of euros for main Italian and European banks, 2010: end-of-year values	69
5.2	Total assets in billions of euros for main Italian and European banks, 2010: end-of-year values	70
5.3	Gross operating income of main Italian and European banks composition, 2008 and 2010	71
5.4	Return on equity: average value and gross domestic product annual growth, banks in Italy 1999–2010	72
5.5	Return on equity: average value	73
5.6	Gross operating income/total assets: composition, banks in Italy 1999–2010	74
5.7	Customer mark-up, average value, Italy 1999–2010	75
5.8	Customer mark-down, average value, Italy 1999–2010	75
5.9	Composition of net commissions/total assets, banks in Italy 1999–2010	76
5.10	Net commissions/total assets, average value, Italy 1999–2010	77
5.11	Cost/income ratio, average value, Italy 1999–2010	78
5.12	Composition of total impaired loans/total loans, banks in Italy 1999–2010	79
5.13	Tier 1 ratio, average value, Italy 1999–2010	80
5.14	Financial leverage, average value, Italy 1999–2010	81
5.15	Italian listed banks: number and market capitalisation weight, 1999–2010	83
5.16	Italian listed banks: price-to-book values, 1999–2010	91
5.17	National comparison: market and economic-financial profitability (CAGR v. ROE)	94
5.18	National comparison: market and economic-financial risk (beta v. loan loss provisions/loans)	95
6.1	The mutual bank network model	112
6.2	The structure of the ICCREA group	113
7.1	The evolution of credit to Italian household sector, as a percentage of GDP, 2005–10	123

7.2 Bad debts to non-financial corporations and consumer households, banks in Italy 2001–10 126
7.3 (Left) Mortgage loans for house purchases. (Right) Index of supply and demand conditions for house purchase loans 128
7.4 Features of mortgage loans for house purchases 129
7.5 Consumer credit by type: personal loans, credit cards, SP, and CQS 132
7.6 Consumer credit by lenders: the role of retail banks and banking groups 135
7.7 Composition of household financial wealth in Italy, 1995–2009 137
7.8 Retail funding compared to total funding in Italy and Euro Area 139
9.1 The asset management value chain 172
9.2 Needs and product solutions for private customers 174
9.3 Assets under management (AUM) by client segments 177

Tables

2.1 Public facilities in support of banks 17
2.2 Measures taken by the Italian authorities, 2008–09 20
2.3 The "Tremonti bonds" facility 23
2.4 EBA-aggregated shortfall required by country 25
2.5 Public debt (percentage of GDP) 27
2.6 Holders of Italian government bonds (31 December 2010) 28
2.7 EBA-Italian banks' shortfalls (31 December 2011) 29
3.1 Financial intermediation ratio, outstanding amount 36
3.2 Financial intermediation ratio, non-financial corporations and households 38
3.3 Percentage composition of financial assets by instruments, households 40
3.4 Percentage composition of financial liabilities by instruments, non-financial corporations 42
3.5 Banking intermediation ratio 44
3.6 Monetary financial institutions' loans 45
3.7 Balance sheet composition, MFIs, excluding ESCB, assets 46
3.8 General government securities as percentage of total assets 47
3.9 Balance sheet composition, MFIs, excluding ESCB, liabilities 48
3.10 Number of credit institutions 49

3.11 Number of credit institutions, the Italian situation, total and breakdown 50
3.12 Number of local banking units 51
3.13 Number of local branch bank units, the Italian situation, total and breakdown 52
3.14 Number of local banking units per 100,000 inhabitants 52
4.1 Number of banking institutions and M&A operations, 1990–2010 57
4.2 Market shares of Italian banking groups and banks 59
4.3 Indicators for the main European banks 60
4.4 Foundations' holdings in the capital of their banks of origin, 2010 62
4.5 Foundation shareholders of the three largest Italian banking groups, 2010 63
5.1 Banking sectors: stock market returns, 1995–2010, compound annual growth rate (CAGR) and annual growth rate, 2000–10 84
5.2 Banking sectors: standard deviation of monthly returns, 1995–2010 86
5.3 Banking sectors: European Monetary Union systematic risk, 1999–2010, market model beta on monthly returns 87
5.4 Italian listed banks: stock market performance, 1999–2010 89
5.5 Italian listed banks: European Monetary Union systematic risk, 1999–2010, market model beta on monthly returns 92
6.1 Organisation model and management of business areas in large banking groups 107
7.1 Total loans and financial assets of banks: an international comparison 120
7.2 Incidence of loans to firms and households on total assets 121
7.3 Compound annual growth rate (CAGR) of total credit to households, loans for house purchase, and consumer credit 122
7.4 Breakdown of percentage of loans to customers resident in Italy, by debtor type, 1998–2011 125
7.5 Mortgage loans for house purchases and consumer credit by banks only, Italy 2003–10 127
7.6 Evolution of consumer credit in Italian households 131
7.7 Italian banking groups with consumer credit specialised financial institutions 133
7.8 Aggregated balance sheets of MFIs 136

8.1 Financing of Italian manufacturing firms, values as percentages of total liabilities 142
8.2 Average number of banks per borrower, by company's credit line. Manufacturing industry 145
8.3 First bank's share of total credit granted. Manufacturing industry 147
8.4 Segmentation thresholds of banks, in millions of euros, 2011 165
9.1 The importance of the asset management industry 175
9.2 The first 10 operators active in Italy, 2005–10 178
9.3 High net-worth individuals, population by country, end of 2010 184
9.4 The Italian private banking market: the potential market of households 185
9.5 Market players and market shares in Italy for private wealth clients 187
9.6 Average number of clients per CRM 189

Box

2.1 EBA Recapitalisation Exercise (8 December 2011) 26

Contributors

Cesare Bisoni is a full professor of Banking and Finance at the Marco Biagi Department of Economics at the University of Modena and Reggio Emilia, where he is a director of CEFIN (Center for Studies in Banking and Finance). He graduated from Bocconi University and completed the Harvard Business School Program of Business Administration of the International Teachers Program. He is the chairman of ADEIMF (Italian Association of Teachers in Banking and Finance), a director of the European Association of University Teachers in Banking and Finance, and a member of AIDEA (Italian Academy of Business Administration and Management). He has been a member of the board of various Italian banks and he is a statutory auditor of UniCredit. His research topics include the institutional aspects of banking systems, bank–firm relationships, bank financial reporting, and bank performance analysis.

Stefano Cosma is an associate professor of Banking and Finance at the Marco Biagi Department of Economics of the University of Modena and Reggio Emilia, where he is a member of CEFIN (Center for Studies in Banking and Finance). He graduated from the University of Modena and obtained a PhD in Business Administration from Cà Foscari University, Venice. He is a member of the European Association of University Teachers in Banking and Finance of ADEIMF (Italian Association of Teachers of Banking and Finance) and of AIDEA (Italian Academy of Business Administration and Management). He is a member of the scientific committee of the Banking and Financial Diploma of the Italian Banking Association (ABI) and is an advisor to Prometeia and various banks. Research topics include corporate and retail lending, consumer credit, behavioural finance, and the economics of banking.

Andrea Ferrari is a full professor of Banking and Finance at the Marco Biagi Department of Economics of the University of Modena and Reggio Emilia, where he was previously the dean of the Faculty of Economics. He graduated from the University of Siena. He is a member of the European Association of University Teachers in Banking and Finance and of ADEIMF (Italian Association of Teachers of Banking and Finance). His research topics include the economics of banking, bank relationship lending, and structured financing. He served as an expert adviser to the public prosecutor in the Parmalat case.

Riccardo Ferretti is a full professor of Banking and Finance in the Department of Communication and Economics of the University of Modena and Reggio Emilia, where he was previously the dean of the Faculty. He graduated from the University of Modena and obtained a PhD in Capital Markets and Financial Management from the University of Bergamo. He was a visiting PhD student at the New York University Graduate School of Business Administration in the Finance Department. He is the managing director of CEFIN (Center for Studies in Banking and Finance). He is a member of the European Association of University Teachers in Banking and Finance and of ADEIMF (Italian Association of Teachers of Banking and Finance). His research topics include the growth of banking firms, bank capital, the efficiency of financial markets, bank evaluation, the cost of capital, loan pricing, behavioural finance, financial communication, and financial education.

Alessandro Giovanni Grasso is a lecturer in Banking and Finance at the Faculty of Economics of the University of Macerata. He graduated from the Catholic University of Milan, where he obtained a PhD in Financial Markets and Institutions. He is a member of CEFIN (Center for Studies in Banking and Finance), of ADEIMF (Italian Association of University Teachers of Financial Intermediaries and Markets) and the European Association of University Teachers in Banking and Finance. Research topics include the private equity industry, the economics of banking and other financial institutions, and the evolution of the pension system in Italy.

Elisabetta Gualandri is a full professor of Banking and Finance at the Marco Biagi Department of Economics of the University of Modena and Reggio Emilia, where she is a director of CEFIN (Center for Studies in Banking and Finance). She graduated from the University of Modena and obtained an MA in Banking and Finance at the University College of North Wales. She is also a director of the European Association of University Teachers in Banking and Finance, and a member of ADEIMF (Italian Association of Teachers in Banking and Finance), of AIDEA (Italian Academy of Business Administration and Management), and of SUERF (The European Money and Finance Forum). She served as an auditor of Banca d'Italia from 2007 to 2012, when she was appointed to the Board of Banca Popolare dell'Emilia Romagna. Her recent research topics include the regulation and supervision of financial intermediaries and markets, financial crisis, Basel III, the financing of innovative small to medium-sized enterprises, and public intervention programmes. She is a co-author for Palgrave Macmillan of *Bridging the Equity Gap for Innovative SMEs* (with V. Venturelli 2008), and *Consolidation in the European Financial Industry* (with R. Bottiglia and G. N. Mazzocco 2010).

Andrea Landi is a full professor of Banking and Finance at the Marco Biagi Department of Economics of the University of Modena and Reggio Emilia, where he was previously dean of the faculty. He graduated from the University of Modena. He is a member of CEFIN (Center for Studies in Banking and Finance), of ADEIMF (Italian Association of University Teachers in Financial Intermediaries and Markets) and of the European Association of University Teachers of Banking and Finance. He is the chairman of the Cassa di Risparmio Modena Banking Foundation, a member of the Strategic Committee of Cassa Depositi e Prestiti, and the chairman of the Scientific and Technological Research Commission of ACRI (Italian Association of Banking Foundations and Savings Banks). His research topics include bank efficiency and performance, financial intermediation theory, and the bank–firm relationships.

Marzia Torresetti is a financial analyst with the Research and Publishing Division of Prometeia, SpA, where she participates in the writing of reports on performance in the Italian and European banking industry (analyses of listed banks and analyses of bank financial statements) and in advisory projects on financial analysis and benchmarking for the industry's major players. She graduated from the University of Bologna.

Valeria Venturelli is an associate professor of Banking and Finance at the Marco Biagi Department of Economics of the University of Modena and Reggio Emilia, where she is a member of CEFIN (Center for Studies in Banking and Finance). She graduated from the University of Modena and Reggio Emilia and obtained a PhD in Financial Markets and Institutions from the Catholic University of Milan. She is a member of ADEIMF (Italian Association of University Teachers in Financial Intermediaries and Markets) and of the European Association of University Teachers in Banking and Finance. She is a co-author for Palgrave Macmillan of *Bridging the Equity Gap for Innovative SMEs* (with E. Gualandri 2008). She acts as an advisor to various public institutions and consulting firms. Research topics include the economics of banking and other financial institutions and valuation methods.

Paola Vezzani is a full professor of Banking and Finance at the Department of Communication and Economics of the University of Modena and Reggio Emilia, where she was previously the dean of Faculty. She graduated from the University of Modena and obtained a PhD in Capital Markets and Financial Management from the University of Bergamo. She was a visiting PhD student at the New York University Graduate School of Business Administration in the Finance Department. She is a member of CEFIN (Center for Studies in Banking and Finance), of AIDEA (Italian Academy of Business Administration and Management), and of the European Association of University Teachers in Banking and Finance. She is a member of the scientific committee of the Banking and Financial Diploma of the Italian Banking Association (ABI). Her research topics include the diversification strategies of banking groups, organizational and business models, analysis of bank performance and efficiency, voluntary disclosure, intangible assets and intellectual capital.

Acronyms and Abbreviations

ABI	Associazione Bancaria Italiana
ADEIMF	Associazione Docenti Economia Intermediari Mercati Finanziari (Italian Association of University Teachers of Financial Intermediaries and Markets)
AIM	Alternative investment market
AIPB	Associazione Italiana Private Banking (Italian Private Banking Association)
ATM	automated teller machine
AUM	assets under management
BARC	Barclays
BBVA	Banco Bilbao Vizcaya Argentaria
BI	Banca d'Italia (Bank of Italy)
BIS	Bank for International Settlements
BNP	BNP Paribas
bps	basis points
BTPs	Buoni del Tesoro Poliennali (Italian long term government bonds)
CA	Crédit Agricole
CAGR	compound annual growth rate
CBs	cooperative banks
CDS	Credit Default Swaps
CEBS	Committee on European Banking Supervisors
CEO	chief executive officer
CIB	corporate and investment banking
COMM	Commerzbank
CONSOB	Commissione Nazionale per le Società e la Borsa
COVIP	Commissione di Vigilanza sui Fondi Pensione
CRD	Capital Requirements Directive
DEUT	Deutsche Bank
EBA	European Banking Authority
EC	European Commission
ECB	European Central Bank
ECOFIN	Economic and Financial Affairs Council of the European Union
ECRI	European Credit Research Institute
EFSF	European Financial Stability Facility

e-MID	Mercato Interbancario dei Depositi
EMU	European Monetary Union
ESCB	European System of Central Banks
ETF	exchange-traded fund
EU	European Union
Euribor	European interbank offered rate
FIR	financial intermediation ratio
FSA	Financial Services Authority
FSAP	Financial Sector Assessment Program
FSB	Financial Stability Board
FSC	Financial Stability Committee
GDP	gross domestic product
HNWI	high net worth individuals
HSBC	Hong Kong and Shanghai Banking Corporation
IAS	International Accounting Standards
ICAAP	Internal Capital Adequacy Assessment Process
ICCREA	Istituto Centrale delle Casse Rurali e Artigiane
IFRS	International Financial Reporting Standards
IMF	International Monetary Fund
ISVAP	Istituto per la vigilanza sulle assicurazioni private e di interesse collettivo
KBC	KBC Group
KID	key information document
LLOY	Lloyds Banking Group
LTCM	Long-Term Capital Management
LTRO	Long-Term Refinancing Operation
LTV	loan to value
MB	mutual banks
MEF	Ministero dell'Economia e delle Finanze (Ministry of Economy and Finance)
MFIs	Monetary Financial Institutions
MIC	Mercato Interbancario Collateralizzato
MiFID	Markets in Financial Instruments Directive
MoU	memorandum of understanding
MSCI	Morgan Stanley Capital International (Price Index)
M&A	mergers and acquisitions
new MIC	Nuovo Mercato Interbancario Collateralizzato
OECD	Organization for Economic Co-operation and Development
OTD	originate-to-distribute (model)
PBV	price-to-book value

RBS	Royal Bank of Scotland
ROE	return on equity
SANT	Santander
SD	standard deviation
SFI	specialised financial institutions
SIFI	systemically important financial institutions
SMEs	small and medium enterprises
SOGEN	Société Générale
SPV	special purpose vehicle
SREP	Supervisory Review and Evaluation Process
UBI	UBI Banca
UBS	Unione Banche Svizzere
UCITS	Undertaking for Collective Investment in Transferable Securities
UK	United Kingdom
US	United States

1
Introduction

Stefano Cosma and Elisabetta Gualandri

The impact of the financial crisis on various banking and financial systems has been severe, even dramatic, and has required interventions of different kinds: bailout operations by governments; regulatory and supervisory rethinking by policy makers and supervisory authorities (Gualandri 2008); and the definition of new strategies and refocusing of their businesses on the part of financial intermediaries.

However, the impact on European banking systems has varied widely, due to differences in the business lines developed, as well as in the degree of involvement in the originate-to-distribute (OTD) model, in the level of national discretion used in the implementation of European Union directives, and in the approach followed by the supervisory authorities, with strategies ranging from having a light touch to more hands-on policies.

The Italian banking system has found itself paying for the consequences of a crisis that originated in the United States, which can be traced in more general terms to the development of the typically Anglo-Saxon OTD model.

The Italian case is particularly interesting because of the crisis's dual-stage impact on the country's banks: it was not as severe as elsewhere in Europe and beyond in the first phase (the subprime phase), but was more intense from 2010 onward (the sovereign debt phase).

At the time of this writing in Spring 2012, the second phase is still ongoing, and future prospects are rather uncertain, both for economies in general and for the banks in the various countries. The time is therefore not yet ripe for overall assessments, but an initial analysis can be made.

The book aims to describe the impact of the crisis on the Italian banking system, focusing on the first phase; the concluding chapter attempts to provide an outline of the banking system's situation within the economic and financial scenario of the second phase of the crisis. We followed the approach of analysing the structure, main features, and functioning of the Italian banking system and of the financial system in general at the beginning of the crisis, in order to understand the reasons why Italy suffered less than other countries during its first phase. A number of these characteristics have mutated from positive to negative factors during the course of the crisis, helping to explain why the country's banks have been hit especially hard in the transition to the second phase.

The second chapter begins this analysis by describing the impact of the financial crisis on the Italian banking system. The following chapters offer an overview of the main characteristics of the banking system and of the factors that initially helped to cushion the effects of the crisis, focusing on those that actually turned out to be weaknesses in the sovereign debt phase. In the final chapter we give an initial assessment of the main consequences of the crisis and outline future prospects for Italian banks by surveying the main strengths and weaknesses of the Italian banking system.

The first step is to assess the impact of the crisis on the Italian banking system and to offer an account of the measures taken by the government and the credit authorities (Chapter 2). For greater clarity, the two main stages of the crisis, the subprime and sovereign debt phases, are examined separately. The Italian banking system's greater resilience during the subprime crisis meant that the amount of public resources required to overcome it was much lower than needed in other countries; no rescue or nationalisation operations at the expense of the public purse were undertaken. Therefore, the limited public facilities made available had no significant impact on the country's huge public debt, and this helped to maintain a fair level of market confidence in the Italian state and banks, until the worsening of the sovereign debt crisis in 2011.

The second phase of the global financial crisis, triggered by the sovereign debt crisis in Greece, has its epicentre in the Euro Area and has had much more serious consequences for Italian banks than the subprime phase did, for a number of reasons. The first factor was the contagious effect of Euro Area sovereign debt risk, as foreign investors fled Italian government bonds in summer 2011. The second reason that Italian banks have been so hard hit has been their poor earnings outlook, due to both the discouraging forecasts for the Italian economy during 2012–13 (after 15 years of disappointing growth rates) and their adherence to the commercial bank operating model, paradoxically the very factor that protected them during the first phase of the crisis.

The second step of our study is to provide an in-depth investigation of the characteristics of the Italian financial system which partially shielded it from the effects of the financial crisis in its first phase. This is done (Chapter 3) by analysing the evolution of the financial aggregates and balance sheet compositions of banks at the European and Italian level. Based on the harmonised statistics produced by the European Central Bank (ECB) (1999), the analysis compares the structural characteristics of banks in some of the main European countries. Apart from Italy, the countries considered were Germany, France, Spain, and the United Kingdom, which were chosen because these countries' banking and financial systems share a number of features and trends.

The analysis reveals that Italian banks have retained a traditional business model based on conventional forms of lending, and have retained a high proportion of traditional funding, which has provided them with stable sources of funds. Their specialisation in traditional banking operations—the use of retail funding to finance loans to corporations and households—was one of the Italian banks' strengths during the initial stages of the crisis. Moreover, the banking sector is less internationalised than those of other countries, and financial innovation is less widespread than in the United States or the United Kingdom. The number of purely financial investments is fairly low. Italian banks have low leverage, which has not grown over the years, in contrast to the situation in other countries. Moreover Italian banks have strong territorial roots, with a large network of branches, reducing the distance between borrower and lender.

Key issues in understanding the impact of the crisis are the consolidation of the Italian banking system over the last two decades and the main features of bank governance (Chapter 4). During this period, changes to the relevant legislation and to the regulatory framework, together with the privatisation of publicly owned banks, which began in the early 1990s, have generated a strengthening of the banks' role within the Italian financial system, as they have led to the creation of large banking groups, capable of competing on a national and international scale and capable of supporting the economic system—enterprises and households—with a wider, more up-to-date offering of financial services. At the same time, the organisational models and procedures adopted within these aggregation processes have made it possible to conserve and exploit the territorial bonds of the local banks targeted by merger and acquisition operations. Chapter 4 also analyses the ownership structures and legal forms of Italian banks, which reflect their territorial connotations. The focus is first of all on the role of the banking foundations, which are major shareholders in the large banks and have assisted in their transformation, enabling them to combine larger size, geographical links, and relative stability in their ownership structures and governance. The financial crisis is continuing to put the corporate governance of the large Italian banks to the test, as they attempt major recapitalisation operations without recourse to public aid. During the second phase of the crisis, clear signs are emerging of a change in the ownership structure of large banks, with a reduction of the historic role of banking foundations as institutional investors and the acquisition of larger capital holdings by sovereign funds. The second aspect analysed in this chapter is the system of mutual banks, which continues to play an important role in serving a clientele of households and medium-sized and small enterprises. This role has been reinforced by the crisis.

For a more detailed understanding of the effects of the crisis on the Italian banking system, Chapter 5 analyses the Italian banks' performance and risk levels for the period 1999–2010, when the evolution of the banks' performance was considerably affected by significant changes with regard to ownership structures, organisational models, scale of operation, risk management techniques, gains in efficiency, and more. The first part of the chapter describes the economic and financial performance of the Italian banking system, providing a short international comparison of the five largest banking groups and then, in greater detail, examining trends—in terms of profitability, efficiency, risk level, and solvency in relation to size and legal form—from a strictly domestic viewpoint. The second part of the chapter investigates the risk-return profile of listed Italian banks compared to their European counterparts and analyses the national banks in greater detail, to reveal the role played by differences in size, business model, and legal form.

The international comparison confirms the hypothesis that Italian banks' risk levels withstood the first phase of the crisis well. The figures reveal a business model more firmly based on traditional lending operations for Italian large banks, with loans to customers exceeding financial investments. A structure of this kind absorbs much more capital and necessarily implies a lower degree of financial leverage than other European large banks in the bank's business and a lower level of risk (or greater capitalisation).

From the point of view of market values, over the period of time considered, Italy's listed banks did not show particularly strong performance in terms of growth in share price, but their results were decidedly better with regard to both overall and systematic risk.

As the overall risk data reveal, during 1999–2010 Italian banks had one of the lowest risk levels of those of any European country. The systematic risk trend of Italian banks was also positive until 2007, when the risk level of European banks had already risen significantly. During 2008–10, Italian banking share betas were hit by the financial crisis with the second highest increase in betas of the banks of the other European states (after that of the Irish banks).

On the profitability side, Italian banks' specifically retail-oriented business generates more than 80 per cent of their total earnings (from interest and commissions on services to customers), in contrast with other European groups, whose balance sheet assets consist mainly of securities and earnings derived above all from trading and fair value valuation of financial assets and liabilities.

The earnings of medium-sized banking groups are more stable, and thus on average they achieve the best performances, without the higher risk and loss of efficiency suffered by both large and small banking groups in times of crisis.

An analysis of banks' degree of diversification, areas of business, and their consequent organisational complexity is of great assistance in understanding the effects of the crisis. To this end, Chapter 6 describes the organisational models that banks adopt for their operations in the banking market and in the various areas of business.

Since 1994, thanks to the deregulation that has opened the way to the adoption of the universal bank institutional model, Italian banks have been engaged in rapid diversification and expansion, both of the range of services delivered and of the product-customer-channel combinations in their chosen market mixes. At the same time, the greater complexity of their operations has obliged them to adopt organisational models capable of recognising and managing the many interdependent relationships created and the higher degree of market uncertainty. This expansion of the range of services has been accompanied by a large-scale consolidation of ownership within the banking system, resulting in a high level of polarisation, with a few large banking groups and some medium-sized banking groups operating alongside a large number of small banks.

Naturally, differences in size also influence the strategic choices, degree of diversification, the organisational structures used for the main areas of business, and banking models, and these differences have exposed banks to different risks and have affected their ability to deal with the financial crisis and the economic effects of the recession.

The large banking groups have opted for a high degree of diversification of services and customers, combined with considerable growth in size, pursued through external expansion. The rapid growth in areas of business and the swift succession of merger and acquisition (M&A) operations by which banks have increased their size have generated problems with regard to the creation of an organisational model capable of managing this complexity. Amongst the largest Italian banks, some have adopted the divisional or universal bank model, while others have taken the form of banking groups.

Small banks have chosen selective diversification, concentrating on the financial needs of their own customers and local areas, and on their existing areas of professional expertise. Small banks that have selectively expanded their operations have tended to maintain a simple, functional organisational model. In some cases, these banks extend their expertise and business models through membership in networks for the joint performance of phases in the production process, or for the more favorable acquisition of products and services for distribution to their customers.

One of the most important features of the Italian banks' intermediation model is the role of the household sector and retail banking. Chapter 7 aims to analyse the role and contribution of banking for households in improving stability and mitigating the effects of the financial crisis. In particular, it examines the composition of Italian banks' retail banking operations, focusing above all on banking services to households, the characteristics of Italian banks' loan portfolios, and the importance of loans to households, with international comparisons. Finally, it takes a more in-depth look at Italian banks' fund-raising characteristics and especially the role of retail funding, with special reference to the household sector.

Retail banking is the traditional credit intermediation model, under which funding is received from households in the form of deposits and used to finance lending to households and small and medium-sized enterprises (SMEs), above all by direct channels. It is founded on a broad customer portfolio and normally on lasting, long-term relationships with customers. The large number of customers tends to stabilise the banking business's volume and margins by providing naturally diversified, granular loan and deposit portfolios.

From the analysis it emerges that the Italian banks' level of financialisation of their capital is low, and their credit intermediation operations are based mainly on a deposit-funded model in which, on the assets side, loans predominate over other areas of business, while on the liabilities side, retail funding (sight deposits, term deposits, and bonds) plays a larger role than wholesale funding and liquidity generated by the securitisation of assets.

Together with a low funding gap (measured by the proportion of loans not financed by retail funding), in general this bank financial equilibrium and operating model mitigated the consequences of the 2007 financial crisis, leading to fewer liquidity and credit rationing problems, especially among the smallest banks.

Another important feature of the Italian banks' intermediation model is the large proportion of assets that derives from corporate lending. Chapter 8 discusses corporate lending and investment banking.

In Italy, banks have always been the main source of external financing for companies, and especially for small and medium-sized enterprises, which make up the connective tissue of the Italian economy. Small and medium-sized enterprises, with informal governance models, generally use fairly simple forms of financing. Their financial structures are based largely on debt, especially short-term bank loans, often supported by the entrepreneur's personal assets. However in recent years the positive development of the bank-firm relationship has involved the evolution not only of corporate lending, but also of corporate and investment banking services. To analyse this situation, Chapter 8 is divided into two parts.

The first investigates the approach taken to corporate banking and the role of the bank-firm relationship and the effect of strong local roots (retained even by the largest groups) on corporate lending during the crisis period.

On average, Italian companies maintain relations with more banks, with a smaller proportion of their borrowing from their chief bank, than is the case in other countries. This kind of bank-firm relationship is known as "multibanking." Despite the development of the bank-firm relationship and the reduction in the number of banks in the last ten years, multibanking has been a point of weakness in the bank-firm relationship, a finding confirmed by a number of studies that examine its effects on the availability of credit in the specific context of the financial crisis, which report that firms which borrowed from a larger number of banks experienced lower credit growth during the crisis period.

In the second part of Chapter 8, the nature of corporate and investment banking in Italy is illustrated, describing the way this sector is served by the country's largest banks, and outlining possible developments in the light of the recent financial crisis. Given the regulatory changes introduced by Basel II and Basel III, corporate and investment banking are destined to become capital-intensive businesses. The chief Italian banks are adapting their organisations to fulfill this requirement.

The rationalisation process involves the raising of the threshold for access to corporate and investment banking services. This represents the definitive victory of the relationship banking model, since it allows the central figure, the client relationship manager, to concentrate on the needs of the natural recipients of corporate and investment banking services, without wasting energy trying to attract firms whose small size means that their interest in this area can at best be only sporadic. In this approach, strong territorial roots are a key factor in the strategic development of customer relationships.

The asset management industry has also been hit by the crisis and is facing major challenges with regard to both returns and the currently ongoing regulatory processes. In Italy, as described in Chapter 9, these activities are mainly in the hands of the banks, with regard to both production and distribution. Therefore, the Italian banking system plays a fundamental role in the evolution of this sector. Moreover, private banking is viewed as a strategic business area of particular interest, since this market is still highly fragmented and therefore offers ample growth potential. The analysis in Chapter 9 is conducted from various perspectives, from the point of view of the trends in supply and demand, for both the mutual investment fund and high net-worth individual (HNWI) segments, with the aim of analysing and evaluating banks' strategic choices with regard to the asset management industry. First, the chapter analyses the size and trend of the market for asset management products and services, and discusses the main underlying factors. This is followed by a closer investigation of the investment fund sector, one of the asset management industry segments that has experienced the largest drop in the amounts of funds managed during recent years, with the aim of identifying the causes of this reduction and possible solutions for overcoming it. The strategic business area of private banking, serving HNWI customers, is also reviewed, to identify elements of similarity or contrast with the asset management industry overall.

The final chapter concludes the survey by identifying the strengths and weaknesses of the Italian banking system and outlining the possible strategies available for surviving the great financial crisis.

2

The Impact of the Financial Crisis on Italian Banks

Elisabetta Gualandri

2.1 Introduction

For a clearer description of the impact of the crisis on the Italian banking system, it is useful to subdivide the period from 2007 to 2011 into two acute phases: the subprime phase of 2007–09, with the turmoil in the financial markets caused by the subprime mortgage crisis, aggravated to dramatic proportions by the failure of Lehman Brothers in September 2008, and the sovereign debt phase from 2010 onward, caused by the sovereign debt crisis affecting first Greece and then the peripheral countries of the European Monetary Union (EMU): Portugal, Ireland, Spain, and Italy. This approach enables us to focus more closely on the first phase, bearing in mind that the second is still ongoing at the time of writing. It also allows a more precise analysis of the crisis's dual-stage impact in Italy: at a lower level in the first period and at a higher level from 2010 onward, with a trend contrasting with that of other countries in Europe and beyond.

Between these two phases there was a short period, from mid-2009 to mid-2010, when there appeared to be the prospects of a worldwide economic and financial recovery; they actually were extremely fragile and were soon to prove illusory. In the second half of 2010, the sovereign debt crisis worsened again, especially in Greece, and it spread to both Spain and Italy during 2011. Towards the end of 2011, the hopes of a European Union (EU)–wide recovery were finally dashed, and the forecasts for 2012 were gradually revised downwards to the point where most countries were expected to go into recession, with Italy one of the most affected of all.

The aim of this chapter is to assess the impact of the crisis on the Italian banking system and to describe the measures taken by the credit authorities and the government.

The chapter also highlights the reasons, including the specific characteristics of the banking system and of the entire Italian financial system in general, that explain why the country suffered less than other nations during the first phase of the crisis. A number of these characteristics mutated from positive to negative factors during the course of the crisis. Some of these features will be discussed in greater detail in subsequent chapters.

2.2 A snapshot of the pre-crisis situation

On the eve of the crisis, the Italian banking system was still feeling the effects of the period of deep restructuring in the 1990s, during which the state significantly reduced its direct ownership of banks and the system underwent intensive consolidation. The wave of mergers and acquisitions that began in the late 1990s continued in the first decade of this century with an increase in concentration, generating significant cost reductions.

The restructuring had helped to improve the efficiency and competition of the Italian banking industry, and before the beginning of the crisis most of Italian banks' standard performance indicators were broadly in line with those of other large European countries. There was further room for improvement in operational costs, which remained high compared to competitors elsewhere in Europe, and in competition, not yet fully reflected in the pricing and quality of core services, partly due to a low level of access to the market by foreign intermediaries, which, according to received wisdom, would have helped strengthen efficiency and competition (International Monetary Fund (IMF) 2006).

In 2005–06, a detailed assessment of the financial system's stability was carried out by the IMF within the Financial Sector Assessment Program (FSAP). In general, the Italian financial system appeared sound, and no major vulnerabilities capable of causing systemic risks were identified, also thanks to an overall strong supervisory framework. The FSAP team concluded: "Italy's financial system appears sound and...the system's strength is supported by a high degree of conformity to supervisory and regulatory standards" (IMF 2006). In the meantime, the governance provisions at the Bank of Italy (BI) had already been strengthened by the reform at the end of 2005 (Law No. 262 of 28 December 2005).

Nonetheless, specific areas of weakness were identified in the macroeconomic environment, and did, in fact, prove to be critical during the crisis: a protracted period of low growth (almost a decade), with an impact on the quality of the banks' loan portfolio and high public debt and fiscal instability, which could pose a potential risk of widening interest rate spreads. With regard to the first factor, the IMF Report stressed that Italian banks suffered from structurally higher non-performing loans compared to other leading European countries. In terms of the high public debt, it was pointed out that Italy's government bond market was the largest in Europe, and a large proportion of domestic debt was in the portfolios of the domestic banks.

Specific features of the Italian system were also identified in the equity and corporate bond markets, comparatively small in relation to the sovereign debt market, which generated a lack of diversity in sources of financing for firms and a lack of investment opportunities for savers. The overall situation of the Italian financial market reflected the predominance of family-owned small and medium-sized enterprises (SMEs) in the economy, the presence of only a small number of big firms, the role of the banking sector as the core funding source for the domestic economy, and the marginal importance of certain institutional investor classes in the asset management industry.

2.3 From the subprime mortgage crisis to the Lehman Brothers crash

The Italian banking and financial system showed more resilience than other national systems in the first wave of the global financial crisis (Financial Stability Board (FSB) 2011): not one bank was rescued or nationalised. The total value of the measures taken by the Italian government was €4.1 billion, or 0.3 per cent of gross domestic product (GDP), the lowest figure of all the Organization for Economic Co-operation and Development (OECD) countries – strikingly so, since total assistance to the banking industry across the EU amounted to 30 per cent of GDP.

Until the Lehman Brothers crash in September 2008, the impact of the crisis on Italian banks was relatively slight in various respects: the stock market value of Italy's largest banking groups fell considerably (about €4.5 billion), but less than that of the main foreign banks; overall profits had dropped, but the banks were not recording losses; and the fall-off in earnings due to write-downs of securities, trading losses, and reductions in commissions was relatively small compared to the serious losses suffered by other countries' banks, thanks to portfolios with lower risk levels and above all fewer toxic securities, and thanks to a strong focus on the traditional banking business. Last but not least, capital had remained overall at levels above the minimum required by the regulation (Draghi 2009a, 2011b).

The reasons can be found on the one hand in the prevailing business model of Italian banks and on the other in the national regulatory and supervisory framework. The business model was mainly traditional and relationship-oriented, relying heavily on lending activities and it had a stable retail funding base. Financial innovation had not developed at the same speed or in the same depth as in other systems. As the ongoing debate on the consequences of financial innovation indicates, the role of financial innovation in fostering economic growth (by improving the efficiency of resource and risk allocation) had been lower than in other countries, but, conversely, the accompanying threat of systemic risk and financial instability was slighter.

The regulatory and supervisory approach was not "light touch," but rather prudent and thorough, aiming to prevent aggressive practices in mortgage lending and to discourage banks from participating in complex securitisation activities and sponsoring structured investment vehicles. Thanks to the principle of national discretion included in the EU regulations within the Capital Adequacy Accord (Basel I at that time), the methods for the calculation of Italian groups' capital ratios set by the Bank of Italy were based on more prudential criteria than those in force in other countries. Moreover, the reform of the Bank of Italy at the end of 2005 had overhauled the entire supervisory function, with measures including the introduction of stress tests. In addition, specialist teams of regulators had been constantly at work in the offices of the largest, most complex banking groups, to investigate specific topics and analyse particular risk profiles (Draghi 2009c).

The Bank of Italy's overall approach helped the country's banks to achieve lower leverage, higher capitalisation, and higher liquidity ratios than their main international competitors.

With the Lehman Brothers crash, the Italian banks were seriously affected by the general loss of faith in the banking system and the consequent lack of liquidity, due both to greater difficulties in the collection of retail funding and, above all, to the freezing of the interbank deposit market. To overcome this crisis of confidence, the Bank of Italy sponsored the creation of MIC (Mercato Interbancario Collateralizzato), a collateralised segment of the e-MID (Mercato Interbancario dei Depositi), the interbank deposit market (see below for details of how this was done). Thanks to this measure, and to the injection of large amounts of liquidity by the European Central Bank (ECB) and the other main central banks, and the general improvement in the perception of banks' risk levels, the situation gradually improved in 2009, and there were also signs of a recovery in the bond market.

In Italy, all the major financial institutions remained profitable over this period, and only a few of them made use of the facilities provided by the government, the so-called Tremonti bonds. The facilities introduced in Italy, to be described in greater detail below, were very low compared to those of other European countries. The public facilities provided to Italian banks amounted to just 0.3 per cent of GDP, by a considerable margin the lowest ratio of the various European and non-European countries. In the United States , the figure was 19.3 per cent; in Great Britain, 64.3 per cent; in Germany, 16.9 per cent; and in France it was 4.4 per cent.

Liquidity ratios and capital adequacy improved during 2009, in this case thanks to both capital increases and the sale of non-strategic assets. Although capital adequacy improved compared to the end of 2008 for the five largest banking groups (on average, Core Tier 1 capital increased from 5.5 to 7.3 per cent) and the financial markets' view of Italian banks' risk level became less pessimistic, a further increase in capital resources was encouraged by the Bank of Italy for the largest banks, in order to strengthen their core capital to cope with domestic vulnerabilities and increase their resilience in adverse macroeconomic conditions, given the high level of financial interlinking. In the meantime, the national economy was starting to look more vulnerable, as the worsening situation combined with the low economic growth of previous years, and was beginning to cause a deterioration of the quality of loans, with growing weight on banks' profits. Non-performing assets rose from 6.5 to 9.1 per cent of total exposures to customers; the ratio of bad debts to total loans outstanding rose by more than 0.6 points to 1.9 per cent (Banca d'Italia 2010a).

Two additional factors started to weigh on Italian banks' performance during 2009. First, they were at a competitive disadvantage compared to the banks of other systems, which had benefited from public facilities and large injections of public capital. Second, in the main countries of the EU, the inflow of large amounts of liquidity provided by the monetary authorities encouraged a return to investments in securities, even those of a highly speculative nature, stimulating a recovery in profitability. Due to their stronger focus on traditional banking activities, Italian banks' profit performance was decidedly flatter. Profits fell by

15.6 per cent and return on equity (ROE) decreased from 4.5 to 3.6 per cent in 2009 as compared with 2008.

2.4 Towards the sovereign debt crisis

As the onset of the sovereign debt crisis drew near, Italian banks continued to experience a deterioration in earnings, hand-in-hand with a worsening in the quality of loans (Draghi 2010a). Moreover, a factor that had been central to the Italian banking system's greater resilience in the first phase of the crisis now became a disadvantage: in this stage, the banks' strong focus on the traditional banking business, meaning that a smaller proportion of their earnings derived from trading and investment banking than was the case in other European banks/groups, made them highly dependent on the interest rate margin and economic trend and reduced the flexibility of their cost structures, leading to lower profitability. The business model that had protected them at the start of the crisis and decreased their exposure to the volatility of the financial markets, with its lower leverage, limited proprietary trading on the securities markets, less use of maturity transformation, and prevalence of variable interest loans, now became a weak point (FSB 2011; Draghi 2011a).

The EU-wide stress test introduced by the Committee of European Banking Supervisors (CEBS) in 2010 (FSB 2011) confirmed that Italy's five largest banking groups had sufficient capital adequacy, with Tier 1 capital ratio above the threshold value of 6 per cent, but the ratios projected for them at the end of 2011 were rather low compared to other EU banks. This finding was attributed to two main factors: lower capital adequacy ratios at the outset (partly due to tighter restrictions on capital deductions and hybrid instruments) and the fact that Italian banks received lower government capital injections than those of other EU countries. Conversely, the banks' leverage ratios were found to be relatively lower.

After the approval of Basel III in December 2010, it became obvious that further recapitalisation and an improvement in the quality of assets would be necessary. Although the implementation of Basel III grants banks a relatively long transition period (until the end of 2018), the need for recapitalisation was made more pressing due to market conditions and due to the requirements of the supervisory authorities. As a consequence Italian banks found themselves between Scylla and Charybdis: they needed to raise funds from the market once again, but were faced with an outlook of unsatisfactory profits (arising from the poor prospects for the Italian economy), which appeared to put constraints on their ability to increase their equity quickly. In some cases, ownership structures were seen as a further obstacle to recapitalisation.

On the other hand, the introduction by Basel III in 2010 of the leverage ratio should pass off without significant consequences, since the limited leverage of Italian banks; in June 2009 the ratio of total assets to core capital averaged 24 for the largest Italian banking groups, compared to 34 for the largest European banks (Draghi 2010a). The Basel Committee will test a minimum Tier 1 leverage ratio of 3 per cent during the parallel run period from 1 January 2013 to 1 January 2017 (Basel Committe on Banking Supervision 2010).

In spite of the stresses described above, until the end of 2010 the sovereign debt crisis had no serious repercussions for Italian banks, thanks to their very limited exposure to the debt of the peripheral countries (Greece, Ireland, Portugal, and Spain): the exposure was about 1 per cent of the assets of the Italian banking system as a whole. In contrast, Italian banks had large amounts invested in Italian sovereign bonds (7.40 per cent of total assets), and this was to serve as detonator for the next phase of the crisis, triggered by sovereign debt, which we discuss in greater detail below.

2.5 Anti-crisis measures and the role of the Italian government

The various countries dealt with the financial crisis with measures of different kinds. The first line of defence was public intervention, followed by action by the supervisory authorities. At the international level, the regulatory framework underwent a thorough overhaul between 2010 and 2011, with the issue of Basel III on capital adequacy, the global liquidity standards with regard to liquidity provisions, the measures on SIFIs (systemically important financial institutions), and the additional capital provisions required by the European Banking Authority (EBA) at the end of 2011.

We will now discuss the anti-crisis measures implemented by the Italian government, in an international context, before focusing on the actions taken by the Bank of Italy in its supervisory capacity.

After the collapse of Lehman Brothers, the main industrialised countries launched measures to support banks and other financial intermediaries. The mechanisms used were of various kinds: the provision of guarantees on banks' liabilities, measures to supply liquidity, rescue packages for banks in serious difficulties, recapitalisation with public funds for banks that were having problems in obtaining external funding, and the extension of the deposit protection schemes.

Table 2.1 records the forms of public intervention undertaken during 2008–11, and thus includes further measures introduced in response to the sovereign debt crisis in countries such as Belgium, France, and Germany. Overall, the amount spent on protecting the banking sector in Europe between December 2008 and November 2011 (capital, guarantees, and other measures) totalled €2356.4 billion, with 174 intermediaries involved (Table 2.1). As of November 2011 the amount net of repayments and renunciations was €1231 billion. In the United States, the amount spent was $2851 billion, assisting 1366 banks (Mediobanca 2011b). The total amount in the United States and Europe totalled more than €4397 billion, with 1540 institutions involved.

The situation in Italy was clearly one of the least serious: only four banks were recapitalised by means of the Tremonti bond facilities. The total value of these measures was €4.1 billion, or 0.3 per cent of GDP, the lowest figure of all the countries considered. For example, the equivalent value in Germany was €45.3 billion; if the additional measures, mainly the provision of guarantees, are added, the overall figure is €418 billion, or 16.9 per cent of GDP. In Great Britain, the cost of the rescue packages was 67.7 per cent of GDP, while in France it was 6.6 per cent. The highest figure was in Ireland: 101.9 per cent of GDP.

Starting in October 2008, the Italian authorities (government and Parliament with the support of the Bank of Italy) introduced a series of measures (Banca d'Italia 2009a, 2009b; FSB 2011; Petrovic and Tutsch 2009), in line with the international initiatives in the sector and, where appropriate, in accordance with the European Commission regulations on state aid. These measures aimed on the one hand to safeguard financial stability and sustain banks' liquidity and on the other to restore the beneficiary banks' capacity to provide medium- to long-term loans, in order to reduce the impact of the financial crisis on the real economy. In contrast with some other countries, in Italy no rescue or nationalisation packages were needed, and some of the measures made ready were never activated, reflecting Italian banks' greater resilience.

The bulk of the Italian measures are based on two laws: Law No. 190 of 4 December 2008, provisions that came into effect on 9 and 13 October 2008 as urgent measures to guarantee the stability of the banking system and the continued availability of credit to enterprises and consumers in the current crisis in international financial markets, and Law No. 2 of 28 January 2009, article 12, on recapitalisation (Banca

Table 2.1 Public facilities in support of banks: types of measures as of November 2011 (all data are in billions of euros, unless indicated as dollars always billions)

Country	Capital	Guarantees	Others	Total	% GDP	Total institutions involved	Amount net of renunciations and repayments November 2011
United States ($)	562.7	1,869.0	419.4	2,851.0	19.3	1,366	1,183.0
United States	402.8	1,337.8	300.2	2,040.8	19.3	1,366	846.8
Austria	8.6	24.3	–	32.9	11.6	8	32.6
Belgium	20.9	169.8	5.5	196.3	55.8	6	125.4
Denmark	7.4	26.3	6.6	40.3	17.2	59	35.8
France	25.3	102.4	0.5	128.2	6.6	8	69.0
Germany	45.3	365.4	7.3	418	16.9	13	122.5
Great Britain	109.0	959.0	80.0	1148	67.7	18	593.9
Greece	2.8	0.5	0.1	3.4	1.5	9	2.9
Ireland	31.5	127.5	–	159	101.9	6	116.8
Island	0.8	–	–	0.8	na	3	0.8
Italy	**4.1**	–	–	**4.1**	**0.3**	**4**	**2.6**
Luxembourg	2.8	7.2	0.2	10.1	24.3	4	6.7
Netherlands	30.1	105.4	8.3	143.8	24.5	14	83.1
Portugal	–	6.2	–	6.2	3.6	7	
Spain	10.3	0.4	9.0	19.7	1.9	21	19.3
Switzerland	45.6	–	–	45.6	11.4	1	
Total Europe	**344.6**	**1,894.4**	**117.4**	**2,356.4**		**174**	**1,231.8**
Total Europe and United States				**4,397.2**		**1540**	**2,141.0**

Source: Processing of Mediobanca R&S (2011b), IMF World Economic Outlook Data Base, September 2011 (GDP value as 2010); ECB, Economic Bulletin Statistics, various issues. (Exchange rate €/$ 1.397: average 2008–10).

d'Italia 2009b). The main measure, involving what have become known as the "Tremonti bonds," came into force on 29 November 2008.

This safety net was intended first of all to strengthen banks' solvency and liquidity, to avoid runs on banks by depositors, and thereafter to maintain flows of credit to the economy. It consisted of four main sets of measures implemented by the Ministry of Economy and Finance (MEF) and the Bank of Italy: liquidity provisions, measures for the recapitalisation of distressed banks, schemes for strengthening and supporting the banking sector to enable it to continue to finance the economy, and the extension of the depositor protection scheme (Table 2.2).

1. **Liquidity provisions.** The measures introduced to prevent a liquidity crisis were of four types: the issuing of government guarantees for bank liabilities by the MEF; the acquisition by the MEF of banks' high-risk positions/impaired assets through temporary swap arrangements; the introduction of a collateralised securities loan facility and the setting up, by the Bank of Italy, of a Collateralised Interbank Market, the MIC. The first three schemes were available until the end of 2009 and only the third was actually utilised, with the Bank of Italy lending Euro Area government securities to Eurosystem banks against investment grade collateral for one month, for an amount of up to €5.4 billion. The last measure was drawn up by the Bank of Italy and the e-MID, the uncollateralised Electronic Interbank Deposit Market, with the aim of providing guarantees to overcome the freezing-up of this market that were caused by banks' loss of confidence in each other. The scheme was improved in 2010 with the creation of the New MIC (New Interbank Collateralized Market), a guaranteed interbank market where funds are traded anonymously and counterparty risk is mitigated by the pooling of collateral.
2. **Recapitalisation of distressed banks.** Under this scheme, the MEF was allowed to subscribe to capital increases by banks or bank holding companies that the Bank of Italy deemed to be undercapitalised. This scheme was available until 31 December 2009 and was never used, meaning that within the Italian banking system not one bank was rescued and nationalised.
3. **Strengthening and supporting of banks.** This scheme is still working and consists of special equity instruments, Tremonti bonds, issued by sound banks, eligible as Tier 1 regulatory capital, and subscribed to by the MEF. The measure is intended to strengthen banks in order to maintain the flow of credit to SMEs, in particular. This is one of the key measures and is described in detail below.

4. **Depositor protection.** The Italian deposit protection scheme was already in operation with one of the highest coverage levels in the EU, but after the Lehman Brothers collapse, as in other countries, the Italian government decided to introduce a supplementary state guarantee to protect depositors against all bank failures for three years (until October 2011). The aim was to avoid runs on banks by depositors. In May 2011, the new directive was introduced, (2009/14/EC, 11 March 2009), replacing the old scheme.

The "Tremonti bonds" facility

Tremonti bonds are hybrid bank recapitalisation instruments, underwritten by the state. They are long-term loans and are included amongst the capital of the beneficiary banks for supervisory and other purposes. The annual interest rate is between 7.5 and 8.5 per cent for the first few years, gradually increasing over time.

Under the complex allocation procedure, which involves controls by the Ministry of the Economy and Finance and the Bank of Italy, the beneficiary bank undertakes to guarantee:

1. maintenance of financing, in particular in favour of SMEs;
2. conditions to support and maintain entrepreneurial initiatives;
3. measures to assist households facing difficulties in mortgage repayments;
4. dividend policy that favours the recapitalisation of the bank;
5. presentation of a report on the actions undertaken to sustain the real economy.

In addition, the beneficiary bank has to sign a code of conduct, which includes limitations on the pay of management and market operators, together with exit bonus caps.

This facility was only used by four banks, which applied to the scheme for €4.1 billion: Banco Popolare, Banca Popolare di Milano, Banca Monte dei Paschi di Siena, and Credito Valtellinese (Table 2.3). This low level of utilisation reflects banks' resilience as well as the conditionality and costs of the facility itself. In terms of cost, in 2009, at the time when the Tremonti bond scheme was launched, interest of 7.5–8.5 per cent, was decidedly high compared to the prevailing market conditions.

During 2011, Banco Popolare repaid the entire loan received, of €1.45 billion, while for the other banks, the final due date in the initial repayment plan was June 2013. The worsening of the crisis in 2011 might lead to an extension of the repayment term and also to further applications,

Table 2.2 Measures taken by the Italian authorities 2008–09

Target	Measure	Eligible institutions	Law and timing	Notes
Liquidity	Government guarantees of bank liabilities. The issuer of guarantees is the Ministry of Economy and Finance (MEF). For each individual bank, the overall maximum amount of transactions guaranteed may not exceed the eligible institution's regulatory capital, including Tier 3 capital. Liabilities that can be included in the calculation of the regulatory capital cannot benefit from the state guarantee. Payment of an appropriate fee.	Solvent banks that have their registered office in Italy. The BI assesses the capital adequacy of a bank and its ability to discharge any obligations it assumes.	Decree-Law 157 of 2008, converted into Law 190/2008. Scheme available until 31 December 2009.	Not utilised.
	MEF is authorised to enter temporary swap arrangements between treasury bills and financial instruments held by Italian banks or liabilities of Italian banks issued after 13 October 2008.	Solvent banks incorporated in Italy, including Italian subsidiaries of foreign banks. Charges to be applied to banks determined according to prevailing market conditions.	Decree-Law 157 of 2008, converted into Law 190/2008. Scheme available until 31 December 2009.	Not utilised.
	Collateralised securities loan facility under which the Banks of Italy (BI) can lend Euro Area government securities to Eurosystem banks against investment grade collateral for a month.		Scheme available until 31 December 2009.	Value of transactions undertaken: close to €5.4 billions; last transaction: March 2009.

	Setting up of a Collateralised Interbank Market (MIC) by e-MID and BI. It is a guaranteed interbank market. Funds are traded anonymously and counterparty risk is mitigated by the pooling of collateral.	Domestic banks which meet the prerequisites set by e-MID.	2009	In October 2010 MIC evolved into New MIC, a triparty repo market in which the Italian Central Clearing Counterpart (Cassa di Compensazione Garanzia) will guarantee trades. Eligible institutions are domestic and international banks with the prerequisites set by e-MID.
Recapitalisation of distressed banks	The MEF was allowed to subscribe to capital increases by banks or bank holding companies that the BI deemed to be undercapitalised. These shares would carry no voting rights, but would have preference in the distribution of dividends, and their purchase would be accompanied by a stabilisation and strengthening plan that would be overseen by the BI.	Italian banks whose capital increases were not completed by 9 October 2008.	Decree-Law 155 of 2008, converted into Law 190/2008 Scheme available until 31 December 2009.	Not utilised.

Continued

Table 2.2 Continued

Target	Measure	Eligible institutions	Law and timing	Notes
To support the strength and ability of the banking sector to finance the economy	Special equity instruments, "Tremonti bonds," issued by sound banks, eligible as Tier 1 regulatory capital, and subscribed to by the MEF. The maximum amount of recapitalisation for an individual eligible institution (or of the eligible institution's group) is set at 2 per cent of their total risk weighted assets. Conditions include an appropriate fee. In addition, a code of behaviour must be signed between the beneficiary and the MEF, containing a number of conditions. The beneficiary banks must also conduct their activity in a manner that does not abuse the assistance received nor may the assistance result in the beneficiary obtaining an advantageous position.	All fundamentally sound banks incorporated under Italian law, subsidiaries of foreign banks, and holding companies of Italian banking groups whose shares are listed on regulated markets.	Decree-Law 185 of 2008, converted into Law 2/2009. The measure entered into force on 29 November 2008.	Amount granted to four banks by 2011: €4.1 billion (1.45 repaid).
Depositor protection	Introduction of a supplementary state guarantee to protect depositors against all bank failures for three years (until October 2011).	Depositors of Italian banks and their subsidiaries in the other EU states, and of the Italian subsidiaries of EU and non-EU banking groups.	Decree-Law 155 of 2008 converted into Law 190/2008.	Not utilised. In May 2011, the new EU Directive 2009/14/CE was introduced, with the Decree-Law 49, which amended the level of coverage and refund term in the existing depositor protection scheme.

Sources: Processing of Banca d'Italia (2008a, 2009a, 2009b); FSB (2011); Petrovic and Tutsch (2009).

Table 2.3 The "Tremonti bonds" facility

Bank	Date	Amount in billions of €	Situation (end 2011)
Banco Popolare	19 June 2009	1.45	Total repayment 14 March 2011
Banca Popolare di Milano	21 September 2009	0.5	Repayment plan over four years (due 30 June 2013)
Banca Monte dei Paschi di Siena	14 December 2009	1.9	Repayment plan over four years (due 30 June 2013)
Credito Valtellinese	30 December 2009	0.2	Repayment plan over four years (due 30 June 2013)

Source: Processing of Mediobanca (2011a, 2011b).

to deal with the recapitalisation demands put forward by the EBA at the end of 2011[1].

2.6 The sovereign debt crisis, 2010–?

The global financial crisis was rekindled in 2010; triggered by the Greek sovereign debt crisis, it was centered on the Euro Area and hit Italian banks much harder than had been the case during the subprime phase.

The general sequence of events

The crisis was initially limited to Greece, after which it spread to Portugal and Ireland, but with no signs of the possible serious involvement of other countries. The picture changed significantly for the whole European banking sector from the middle of 2011 onwards, due to the failure to find a solution to the Greek crisis and the decision to require private creditors to share the "haircut." This resulted in a worsening of the sovereign debt crisis of the peripheral EU states, especially Spain and Italy.

The main cause of the general deterioration was apparently the holding of sizeable amounts of debt issued by foreign sovereigns. The Bank for International Settlements, BIS, (2011b) suggests that banks were exposed to the public sector in all foreign countries at the end of 2010 by amounts ranging from 75 per cent of Tier 1 capital for Italian, US and German banks to over 200 per cent for Swiss, Belgian, and Canadian banks. Exposure to those countries worst hit by the sovereign debt tensions was significantly smaller, but on occasion was quite significant—for instance, German, French and Belgian banks' exposures were around 20 per cent of their Core Tier 1 capital.

Banks all over Europe have been affected by the main transmission channels by which the sovereign risk impacts on banks' funding (cost and availability). These effects can also be triggered or reinforced by the international transmission of stresses (BIS 2011b):

1. direct effects on bank balance sheets and profitability through their holdings of sovereign debt and their derivatives positions with sovereign bonds
2. reduction in the value of the collateral that banks can use to obtain wholesale funding and central bank refinancing
3. negative impact of sovereign downgrades, felt in two ways: the first is on the cost of bank funding (debt and equity); the second consists of downgrades of domestic banks following on from sovereign downgrades (usually sovereign ratings represent a ceiling for the rating of domestic banks).

The reactions to the publication in July 2011 of the results of the stress tests promoted by the EBA on 70 large EU banks were conflicting. In response to the worsening of the crisis during the summer, the EBA issued additional capital requirements in its Recapitalisation Plan of 26 October 2011, subsequently revised on 8 December (Table 2.4 and Box 2.1). Shortfalls were mainly due to two factors: the deepening of the sovereign debt crisis since the summer and the creation an exceptional, temporary buffer raising the Core Tier 1 capital ratio to 9 per cent (Box 2.1).

The results of the stress tests and the additional capital requirements did not reassure investors: as a consequence, large European banks started to suffer significant strain, which produced a general worsening of systemic risk indicators at the international level.

The case of Italian banks

Towards the end of 2010, Italy's sovereign risk started to rise, with negative impacts on the wholesale funding markets. Early in 2011, the cost of borrowing for Italian banks was about 70 basis points higher than that for German intermediaries. During the summer of 2011, the risk crisis worsened, as it also did in Spain; high and excessively volatile yields on sovereign securities led markets to fear that public debt might not be

Table 2.4 EBA-aggregated shortfall required, by country (8 December 2011)

Country	**Total amount (millions of €)**	**of which: sovereign buffer**
AT (Austria)	3,923	112
BE (Belgium)	6,313	4,774
CY (Cyprus)	3,531	2,457
DE (Germany)	13,107	7,563
DK (Denmark)	–	22
ES (Spain)	26,170	6,561
FI (Finland)	–	–
FR (France)	7,324	3,512
GB (United Kingdom)	–	–
GR (Greece)	*30,000*	–
HU (Hungary)	–	33
IE (Ireland)	–	815
IT (Italy)	15,366	9,674
LU (Luxembourg)	–	–
MT (Malta)	–	1
NL (Netherlands)	159	183
NO (Norway)	1,520	–
PL (Poland)	–	–
PT (Portugal)	6,950	3,718
SE (Sweden)	–	2
SI (Slovenia)	320	4
Total	114,685	39,428

Source: EBA (2011) EU Capital Exercise Recommendation and final results of bank recapitalisation plan as part of co-ordinated measures to restore confidence in the banking sector, London, 8 December 2011.

sustainable, especially in economies with a high debt/GDP ratio, such as Italy's. The general perception of the sovereign risk was aggravated by the difficulties and uncertainties surrounding European governance.

In Italy's case, previously, the small size of the increase in the deficit and public debt as a result of the crisis compared to that of other countries, and the high level of private savings, had reassured the markets concerning the sustainability of refinancing the public debt, the highest in relation to GDP (126.8 per cent in 2010) of the industrialised countries, with the exception of Japan. Of the Euro Area countries with high debt/GDP ratios, Italy was one of those that reduced their debt the least during the early stages of the single currency. All the same, as Table 2.5 shows, the growth in the ratio between 2007 and 2010 was one of the lowest (2010/2007 +12.4 per cent). The countries with the highest increases in public debt as a percentage of GDP were the ones that

Box 2.1 EBA Recapitalisation Exercise (8 December 2011)

The European Banking Authority (EBA) conducted an EU-wide recapitalisation exercise, examining the situations of 58 large banks from 20 European countries (as well as Greece, for which the data of the banks involved have not been disclosed) and drawing up recommendations on 26 October 2011 and then on 8 December (with regard to the situation at 30 September 2011). The aim was to strengthen European banks' position in an environment of heightened systemic risk that arose from the sovereign debt crisis. Higher capital levels were expected to increase the resilience of the banking sector and therefore to support banks in maintaining their ability to lend to the real economy within the EU. Bank funding was in truth severely affected, as from July 2011 onwards the markets ground to a halt; this has triggered considerably deleveraging, which posed a serious threat to prospects for growth.

The strengthening of capital positions was required for two main reasons:

1. to build up an exceptional, temporary capital buffer against sovereign debt exposure (to reflect market prices at the end of September 2011)
2. to create an exceptional, temporary buffer so that the Core Tier 1 capital ratio would reach the level of 9 per cent (as required by the European Council on 26 October). This measure formed part of a broader European package, agreed and confirmed during the meeting of the Economic and Financial Affairs Council of the EU (ECOFIN) on 30 November, to address the current situation in the EU by restoring stability and confidence in the markets

Banks required to strengthen their capital position were asked to submit plans for achieving the target capital levels to their national supervisory authorities by January 2012 and to meet the buffer requirement by June 2012.

undertook the biggest banking sector rescue operations at taxpayer's expense, such as Ireland, the United Kingdom, and the United States. With regard to the public sector deficit as a proportion of GDP, a key sustainability indicator, the figure in 2010 was 4.6 per cent in Italy, almost in line with the German figure of 4.3 per cent, but lower than those for France, 7.1 per cent; Spain, 9.3 per cent; Portugal, 9.8 per cent; and Ireland, 31.43 per cent (Banca d' Italia, 2011b, p. 13).

In summer 2011, given the stalemate in the drawing up of new rules on governance for the EU, the ineffectuality of the instruments at Europe's disposal for dealing with the sovereign debt crisis, and a domestic political situation clearly no longer able to handle the emergencies triggered by the fresh deterioration in the situation, the markets' perception of Italy's risk level soared. The main causes for concern were the huge level

Table 2.5 Public debt (percentage of GDP)

Location	2002	2007	2010	Change (2007–2002)	Change (2010–2007)
Euro Area	72.5	71.6	92.7	–1.2%	29.5%
Germany	62.2	65.3	87.0	5.0%	33.2%
France	67.3	72.3	94.1	7.4%	30.2%
Italy	119.4	112.8	126.8	–5.5%	12.4%
Spain	60.3	42.1	66.1	–30.2%	57.0%
Netherlands	60.3	51.5	71.4	–14.6%	38.6%
Belgium	108.4	88.1	100.7	–18.7%	14.3%
Greece	117.6	112.9	147.3	–4.0%	30.5%
Portugal	65.0	75.4	103.1	16.0%	36.7%
Ireland	35.2	28.8	102.4	–18.2%	255.6%
Japan	152.3	167.0	199.7	9.7%	19.6%
United Kingdom	40.8	47.2	82.5	15.7%	74.8%
United States	56.8	62.0	93.6	9.2%	51.0%
Total OECD	71.6	73.1	97.6	2.1%	33.5%

Source: Processing of BIS, 81th Annual Report, 2011.

of public debt, the large amounts of funding that would be needed to refinance it in the future, and the almost certain knowledge that the country was facing a recession.

As a consequence, Italian banks were affected by the increased sovereign risk in a number of ways: funding, with a rise in retail funding costs, was rendered more problematic by the lasting tension in the interbank market; the value of the guarantees provided for refinancing; and the conditions of access to capital markets for the recapitalisation operations that were required of some of the largest banks by the new EBA rules.

Table 2.6 shows holdings of Italian government public bonds at the end of 2010; at that time, domestic monetary financial institutions (MFIs) had 18.5 per cent of the total amount in their portfolios (with the Bank of Italy holding around 2%). Due to these large holdings, the increase in sovereign risk had further adverse repercussions for the domestic banks, which were now under significant strain, with an increased risk premium reflected by the widening of credit default swap (CDS) spreads and the rise in expected default frequencies derived from the stock market. The increase in risk premiums and the decline in expected earnings, deriving in part from the general economic conditions, cut Italian banks' market-to-book ratios to very low levels by the end of 2011 (Banca d'Italia 2011b).

Table 2.6 Holders of Italian government bonds (31 December 2010)

Counterparties	Amount (millions of €)	% of total
Domestic monetary financial institutions	282,228	18.5
Other domestic financial institutions	55,763	3.7
Domestic institutional investors' insurance and pension funds	159,329	10.5
Domestic private investors	214,361	14.1
Total domestic	718,829	47.2
Foreign investors	803,732	52.8
Total	**1,522,561**	**100.00**

Source: Processing of Banca d'Italia (2011c) Supplementi al Bollettino Statistico, Indicatori monetari e finanziari, Conti finanziari, Nuova serie, Anno XXI—8 Novembre 2011, N. 58 (Tavola 3).

The EBA's additional capital requirements arose from the banks' large holdings of the national public debt. On average, the additional capital requirements due to sovereign risk were particularly high for Italian banks (Table 2.4).

The situation varied widely amongst the five banks assessed (Table 2.7); for Intesa Sanpaolo, Italy's largest banking group, no capital deficit was reported, while for UniCredit the figure produced was €7,974 millions (virtually half of the total required from the five Italian banks), one-third of which was due to sovereign risk. By the beginning of 2012 UniCredit had already completed the necessary recapitalisation, while the other banks had submitted the relevant plans to the Bank of Italy.

The Italian banks began to have recourse to Eurosystem refinancing on a large scale from summer 2011, offsetting the slowdown in fundraising from foreign counterparts, while deposits from resident households remained almost stable. On 21 December, Italian banks' total drawings on the ECB's three-year Long-Term Refinancing Operation (LTRO) was €116 billion (€60 billion net) out of an EU-wide total drawings of €490 billion (€210 billion net). The expectation is that this has enabled the Italian banks to obtain 90 per cent of the liquidity required for 2012, including their scheduled bond and loan repayments.

The "Save Italy" decree

In December 2011, new measures for the stability of the banking system were decided, with the so-called "Save Italy Austerity Plan," introduced by Decree-Law No. 201 of 6 December 2011 (converted into statute by

Table 2.7 EBA-Italian banks' shortfalls (8 December 2011)

Name	Total amount (millions of €)	Shortfall to 9% before application sovereign capital buffer (millions of €)
Intesa Sanpaolo S.p.A	0	0
UniCredit S.p.A	7,974	5,741
Banca Monte dei Paschi di Siena S.p.A	3,267	0
Banco Popolare, S.C.	2,731	2,357
Unione di Banche Italiane (UBI Banca)	1,393	526

Source: Processing of EBA (2011) EU Capital Exercise, Recommendation and final results of bank recapitalisation plan as part of co-ordinated measures to restore confidence in the banking sector, London, 8 December 2011.

Law No. 214 of 22 December), which contained "urgent measures for growth, equity and the consolidation of public finances." This legislation reintroduces the mechanism for the provision of guarantees on the liabilities of Italian banks by the MEF (Italian Ministry of Economy and Finance), to remain in force until 30 June 2012. The loans concerned were for periods from three months to five years; the time period was seven years for the bank bonds covered by the guarantees that were issued after the decree came into force. Guarantees were granted further to an assessment by the Bank of Italy of the capital adequacy of the applicant bank and its ability to meet its obligations.

The aim of the guarantees was to restore the beneficiary banks' capability for providing medium- and long-term loans. After the first six months, the operations undertaken and their effects on the economy were to be evaluated by the MEF and the Bank of Italy, and the results were to be reported to the European Commission (2010, 2011). The need for an extension of the guarantee programme would then be assessed. The rules stated that the total amount of the guarantees provided for each bank must not exceed its regulatory capital.

2.7 The role of supervision in combating the crisis

Within the Italian supervisory architecture, the Bank of Italy is responsible for the financial stability of financial intermediaries, with two exceptions: insurance companies, whose authority is ISVAP (Istituto per la vigilanza sulle assicurazioni private e di interesse collettivo), and pension funds, whose authority is COVIP (Commissione di Vigilanza sui Fondi Pensione). CONSOB (Commissione Nazionale per le Società e la Borsa) is the securities market regulator.

As a consequence of the crisis, co-ordination at the national level was established in March 2008, and a Memorandum of Understanding (MoU) for co-operation on financial stability was signed by the MEF, BI, CONSOB, and ISVAP. The bodies involved agreed to cooperate and to exchange information and assessments, with the aim of strengthening financial stability and preventing and managing financial crises that have potentially systemic effects. This agreement was on a voluntary basis and its terms reflected the individual area of competence of each body. The MoU also established a Financial Stability Committee (FSC) consisting of these bodies, tasked with financial stability issues, developing emergency plans, and conducting crisis simulation exercises. The FSC is under an obligation to hold meetings at least twice a year, but there have been several unscheduled meetings since 2008, especially during times of stress on the financial markets (FSB 2011).

Moving on to examine the supervisory policy implemented by the Bank of Italy in response to the crisis, as we have already seen, the Bank of Italy has a tradition of strict implementation of EU directives, with restrictive use of national discretion. It has also performed its supervisory activities thoroughly and pervasively, abjuring the light-touch approach. This practice helped to contain the effects of the crisis, in response to which the Bank of Italy strengthened its monitoring activity and intensified its supervisory operations.

A major improvement in terms of prudential supervision arose from the entry into force of Basel II in 2008. The Bank of Italy issued a New Guide for Supervisory Activity in mid-2008, covering methods and procedures; it was revised as the basis for the Supervisory Review and Evaluation Process or SREP (Pillar 2, Basel II). The focus of the Guide is mainly risk analysis, with a unitary approach encompassing off-site and on-site supervision.

In 2008, when the crisis was at its peak, the Bank of Italy adopted an integrated approach of on-site supervision, off-site supervision, and a programme of stress tests (Banca d'Italia 2009a), with the aim of monitoring variations in risk and identifying possible critical situations well in advance, so that banks could be required to take the necessary corrective measures. The approach is firm-wide and risk based, and its application is modulated to suit the size, complexity, and specific areas of vulnerability or weakness of the individual bank. For the main groups, in particular, the audit of capital resources and risk management systems is extended to the entire Internal Capital Adequacy Assessment Process (ICAAP).

The programme of stress tests to be performed on annual basis, involves experts from various areas in the design of the tests and the analysis of results. Within it, two complementary approaches are combined (FSB 2011, p. 12): a top-down approach for the analysis of exposure to banking book risks (credit and interest rate risks), giving consideration to possible feedback effects and contagion channels; and a bottom-up approach for the analysis of credit risk, market risk, and liquidity risk, using the internal data and methods of major banking groups, which are capable of capturing risks even in firms with complex trading activities and liquidity structures.

The two main areas of analysis and intervention have been liquidity provisions and capital adequacy (Gualandri et al. 2009).

As far as the first area is concerned, special attention started to be paid to liquidity provisions even before the general focus on international liquidity standards, with the introduction early in 2009 of specific measures: weekly monitoring of net liquidity positions, simulations based on stress scenarios, frequent contacts with market participants, checks on operating arrangements and procedures, and targeted inspections. The Bank of Italy issued a regulation in December 2010 on the improvement of banks' liquidity risk management, in line with the EU Directive 2009/111/EC. To improve the situation in the interbank deposits market, as already mentioned, the Bank of Italy joined the e-MID to promote MIC (now known as New MIC), the collateralised segment of the interbank deposit market. Convergence with the Basel liquidity standards is being achieved in accordance with a gradual schedule.

With regard to the second area, the Bank of Italy has paid very close attention to capital adequacy since the beginning of the crisis, with constant assessment of the capital levels of banks and banking groups in relation to both the amount of risk taken on and the quality structure of capital. Priority is also given to monitoring the trend in loan quality. On several occasions, the Bank of Italy has urged the banks, especially the largest intermediaries, to proceed with recapitalisation without delay, both to bring them gradually into line with the new international standards and to reinforce Italian banks' capital adequacy; significant recapitalisations were planned and partly completed during the early months of 2011. In some cases, the worsening of the sovereign debt crisis and the EBA's requirements rendered these operations insufficient.

Moreover, partly in response to the SREP included in Pillar 2 of the Basel Accord, the supervisory authorities have performed an in-depth analysis of banks' internal corporate governance organisations of large banks and groups in particular.

The analysis revealed the need to strengthen risk management capacity in a large number of cases, and the Bank of Italy requested banks to simplify their organisational structures, eliminate duplication and overlaps, and the improve their information systems.

As regards compensation and incentive systems, supervisory activity focuses on verifying compliance with principles issued by the Bank of Italy in March 2011 with the implementation of the Capital Requirements Directive (CRD III) that includes some provisions of Basel III.

2.8 Conclusions

At the time of writing, Spring 2012, it is clear that the global financial crisis has hit the Italian banking system harder during its second phase than in its first. The sovereign debt crisis in 2011 affected Italian banks by different channels and has resulted in an increased risk premium, reflected by the widening of credit default swap spreads. The worsening of general economic conditions has aggravated the situation and had slashed Italian banks' market-to-book ratios to very low levels by the end of 2011.

The business model that was based on a strong focus on traditional banking business, which protected Italian banks in the first phase of the global financial crisis, has thus become a weak point in the second phase.

The prospects for Italian banks must be viewed in three main contexts: the development of the global financial crisis, the specific economic and financial situation in Italy, the perspectives of the Italian banking system itself. The first context is in relation to the future development of the global financial crisis, which depends on a number of interconnected factors:—the time taken and the methods adopted to solve the Greek crisis, and the consequent impact on the Euro Area as a whole; the evolution of the sovereign debt crisis. These two factors are themselves inextricably linked to the evolution of governance within the European Monetary Union (procedures and times). Obviously, the safeguarding of Euro Area banks depends first and foremost on the restoration to a sound footing of the finances of the sovereign states, by effective, credible means. While it is essential for the banks to take the recapitalisation measures demanded by tough market conditions, this may count for nothing if the spread of sovereign debt contagion is not halted.

The second context, partly interdependent with the first, relates to the Italian system and particularly two issues: the reduction of the public debt and the nation's ability to respond to its current difficulties with appropriate reforms and to return to sustained growth.

The third context concerns the Italian banking system itself and its capacity to reinforce its weak points. The chapters which follow will analyse the main features of the Italian banking system, which are of particular importance because some of these features have proved to be sources of greater resilience in the first phase and of weakness during the second phase of the crisis.

Note

1. In June 2012, the government decided to provide a further facility for a maximum of €2 billion euro to Banca Monte dei Paschi di Siena, needed to meet the requirement for a 9 per cent Core Tier 1 ratio introduced by the EBA (8 December 2011). The total amount of Tremonti Bonds applied for by BMPS rose to a maximum of €3.9 billion.

3

Main Features of the Italian Financial System

Valeria Venturelli

3.1 Introduction

During the last few years, the main countries' financial systems have undergone profound changes in terms of both the structural characteristics of the systems themselves and the financial behaviours of operators. Common trends linked to the development of financial markets, the growing role of institutional investors, the consolidation of banking systems, and the formation of large banking conglomerates have emerged; however there are still differences among financial systems, which can lead to variations in the magnitude of the consequences of the financial crisis. Therefore, at the European level, discussion of the convergence of banking models must be accompanied by an attempt to identify the distinctive features of the "ideal" financial system. The crisis has revealed that the banking sector of a country can be considered sound and thus an aid to economic growth and prosperity if it is founded on a number of key principles (Vaciago and Zadra 2009):

1. It must focus above all on financing the economy and the private sector.
2. It must be supported by a high level of retail funding.
3. It must be supported by a solid assets structure.
4. Banking services must be provided through distribution channels (i.e. branches) that ensure good geographical coverage and accessibility to the clientele.

This chapter aims to identify the characteristics of the Italian financial system that partially shielded it from the effects of the financial crisis in its first phase. This will be done by analysing the evolution of the financial aggregates and balance sheet compositions of banks at the European and Italian level. Based on the harmonised statistics produced by the European Central Bank (ECB), we compare the structural characteristics of some of the main European countries. Apart from Italy, the countries considered are Germany, France, Spain and the United Kingdom, chosen because these countries' banking and financial systems share a number of features and trends. We also assess the average data for the financial systems of Euro Area countries. The chapter consists of three main parts. The first part identifies the current trends in the financial systems under consideration, by examining the main indicators that reveal the evolution and determinants of financial intensity. This analysis is completed by an assessment of the portfolio composition and financial structures of non-financial sectors, with a particular focus on the financial strategies of households and non-financial corporations. The next part examines the situation of the banking sectors in the various countries by establishing the size of monetary financial institutions (MFIs) and by analysing the breakdown of their balance sheets. The final part of the chapter provides a comparative analysis of the main structural and composition indicators of banking sector activities. This is followed by the main conclusions.

3.2 The Italian financial system: structure and evolution in the international context

To assess the characteristics of the evolution of the Italian banking system from an international perspective, we may start by analysing the size of the banking system in a number of countries including Italy, measured as the ratio of an economy's financial assets in relation to its gross domestic product (GDP), its financial intermediation ratio (FIR). Since 1999 (Table 3.1) there has been an increase across the board in the various economies' financial depth, and in particular an upward trend in the weight of the financial sector, and banking first and foremost. Of the countries examined, the United Kingdom has the largest financial sector, followed by France. In Italy and Germany, the financial system is smaller.

Financial systems' level of internationalisation, the proportion of securities held by non-residents, has also increased; globalisation is affecting both the real and the financial economies, and this helps to explain the contagion experienced during the current crisis. The United Kingdom is the country most open to foreign investors (it is no coincidence that London is the centre of the international banking industry),

Table 3.1 Financial intermediation ratio (FIR), outstanding amount

Location	1999	2002	2005	2006	2007	2008	2009	2010
Financial assets[a]/GDP								
Euro Area	7.99	7.59	8.81	9.33	9.65	9.27	9.99	10.13
Italy	6.22	5.97	6.75	6.96	6.82	6.72	7.10	7.04
Germany	3.60	3.83	3.96	3.81	3.81	3.88	4.14	4.14
France	8.29	7.48	8.86	10.28	10.88	10.06	10.83	11.03
Spain	6.11	6.08	7.54	8.21	8.48	8.13	8.57	8.53
UK	6.56[b]	6.14	8.33	9.48	10.17	14.80	15.29	14.72
Financial assets rest of the world/GDP								
Euro Area	1.06	1.18	1.49	1.60	1.71	1.63	1.73	1.81
Italy	1.05	1.01	1.23	1.35	1.39	1.32	1.41	1.40
Germany	0.54	0.79	0.95	1.06	1.04	1.11	1.18	1.25
France	1.52	1.58	2.35	2.64	2.78	2.61	2.75	2.83
Spain	1.17	1.39	1.83	2.02	2.14	2.04	2.22	2.16
UK	1.98[b]	1.97	2.90	2.99	3.38	4.14	4.59	4.49
Financial assets of financial sector[c]/GDP								
Euro Area	4.14	4.06	4.84	5.19	5.49	5.44	5.81	5.86
Italy	2.45	2.40	2.90	3.06	3.05	3.13	3.41	3.43
Germany	2.58	2.69	2.85	2.81	2.78	2.84	3.01	3.00
France	4.07	3.94	4.78	5.27	5.75	5.66	5.85	5.92
Spain	2.69	2.61	3.44	3.75	4.13	4.28	4.56	4.47
UK	3.71[b]	3.69	5.32	6.42	7.09	11.32	11.03	10.57
Financial assets of monetary financial institutions/GDP								
Euro Area	2.56	2.60	2.96	3.12	3.36	3.50	3.57	3.52
Italy	1.54	1.58	1.85	2.09	2.15	2.30	2.47	2.46

Germany	2.07	2.13	2.17	2.13	2.13	2.19	2.27	2.21
France	2.76	2.72	3.19	3.46	3.84	4.01	4.00	4.01
Spain	2.06	2.02	2.54	2.69	2.99	3.19	3.37	3.29
UK	2.03[b]	2.20	3.11	4.11	4.66	8.65	7.64	7.19
Financial assets of non-financial sector[d]/GDP								
Euro Area	3.85	3.53	3.97	4.14	4.16	3.83	4.18	4.27
Italy	3.77	3.57	3.86	3.90	3.77	3.59	3.69	3.61
Germany	1.02	1.14	1.11	1.00	1.03	1.04	1.13	1.13
France	4.21	3.53	4.08	5.01	5.12	4.40	4.98	5.11
Spain	3.42	3.47	4.10	4.46	4.35	3.85	4.01	4.07
UK	2.84[b]	2.45	3.01	3.06	3.08	3.48	4.26	4.15

[a]If not diversified Total financial assets (liabilities) includes the rest of the world.

[b]Data from 2000 for UK.

[c]The financial sector includes insurance corporations and pension funds, MFIs, and other financial intermediaries, including financial auxiliaries.

[d]The non-financial sector includes non-financial corporations, households, non-profit institutions serving households, and general government.

Source: Processing of European Central Banks – Statistical Data Warehouse – Euro Area Accounts.

followed by France and Spain. The involvement of non-residents in the Italian financial sector has also increased. The liberalisation of flows of capital in the 1990s was the decisive factor here.

The differences among the financial systems reflect the different roles not only of the rest of the world, but also of the other institutional sectors. The sharpest differences are in the weight of financial corporations: in 2010 the ratio of the financial assets of the financial sector was 3.4 times GDP in Italy, compared to 10.6 times in the United Kingdom. Italy's financial sector is therefore smaller, due above all to the smaller scale of its financial corporations; Italy and the United Kingdom are at opposite ends of the scale in terms of the weight of the financial assets of their insurance firms and pension funds in relation to gross domestic product.

The financial crisis interrupted the upward trend in the value of financial assets: from 2008 onwards, financial assets increased at lower rates than during the previous period, and this applies in particular to the level of financial intensity of the financial sectors and monetary financial institutions. The very recent growth in the financial intensity of non-financial sectors is due to the rise in loans to these sectors (Table 3.2).

Table 3.2 Financial intermediation ratio (FIR), non-financial corporations and households

Location	1999	2002	2005	2006	2007	2008	2009	2010
Financial liabilities of households/GDP								
Euro Area	0.54	0.57	0.64	0.66	0.67	0.68	0.72	0.72
Italy	0.34	0.40	0.48	0.51	0.53	0.55	0.58	0.60
Germany	0.73	0.72	0.70	0.67	0.64	0.62	0.64	0.61
France	0.45	0.46	0.52	0.55	0.58	0.58	0.63	0.65
Spain	0.51	0.59	0.78	0.85	0.88	0.88	0.90	0.90
UK	0.46[a]	0.54	0.68	0.72	0.74	0.85	0.98	0.91
Financial liabilities of non-financial corporations/GDP								
Euro Area	2.61	2.27	2.61	2.82	2.93	2.59	2.83	2.87
Italy	2.04	1.97	2.18	2.26	2.30	2.32	2.28	2.21
Germany	0.94	1.05	0.98	0.97	0.99	1.05	1.11	1.07
France	3.57	2.84	3.34	3.76	3.95	3.14	3.61	3.70
Spain	2.50	2.65	3.34	3.75	3.80	3.34	3.41	3.39
UK	1.79[a]	1.41	1.82	1.90	1.88	1.95	2.43	2.36

[a]Data from 2000 for UK.

Source: Processing of European Central Bank – Statistical Data Warehouse – Euro Area Accounts.

The expansion in lending has been fuelled above all by the trend in credit granted to households and non-financial corporations. If we turn to the breakdown of loans to non-financial corporations by sector, the most signification finding for the period under consideration is the growth in loans to households, which is constantly above the rate of growth of gross domestic product for all the years in the period and for all financial systems except that of Germany, rising from 0.54 in 1999 to 0.72 in 2010 for the Euro Zone countries (Table 3.2).

Compared to other countries in the Euro Area, the trend in lending to Italian households is more accentuated, and the levels of the ratio between this figure and GDP are also different. Italian households have lower levels of debt, although the differential compared to European households in general is falling. On the international scene, Italian non-financial corporations are the only ones that have reduced their borrowing levels since 2008; this helps to explain the slight reduction in the financial intermediation ratio (FIR) of non-financial sectors, which decreased from 3.77 in 1999 to 3.61 in 2010 (Table 3.1).

To establish the extent to which the changes in financial intensity reflect structural changes in the balance sheets of the main economic players, it is worth investigating the financial accounts of the main institutional sectors (households and non-financial corporations). During the period under consideration, the growth in the volume of financial intermediation was accompanied by major changes in the composition of private investors' financial portfolios, which affected bank funding and lending trends.

There are differences in the percentage breakdown of households' financial assets. An analysis of the composition of households' portfolios reveals (Table 3.3) that in all the countries analysed, with the sole significant exception of the United Kingdom, banks account for a large proportion of financial investments, reflected by the high figure of the sum of deposits and bonds; this has been particularly true for Spain and Italy since 2008, with a rise in the percentage of households' financial assets held in bank deposits.

The distinctive feature of the Italian situation is the role of direct investment in securities, which historically originates from the role of household savings in supporting government borrowing, due to the high public debt/GDP ratio. Investment in government bonds has been superseded by investment in bank bonds, in response to the drop in interest rates. A high level of direct investment in bonds has been due to both the search for higher returns than those provided by government

Table 3.3 Percentage composition of financial assets by instruments (outstanding amount), households

Location	1999	2002	2005	2006	2007	2008	2009	2010
Currency and deposits/Total financial assets								
Euro Area	30.8	33.2	31.7	31.1	31.8	35.9	35.4	35.2
Italy	24.3	25.2	25.1	25.9	27.2	29.4	30.3	30.5
France	44.0	48.8	45.3	29.1	28.6	31.5	29.5	29.1
Spain	36.4	42.3	36.8	36.1	38.0	47.0	47.0	48.3
UK	20.4[a]	26.9	25.9	25.9	27.1	31.9	28.7	28.0
Securities other than shares, excluding financial derivatives/Total financial assets								
Euro Area	7.6	9.2	7.9	7.6	7.7	8.5	8.0	7.4
Italy	16.0	20.8	19.8	18.8	19.6	20.9	20.8	19.7
France	3.3	3.9	2.6	1.6	1.7	1.9	1.9	1.6
Spain	2.4	2.5	2.1	2.6	2.6	2.4	2.8	3.2
UK	1.5[a]	2.0	1.5	0.9	0.8	1.0	0.7	0.7
Shares and other equity[b]/Total financial assets								
Euro Area	23.7	17.7	19.6	20.7	20.2	16.1	16.0	16.0
Italy	29.1	25.3	25.4	26.5	25.5	25.4	22.4	21.5
France	27.8	22.0	27.1	20.8	21.2	15.5	17.5	18.3
Spain	29.5	24.1	30.7	33.0	31.8	23.6	23.8	22.3
UK	17.9[a]	11.5	12.3	11.5	10.7	8.9	11.3	11.3
Mutual funds shares/Total financial assets								
Euro Area	11.7	10.6	10.4	10.1	9.4	7.8	8.1	8.1
Italy	17.2	12.2	10.7	9.8	8.5	5.2	6.1	6.6
France	14.2	13.7	13.0	9.3	8.2	7.9	7.5	7.2
Spain	16.7	12.0	12.7	11.5	10.7	8.7	8.4	7.1
UK	4.9[a]	4.0	4.0	4.3	4.1	2.2	2.5	3.1
Technical reserves/Total financial assets								
Euro Area	22.9	26.1	27.6	27.6	28.0	28.7	29.6	30.2
Italy	10.5	13.4	15.9	16.1	16.0	15.7	17.2	18.3
France	3.7	4.2	4.2	34.0	35.1	37.3	37.0	36.9
Spain	12.0	15.7	14.4	13.5	13.5	14.6	14.9	15.1
UK	52.4[a]	52.2	53.5	53.9	54.2	52.0	53.2	53.4
Other[c]/Total financial assets								
Euro Area	3.3	3.1	2.9	2.9	2.8	3.0	2.9	3.0
Italy	2.9	3.1	3.1	3.0	3.1	3.3	3.2	3.4
France	6.9	7.4	7.8	5.2	5.3	5.9	6.6	7.0
Spain	3.0	3.4	3.3	3.4	3.4	3.6	3.3	4.0
UK	2.9[a]	3.4	2.9	3.4	3.1	4.1	3.5	3.4

[a]Data from 2000 for UK.
[b]Listed and unlisted.
[c]Derivatives + Loans + Other accounts.

Source: Processing of European Central Bank – Statistical Data Warehouse – Euro Area Accounts. Breakdown of values not available for Germany.

bonds and by banks' supply policies, since they have encouraged their clientele to favour bank bonds offered on the domestic market.

In 2010, institutional investors (mutual funds, pension funds, and insurance companies) overall in the Euro Area managed more than 38 per cent of households' financial assets; this figure was boosted by the trend in the reserves held by insurance companies and pension funds, while the level of investment in mutual funds decreased. The trend in asset management in Italy shows a contrast: the most significant figure is the shift of increasing amounts of financial investment towards technical reserves, which accounted for 18.3 per cent of financial wealth in 2010, compared to 10.5 per cent in 1999. This figure reflects a preference for financial products that provide a stable return and offer a good yield on the capital invested in the medium- to long-term. The Italian situation with regard to mutual funds also reveals a sharper reduction in this type of investment, with the proportion of financial assets directed to mutual funds continuing to fall even in the most recent period.

The countries at either end of the scale with regard to the weight of technical reserves are the United Kingdom at one extreme and Italy and Spain at the other.

The breakdown of corporations' balance sheet liabilities (Table 3.4) reveals, that, due to the write-down in market values, equity becomes the most important item, especially in the United Kingdom and France. Bank loans, like commercial accounts payable ("other" in the aggregate), are significantly high in Italy and Spain. For these countries, bank loans are by far the most widely used source of finance, compensating for firms' reluctance to turn to the equity market. The highest level of financing through bond issues is found in the United Kingdom.

An analysis of the financial preferences of households and corporations provides pointers as to what appear to be the main changes underway in the behaviour of private investors and borrowers. To put it extremely briefly, the analysis of private players' financial portfolios indicates the relative importance of the role of banks in households' financial asset management decisions and in financing strategies for non-financial corporations; banks prove to be important for all the countries investigated, but especially so for Italy.

The banking circuit continues to handle a large proportion of financial intermediation within the Euro Area, partly as a result of the negative impact of the crisis on the financial markets and on households' willingness to accept investment risks. In Italy, the size of banks' role in asset management has also benefited from their ability to convince retail investors to buy their own bonds.

Table 3.4 Percentage composition of financial liabilities by instruments (outstanding amount), non-financial corporations

Location	1999	2002	2005	2006	2007	2008	2009	2010
Loans/Total financial liabilities								
Euro Area	23.9	32.2	29.0	28.0	28.9	34.5	32.7	31.9
Italy	25.2	28.8	28.6	29.0	30.8	32.0	33.5	34.0
France	16.7	24.1	21.2	19.8	20.1	26.8	23.3	22.7
Spain	20.4	32.3	31.0	32.0	34.2	40.3	40.2	40.5
UK	19.0[a]	28.3	28.4	29.6	29.6	37.8	32.5	31.5
Securities other than shares/Total financial liabilities								
Euro Area	2.2	3.3	3.0	2.7	2.5	2.9	3.2	3.3
Italy	0.8	1.7	2.1	2.2	2.0	1.9	2.4	2.8
France	4.2	6.5	5.3	4.4	3.7	4.9	5.4	5.6
Spain	1.4	0.7	0.4	0.3	0.3	0.4	0.5	0.5
UK	7.8[a]	10.9	9.9	9.9	9.4	10.1	10.9	9.3
Shares and other equity[b]/Total financial liabilities								
Euro Area	59.0	47.3	52.5	54.7	54.3	46.1	48.7	49.6
Italy	52.1	47.1	49.2	49.7	47.6	46.9	44.9	43.5
France	67.4	54.5	60.5	63.7	64.3	53.3	57.9	58.3
Spain	56.3	46.2	50.1	49.9	48.2	41.1	42.3	41.1
UK	68.3[a]	54.9	56.9	56.1	56.7	47.5	52.3	55.1
Other[c]/Total financial liabilities								
Euro Area	14.9	17.2	15.5	14.6	14.3	16.4	15.4	15.1
Italy	21.8	22.4	20.1	19.1	19.6	19.2	19.2	19.7
France	11.6	14.8	13.0	12.0	11.8	15.0	13.4	13.4
Spain	21.9	20.8	18.6	17.8	17.2	18.2	17.0	17.9
UK	4.9[a]	5.9	4.8	4.4	4.2	4.6	4.3	4.1

[a]Data from 2000 for UK.
[b]Listed and unlisted.
[c]Other: Currency and deposits, derivatives, technical reserves, other accounts.

Source: Processing of European Central Bank – Statistical Data Warehouse – Euro Area Accounts. Breakdown of values not available for Germany.

There does not appear to be any end in sight to the slump in investment in mutual funds. The figure for Italy seems to indicate that the reasons for these difficulties affecting the fund industry lie partly in strategies within the distribution network, which have to some extent undermined investors' faith in this form of investment.

One finding common to both the Euro Area and Italy is the gradual, progressive shift in financial portfolios towards insurance-pension fund investments, reflecting investors' search for stable forms of investment capable of safeguarding their future spending power in view of the ongoing cuts in public pension provision.

Italian households' portfolios continue to be unusual with regard to the role of direct investments in securities. During the last few years, bank bonds have gradually replaced government securities in households' investment plans. The continued high level of direct investment in bonds has been partly due to banks' marketing policies, since they have encouraged their clientele to favour bank bonds offered on the domestic market.

For corporations, bank loans are by far the most widely used source of finance, compensating for the tendency to avoid recourse to the stock market of recent years. Although the extent of their use is significantly lower than in the Euro Area as a whole, corporate bonds are a particularly dynamic, although still relatively minor, sector in Italian corporations' financing strategies.

3.3 Evolution and composition of monetary financial institutions' balance sheets

While the analysis of private players' financial portfolios has underlined the importance of the role of banks in households' financial asset management decisions and in financing strategies for non-financial corporations, there are still major differences between the banking intermediation rates in the various systems examined. Therefore, in this section it is of interest to identify the aspects in which the Italian banking market differs from those of the other national systems. The difference can be assessed by measuring the size of each country's banking sector, and in particular by studying the composition of the balance sheets of the MFIs within the various systems. The variations from country to country reflect the strategies adopted by the various intermediaries over time, which can only be explained with reference to a large number of factors, such as the business models prevalent in each country, social and cultural factors, characteristics of the clientele, etc.

The banking intermediation rate, which measures the size of the banking sector, can be measured by means of the ratios of loans and deposits to GDP. Both ratios of Loans/GDP and Deposits/GDP reveal that the Italian system has a lower banking intermediation rate than the Euro Area as a whole, and a lower ranking compared to a number of the other countries considered here (Table 3.5).

For loans, the Euro Area ratio was 1.33 in 2010, higher than the Italian figure (1.28). However, some countries have a loans to GDP ratio higher than the European average, especially Spain (1.85) and the United

Table 3.5 Banking intermediation ratio[a]

Location	1999	2002	2005	2006	2007	2008	2009	2010
Total loans/GDP								
Euro Area	1.02	1.05	1.13	1.18	1.24	1.28	1.32	1.33
Italy	0.74	0.81	0.89	0.95	1.10	1.14	1.21	1.28
Germany	1.31	1.30	1.22	1.18	1.15	1.17	1.20	1.19
France	0.79	0.83	0.92	0.97	1.05	1.10	1.13	1.17
Spain	0.88	1.02	1.38	1.59	1.73	1.79	1.83	1.85
UK	1.15	1.23	1.46	1.54	1.58	1.51	1.81	1.75
Total deposits/GDP								
Euro Area	0.82	0.84	0.92	0.95	1.01	1.08	1.14	1.17
Italy	0.52	0.54	0.55	0.58	0.68	0.73	0.80	0.92
Germany	1.00	1.01	1.05	1.06	1.09	1.15	1.21	1.21
France	0.67	0.66	0.74	0.73	0.77	0.80	0.87	0.92
Spain	0.78	0.87	1.10	1.27	1.41	1.56	1.64	1.67
UK	0.97	0.97	1.17	1.28	1.27	1.30	1.66	1.64

[a]Loans and deposits do not include operations with monetary financial intermediaries.

Source: Processing of European Central Bank – Statistical Data Warehouse – Money, banking and financial markets.

Kingdom (1.75). France and Italy differ from the other countries in that since 1999 they have always had banking intermediation ratios significantly lower than the European average figure. For Italy, the phenomenon is explained by households' lower level of use of bank loans (Table 3.6); the household loans to GDP ratio for Italy in 2010 was 0.38 compared to a Euro Area average of 0.56. A higher proportion of Italian banks' lending is to non-financial corporations. The lower ratio in France is due to the fact that French firms tend to be less dependent on bank loans; this applies not only to large corporations but also to smaller enterprises. In France, companies are able to reduce their use of bank lending because of the greater importance of commercial credit and, in the case of large corporations, more reliance on the stock and bond markets (Table 3.4). The trend in the loans/GDP ratio in Germany (Table 3.6) is the result of the decrease in lending to government and a slowdown in loans to the household sector. It should be noted that in the United Kingdom the increase in the loans/GDP ratio is mainly the outcome of the increase in the aggregate of loans granted to other financial sectors (non-monetary financial institutions, insurance companies, and pension funds).

On the liabilities side of MFIs' balance sheets (Table 3.5), the ratio between deposits and GDP at the European level was 1.17 in 2010, with both Italy and France on the one side (0.92) and Spain (1.67) on the other side, with the lowest and highest values respectively. In Italy, more than in other countries, this figure is the outcome of the large-scale

Table 3.6 Monetary financial institutions' loans

Location	1999	2002	2005	2006	2007	2008	2009	2010
Loans of Households/GDP								
Euro Area	0.44	0.46	0.52	0.54	0.54	0.53	0.55	0.56
Italy		0.22	0.27	0.29	0.30	0.30	0.33	0.38
Germany		0.66	0.64	0.62	0.58	0.57	0.59	0.57
France		0.35	0.41	0.44	0.46	0.48	0.50	0.52
Spain		0.49	0.68	0.76	0.80	0.81	0.83	0.83
UK	0.64	0.67	0.72	0.74	0.66	0.55	0.76	0.81
Loans of Non-financial corporations/GDP								
Euro Area	0.39	0.41	0.42	0.45	0.49	0.53	0.52	0.51
Italy		0.42	0.45	0.49	0.53	0.56	0.57	0.57
Germany		0.39	0.35	0.34	0.35	0.38	0.38	0.36
France		0.36	0.36	0.37	0.41	0.44	0.44	0.43
Spain		0.47	0.64	0.77	0.86	0.89	0.89	0.86
UK	0.25	0.25	0.29	0.32	0.33	0.33	0.38	0.33
Loans of General government /GDP								
Euro Area	0.11	0.10	0.10	0.09	0.09	0.09	0.09	0.10
Italy	0.06	0.04	0.04	0.04	0.14	0.15	0.16	0.17
Germany	0.25	0.22	0.20	0.18	0.16	0.15	0.15	0.18
France	0.09	0.08	0.09	0.09	0.09	0.09	0.11	0.11
Spain	0.05	0.05	0.05	0.04	0.04	0.05	0.06	0.07
UK	0.01	0.01	0.02	0.01	0.01	0.01	0.01	0.01
Loans of Other sectors[a]/GDP								
Euro Area	0.06	0.07	0.08	0.09	0.11	0.12	0.13	0.13
Italy		0.13	0.12	0.13	0.13	0.13	0.15	0.16
Germany		0.02	0.03	0.04	0.05	0.07	0.08	0.08
France		0.04	0.06	0.07	0.09	0.09	0.08	0.10
Spain		0.02	0.01	0.02	0.03	0.04	0.06	0.08
UK	0.26	0.30	0.43	0.47	0.57	0.62	0.66	0.60

[a]Non-monetary financial institutions, insurance corporations, and pension funds.

Source: Processing of European Central Bank – Statistical Data Warehouse – Money, banking and financial markets.

reorganisation of Italian investors' financial portfolios that began in the 1980s, and the peculiarities of the taxation of financial income; here, the competition between government bonds and bank bonds is the crucial factor.

Italy's lower figures for both funding and lending confirm that its banking sector is still small compared to those of the main European countries.[1] In other words, Italy's banking sector is small by international standards (the financial accounts also indicate this).

The composition of the assets and liabilities sides of MFIs' balance sheets reveals a great deal of information about the structure of banking sectors and show the reasons for the varying effects of the financial crisis.

On the assets side (Table 3.7), first it is important to underline the predominance of loans to ordinary customers in the case of Italian banks, accounting for more than 50 per cent of total assets, a value higher than the Euro Area average (38 per cent) and higher than the figures

Table 3.7 Balance sheet composition, MFIs (excluding European System of Central Banks – ESCB) assets

Location	1999	2002	2005	2006	2007	2008	2009	2010
Loans to ordinary customers (excluding MFIs) as % total assets								
Euro Area	41.1	40.4	38.5	38.4	37.7	36.9	37.8	38.0
Italy	51.0	50.8	48.7	49.0	50.1	48.6	49.0	52.2
Germany	46.5	43.4	39.8	38.3	36.9	36.7	38.7	35.7
France	29.9	30.9	28.8	28.3	28.0	27.5	27.8	28.9
Spain	49.1	53.2	56.9	62.1	60.7	57.2	56.1	56.5
UK	36.1	35.8	31.6	30.7	32.4	31.4	31.6	32.3
Loans to MFIs as % total assets								
Euro Area	22.1	21.4	19.4	19.0	19.6	19.8	19.0	17.1
Italy	12.9	17.4	18.1	19.5	18.4	18.7	17.6	11.9
Germany	21.9	22.4	21.9	21.2	22.5	23.5	22.4	19.9
France	27.8	26.7	22.9	22.0	23.6	23.7	23.8	22.4
Spain	20.2	16.0	13.5	12.5	12.0	11.4	10.1	9.0
UK	11.1	13.2	17.2	19.1	11.1	10.0	14.7	11.9
Securities other than shares as % total assets								
Euro Area	14.8	14.2	14.8	13.8	13.4	14.5	16.2	15.3
Italy	14.2	10.9	12.0	10.9	10.0	12.1	14.4	17.0
Germany	14.5	14.7	16.2	16.0	15.3	15.7	17.1	14.3
France	14.8	14.7	15.3	14.7	14.2	14.7	14.8	13.9
Spain	14.1	13.3	12.3	7.6	9.8	13.5	16.7	16.0
UK	7.2	5.4	4.1	4.1	3.5	4.9	4.5	4.7
Shares and other equity as % total assets								
Euro Area	4.2	4.4	4.3	4.5	4.4	3.8	4.0	3.8
Italy	4.3	4.7	5.6	5.9	6.4	5.6	5.7	5.5
Germany	4.6	4.9	4.9	5.1	4.4	4.1	4.0	3.5
France	4.9	5.2	5.1	5.6	5.3	4.6	5.1	5.4
Spain	4.1	4.6	4.3	4.6	4.5	3.6	3.8	3.6
UK	1.6	1.9	2.1	2.5	2.3	3.4	4.1	3.9
Other[a] as % total assets								
Euro Area	17.8	19.7	23.0	24.3	24.9	25.0	22.9	25.7
Italy	17.6	16.2	15.6	14.7	15.1	15.1	13.3	13.4
Germany	12.6	14.7	17.2	19.3	20.9	20.0	17.8	26.7
France	22.6	22.5	28.0	29.3	29.0	29.5	28.4	29.3
Spain	12.5	12.9	13.0	13.2	13.0	14.2	13.4	14.8
UK	43.9	43.6	44.9	43.7	50.5	50.2	45.1	47.3

[a]Other: Money market funds shares/units, fixed assets, external assets, remaining assets.

Source: Processing of European Central Bank – Statistical Data Warehouse – Money, banking and financial markets.

for the other countries considered, with the sole exception of Spain in 2010. With regard to ordinary customers, as we have already seen (Table 3.6), Italian banks' loans portfolios are oriented less towards the households and general government sectors and more towards lending to non-financial corporations.

Compared to European banks, except for the last year, Italian banks' assets include fewer securities (Table 3.7), but not fewer government bonds (Table 3.8), present in a growing proportion since 2008. At the end of 2010, Italian banks had larger percentages of their total balance sheet assets invested in government securities, 6.5 per cent of total assets, compared to a Euro Area average of 4.7 per cent (Table 3.8).

Compared to European banks in general, Italian banks have a larger proportion of shares and other equity amongst their assets (Table 3.7). This is because of the size of their holdings in other banks, deriving from the importance of banking groups. Although the universal bank model is allowed under Italian law, many banks are structured on a group basis. Moreover, in Italy there have been more acquisitions in the banking sector than mergers. Conversely, Italian banks' holdings in non-financial corporations are lower than the European average and than the values seen in Germany.

The differences in the composition of banks' liabilities are equally noteworthy (Table 3.9). On the Italian banking market, as in Germany and Spain, direct funding (deposits by ordinary customers and bonds) accounts for more than 50 per cent of total liabilities, while for France this figure is 36.7 per cent, with a Euro Zone average of 48.3 per cent. Italian and German banks issue the highest proportion of bonds, with an average of around 20 per cent (15 per cent for the Euro Zone as a whole, 13 per cent in France and Spain).

Italian banks' level of capitalisation is also above the European average. At the end of the period examined, the "capital and reserves"

Table 3.8 General government securities (other than shares) as percentage of total assets

Location	1999	2002	2005	2006	2007	2008	2009	2010
Euro Area	7.3	6.0	6.1	4.9	4.1	3.9	4.8	4.7
Italy	11.0	7.3	7.1	6.2	5.4	4.8	5.6	6.5
Germany	4.0	3.7	4.3	3.9	3.3	2.9	3.6	3.9
France	7.3	5.9	6.2	5.2	4.7	4.5	4.8	4.2
Spain	11.0	9.4	6.7	3.4	3.1	3.4	5.2	4.9
UK	0.7	0.5	0.2	0.0	0.0	0.3	0.7	1.2

Source: Processing of European Central Bank – Statistical Data Warehouse – Money, banking and financial markets.

Table 3.9 Balance sheet composition, MFIs, excluding ESCB, liabilities

Location	1999	2002	2005	2006	2007	2008	2009	2010
Deposits of ordinary customers (excluding MFIs) as a % total liabilities								
Euro Area	33.2	32.2	31.3	31.0	30.7	31.1	32.7	33.3
Italy	35.9	34.1	30.8	30.2	31.2	31.3	32.7	38.0
Germany	35.5	33.9	34.2	34.5	35.0	36.2	39.0	36.3
France	25.1	24.5	23.3	21.2	20.3	20.0	21.4	22.6
Spain	43.4	45.6	45.3	49.5	49.6	49.6	50.2	51.2
UK	32.4	30.1	26.8	26.8	27.7	28.6	30.8	32.0
Deposits MFIs as a % total liabilities								
Euro Area	23.2	22.0	20.5	20.2	20.6	21.5	20.2	17.9
Italy	17.1	19.2	20.2	22.2	22.0	22.5	20.7	16.7
Germany	22.7	23.1	22.9	22.9	23.4	23.2	21.4	18.0
France	28.7	26.4	22.6	21.4	22.5	24.4	23.5	21.0
Spain	22.4	19.0	17.7	15.2	15.5	15.3	15.0	13.0
UK	11.9	14.3	18.3	20.4	12.1	11.3	13.3	10.6
Securities other than shares as a % total liabilities								
Euro Area	16.3	15.9	16.2	16.3	15.7	15.2	15.8	15.0
Italy	16.5	17.8	18.6	18.9	18.0	20.0	21.8	21.2
Germany	23.3	22.9	23.5	22.9	21.6	20.4	20.2	17.0
France	12.9	12.8	12.4	13.0	13.8	14.1	13.6	14.1
Spain	5.1	5.6	11.7	13.9	14.1	11.7	12.7	12.4
UK	5.9	5.2	4.9	5.1	5.9	6.5	7.2	7.2
Capital and reserves as a % total liabilities								
Euro Area	5.5	5.9	5.6	5.6	5.7	5.6	6.2	6.4
Italy	7.2	7.1	7.4	6.8	7.8	7.5	7.8	9.2
Germany	4.2	4.6	4.4	4.7	4.6	4.8	5.1	4.6
France	6.8	6.8	5.8	6.0	5.5	5.4	5.9	6.1
Spain	7.3	8.2	7.5	7.2	6.9	7.1	7.8	8.1
UK	9.1	8.9	7.7	7.8	7.1	6.4	7.7	8.1
Other[a] as a % of Total liabilities								
Euro Area	21.8	24.0	26.4	26.9	27.3	26.6	25.2	27.4
Italy	23.3	21.8	23.1	21.9	21.1	18.8	16.9	14.8
Germany	14.4	15.6	15.0	15.0	15.3	15.4	14.4	24.2
France	26.6	29.5	35.9	38.4	37.9	36.1	35.6	36.2
Spain	21.7	21.6	17.7	14.2	13.9	16.3	14.3	15.2
UK	40.8	41.5	42.3	39.9	47.3	47.2	41.0	42.0

[a]Other: External liabilities, money market funds shares/units, remaining liabilities.

Source: Processing of European Central Bank – Statistical Data Warehouse – Money, banking and financial markets.

aggregate in Italy represented 9.2 per cent of total liabilities, compared to a European average of 6.4 per cent (Table 3.9). The "capital and reserves/total assets" ratio might become a compulsory prudential measurement in the future, alongside the capital coefficient of the Basel accords, which weights assets with their respective degrees of risk. The ratio is particularly low in Germany (4.6 per cent in 2010).

In the European comparison, Spain is the country with the highest proportion of deposits by ordinary customers, and this explains Spanish banks' lower level of use of interbank funding and bond issues (Table 3.9). At the other extreme, French banks have an incidence of customer deposits well below the figure for the area as a whole, compensated by a high degree of use of interbank market, which is still one of the main forms of investment and funding used.

3.4 Evolution of banking sectors: structural indicators

Other factors underlying the specific characteristics of different countries' banking sectors are of a structural nature. This section analyses a number of structural indicators of the banking sector in the Euro Zone and in the countries under examination. The comparison clearly reflects the deep-seated restructuring process that has taken place, with varying levels of intensity in the different countries, affecting the number of banks, their size, and the coverage of their distribution networks.

At the structural level, the major transformation in the European banking sector during the last few decades has been one of consolidation, still ongoing today, although at a slower pace. This process, which derives from the attempt to achieve cost savings by increasing the efficiency of production and distribution organisations, has been intensive and has occurred in all countries, leading to a reduction of almost one-fourth in the number of European credit institutions during 1997–2009, with the disappearance of more than 2,100 of them (Table 3.10).

However, the aggregate figures for credit institutions overall conceal major differences with regard to the institutional categories of banks involved in the consolidation process.[2] In France, as a result of the concentration of ownership, the banking sector currently consists mainly

Table 3.10 Number of credit institutions

Location	1997	2000	2005	2006	2007	2008	2009
EU15	9,624	8,433	7,037	6,921	6,887	6,683	6,961
Italy	909	861	792	807	821	818	801
Germany	3,420	2,742	2,089	2,050	2,026	1,989	1,948
France	1,258	1,099	854	829	808	728	712
Spain	416	368	348	352	357	362	352
UK	537	491	394	394	396	391	389

Source: Processing of European Central Bank, Report on EU Banking structure, several issues.

of two categories: the large commercial banks and the large mutualistic networks, both operating as universal banks. In this system, the reduction has been mainly in the number of specialist intermediaries in the last few years. In Germany, the period under consideration has witnessed a major fall in the number of credit institutions (–43 per cent); savings and cooperative banks have been the categories most affected by the consolidation process. However, the German banking sector is still dominated by publicly owned institutions, mainly the *Sparkassen-Finanzgruppe* (German Savings Banks Finance Group), competition between which is restricted by the regional principle. Alongside them, and similar in the importance and geographical coverage of their intermediation operations, are the cooperative banks, which, however, are active on a smaller scale than the savings banks. The importance of the German public and cooperative banking circuits is the reason that commercial banks have found it so difficult to grow their business in the domestic market. In Spain, the reduction in the number of banks has been sharp (–15.4 per cent), although less than the average decrease for the area, and the degree of consolidation has varied considerably among the various types of bank. The numbers of Bancos (commercial banks) and Cooperativas de Credito (cooperative banks) have fallen more than that of savings banks (Cajas de Ahorros).

In Italy, the period has seen the launch of major integration projects involving the largest Banche Popolari (cooperative banks), continuing even during 2009 and 2010 (Table 3.11).

The bank ownership concentration process has been associated with different trends with regard to branch network sizes within the various European banking sectors (Table 3.12). Over the period, bank networks have shrunk within the area on average, while at the individual country levels networks have been pruned in Germany and the United Kingdom

Table 3.11 Number of credit institutions, the Italian situation, total and breakdown

	1997	2000	2005	2006	2007	2008	2009	2010
Banks (total)	935	841	783	793	806	799	788	760
Commercial banks	222	234	242	245	248	247	248	234
Banche Popolari (cooperative banks)	69	44	36	38	39	38	37	36
Mutual banks	583	499	439	436	440	432	421	415
Other	61	64	66	74	79	82	82	75

Source: Processing of Bank of Italy, Economic Bulletin, several issues.

Table 3.12 Number of local banking units

Location	1997	2000	2005	2006	2007	2008	2009
EU15	202,297	199,027	186,206	197,886	199,954	201,266	193,437
Italy	25,265	28,189	31,504	32,334	33,230	34,168	34,035
Germany	63,186	56,936	44,044	40,282	39,777	39,531	39,411
France	25,464	25,657	27,075	40,013	39,560	39,634	38,479
Spain	38,039	39,311	41,979	43,691	45,500	46,065	44,431
UK	16,344	14,225	13,130	12,880	12,425	12,360	12,360

Source: Processing of European Central Bank, Report on EU Banking structure, several issues.

but have expanded in France, Spain, and Italy. The figures for the most recent period (2007–09) reveal some stabilisation of the situation for the area on average, but different densities of cover and growth trends from country to country.

Italy and France are very similar in terms of the density of coverage of their distribution networks: these countries' bank branch numbers as percentages of the total Euro Area branches in 2010 were 18 per cent and 20 per cent, respectively. The trend in branch numbers for both countries has been upward. In France, the increase in branch numbers is due to the expansion of cooperative bank networks, only partially compensated by the rationalisation deriving from the concentration processes implemented by the private banks. For Italy, the rise in the number of branches is the outcome of strategies adopted by several categories of bank (mainly Banche Popolari – cooperative banks) with the aim of reinforcing their territorial roots (Table 3.13). However, in spite of the context of increasing banking sector consolidation, the growth in the network has been generated by the drive to make up the gap in territorial coverage compared to the European average. The United Kingdom continues to have the smallest number of bank branches (Table 3.12).

On average, the density of coverage of bank branch networks (Table 3.14) within the European Union does not appear to have changed significantly during the period considered; it is only in Germany and the United Kingdom that there is a clear reduction in the number of branches per capita. Although the reduction in the number of institutions reflects a certain degree of convergence in approaches across the various countries, there is still a large degree of variation with regard to branch network structures.

In general, all banking sectors have experienced a consolidation process, implemented by different procedures and with different intensities

Table 3.13 Number of local branch bank units, the Italian situation, total and breakdown

Item	1997	2000	2005	2006	2007	2008	2009	2010
Total number of branch banks	25,251	28,194	31,504	32,337	33,225	34,139	34,036	33,663
Commercial banks	18,127	20,318	24,045	24,618	26,272	26,808	26,431	25,542
Banche Popolari (cooperative banks)	4,357	4,794	3,746	3,839	2,876	2,997	3,059	3,452
Mutual banks	2,657	2,954	3,605	3,752	3,922	4,109	4,243	4,373
Other	110	128	108	128	155	225	303	296

Source: Processing of Banca d'Italia, Economic Bulletin, several issues.

Table 3.14 Number of local banking units per 100,000 inhabitants

Location	1997	2000	2005	2006	2007	2008	2009
EU 15	54	52	48	51	51	51	49
Italy	45	49	54	55	56	57	56
Germany	77	69	53	49	48	48	48
France	43	42	43	63	62	62	60
Spain	97	98	97	99	101	101	97
UK	28	25	22	21	20	20	20

Source: Processing of European Central Bank, Report on EU Banking structure, several issues.

and overall aims. In Italy, the banking system, after the period of consolidation and reorganisation, is structured as follows:

- large "universal" groups, covering the whole country and capable of expanding abroad
- strong medium-sized banks with local roots, often Banche Popolari – cooperative banks
- a network of mutual banks
- small-sized, independent non-banking intermediaries with niche markets: asset management firms, financial companies

This restructuring of the Italian banking sector has been associated with large-scale territorial reorganisation. In the second half of the 1990s, the combined effect of greater competition and the high level of insolvency triggered an almost systemic crisis in the banking sector in the south of the country. As a result, southern Italian banks lost their independence. At the same time, there were also sweeping transformations in the banking sector's ownership structure. Starting in the early 1990s, deep-seated changes occurred, with a sharp drop in the market share of the state-owned banks. In the banks incorporated as limited liability companies, the main scenario has been that of a stable core of shareholders, often linked to the original foundation or foundations, which have large holdings and are a crucial part of the shareholder base, meaning that these banks cannot be viewed as true "public companies" (see Chapter 4). This model has acted as a brake on hostile takeovers, especially from abroad, but has not prevented consolidation on the domestic market or foreign acquisitions. It is also probably one of the key explanations for Italian bank managements' more cautious approach to the market.

3.5 Conclusions

The introductory section listed the key prerequisites a banking sector must meet if it is to serve as one of the drivers of a country's economic growth. Amongst the main criteria are a strong orientation towards lending to the private sector, a moderate maturity transformation activity, a solid capital base, and a distribution network providing effective territorial coverage, capable of delivering services close to customers.

If we compare the fundamental characteristics of the Italian banking sector with our "shopping list," the results seem to be reassuring. Compared to their European colleagues, Italian banks have

- a fairly low level of investment in financial assets, compared to investment in the real economy. As we have seen, Italian banks show a preference for conventional forms of lending. Their specialisation in traditional banking operations – use of retail funding to finance loans to corporations and households – was one of Italian banks' strengths during the initial stages of the financial crisis. Moreover, the banking sector is less internationalised than those of other countries and financial innovation is less widespread than in the United States or the United Kingdom. The number of purely financial investments is fairly low
- a high proportion of traditional funding. Bank funding sources are stable
- a low leverage indicator, which has not grown over the years, in contrast with the situation in other countries

- strong territorial roots, with a large network of branches, reducing the distance between borrower and lender

Therefore, Italian banks' strong points lie in their business mix, the quality of their assets, and their capital adequacy.

There are also a number of more context-related factors, deriving from the economic system of the country as a whole, which helped to mitigate the effects of the crisis. These include

- stricter supervisory approach than in countries where a soft-touch approach was adopted, which prevented the exponential growth of a shadow banking system
- the low level of indebtedness of Italian households

In the writer's opinion, these are the main reasons why the consequences of the 2007 financial crisis for Italian banks were fairly low-key. We can ask, if the Italian banking sector withstood the crisis better than the banks of other countries, why are Italian banks in greater difficulty now? The point is the general underestimation of the sovereign debt risk and the high proportion of Italian banks' assets invested in government bonds, which, for many reasons, can no longer be considered as the equivalent of a risk-free investment. More detail on this topic will be found in Chapter 2.

Notes

1. For an analysis of the possible explanations, see De Bonis and Stacchini (2009).
2. For further details see European Central Bank, Report on EU Banking structure (2010) and ABI-PROMETEIA (2006).

4
Consolidation and Governance of Italian Banks

Andrea Landi

4.1 Introduction

During the last two decades, the Italian banking system has undergone profound transformations affecting all aspects of banks' ownership structures, their size and geographical coverage, and the assortment of products and services they offer, as well as introducing more advanced techniques for the management of their operations and relative risks.

Similar in many respects to those that have taken place in the other main developed countries, these changes have mainly been the outcome of the modifications to the legal framework, which began in the 1980s and led to the sweeping privatisation and deregulation of credit and financial activities, with the gradual breakdown of geographical and specialisation barriers.

The opening up of local and national markets to competition has been accompanied by the increasing integration, in the same operating context, of the main areas of financial business (commercial banking, capital market activities, and insurance), encouraging and extending the progress achieved in the fields of information technology (IT) and communication technology. The large investments made in IT systems have created new opportunities for innovation in banks' products, distribution channels, and management techniques. The scale of these investments has in turn led to increases in the size and degree of diversification considered necessary for a bank to achieve greater efficiency and higher returns on capital.

This chapter will describe the consolidation of the Italian banking system over the last two decades (Section 4.2). During this period, changes to the relevant legislation and the regulatory framework, together with the privatisation process, have generated a strengthening of the banks' role within the Italian financial system, as they have led to the creation of large banking groups capable of competing on a national and international scale and supporting the economic system – enterprises and households – with a wider, more up-to-date offering of financial services. At the same time, the organisational models and procedures adopted within these aggregation processes have made it possible to conserve and exploit the territorial bonds of the local banks targeted by the merger and acquisition operations.

This territorial connotation of the operation of Italian banks is reflected in their ownership structures and legal forms. On the one hand, the banking foundations (discussed in detail in Section 4.3) are major shareholders in the large banks, while on the other, the system of mutual banks continues to play an important role in serving a clientele of households and small and medium-sized enterprises (SMEs) (Section 4.4).

4.2 Consolidation in the banking system

In Italy, change within the banking system received a decisive boost from the privatisation of the publicly owned banks, which began in the early 1990s. The transformation of the savings banks and public banking institutions into limited companies led to initial forms of ownership that influenced the consolidation processes of the large banking groups, as well as the types of governance adopted. As shown below, the birth of the banking foundations paved the way to the privatisation of a large slice of the country's banking system while ensuring that the new shareholders would include long-term institutional investors capable of supporting the consolidation and reinforcement of the private banking groups.

The most visible effects of the transformation of the Italian system are the increase in banks' size and the correlated concentration of ownership in the banking and financial services market. Within two decades, the number of banks operating on the Italian market was reduced by about one-third, from 1156 in 1990 to 760 in 2010. As Table 4.1 shows, consolidation amongst Italian banks accelerated significantly during the first decade, when the privatisation of the public banks marked the start of a phase of system-wide consolidation, leading to the formation of a number of large banking groups.

One fundamental feature of the banking consolidation process during these years was the change in ownership in the banking system in southern Italy. The recession of 1990–91, and the subsequent cutback in public support for the economy in the south of the country, aggravated

Table 4.1 Number of banking institutions and M&A operations, 1990–2010

Year	Number of banks	of which banche popolari	of which mutual banks	Mergers	Acquisitions
1990	1156		715	19	4
1991	1108		708	33	5
1992	1073		700	20	1
1993	1037		671	38	6
1994	994		643	42	10
1995	970		619	47	19
1996	937		591	37	19
1997	935		583	24	18
1998	921	56	562	27	23
1999	876	49	531	36	28
2000	841	44	499	33	25
2001	830	44	474	31	9
2002	814	40	461	18	11
2003	788	38	445	20	9
2004	778	37	439	10	7
2005	784	36	439	4	7
2006	793	38	436	6	4
2007	806	38	440		
2008	799	38	432		
2009	788	38	421		
2010	760	37	415		

Source: Processing of Banca d'Italia, Annual Report, various issues.

firms' already fragile financial structures, exposing the inefficiencies in the management of most of the southern banks.

Encouraged by the supervisory authorities, the banks of central-northern Italy undertook a major rescue operation of the southern system, acquiring ownership of the main banks operating in the south of the country. Large southern banks such as Banco di Napoli and Banco di Sicilia entered the orbits of the northern banking groups, which by means of these acquisitions not only restored normal operation on the financial circuit in the south of the country but also consolidated their own coverage of the entire country. This laid the foundations for the formation of a smaller core of large banking groups with territorial roots, capable of competing in terms of size and efficiency with their main international competitors.

In 1996–2001 alone, consolidation operations in the south of Italy involved banks handling almost three-fourths of the regions' banking business, while the number of non-mutual banks fell from 83 in 1996 to 48 in 2001, more than half of them (26) belonging to large banking groups based in the centre-north of the country. While emphasising this major transfer of ownership, Panetta (2003) reveals that, in spite of the reduction in the number of banks, and especially the reduction of independent intermediaries, the availability of banking services in the south of the country actually increased. Other studies have given a less positive assessment of the M&A processes involving the southern Italian banks. Bongini and Ferri (2005) and Mattesini and Messori (2004) highlight the continued difficulties of banks based in the centre and north of the country in delivering services to firms in the south, due to a reduction in relationship lending. Alessandrini and Zazzaro (2007) attribute these difficulties to the distances between the northern banks' decision-making centres and firms located in the south.

The years from 2005 to 2010 witnessed a second round of banking consolidation, further reinforcing the market position of the main Italian banks to the point where they were amongst the largest in Europe. The Intesa Sanpaolo Group, formed by the merger of Banca Intesa and the San Paolo IMI Group, became operational on 1 January 2007. The incorporation of Capitalia into UniCredit, which took place in the same year, reinforced the group's geographical coverage of the country and marked a further concentration of the national banking market. In 2008 Monte dei Paschi di Siena, Italy's third-largest banking group by total assets, grew further, by acquiring Antonveneta.

During these years, the main "banche popolari" were also involved in the consolidation process: the merger in 2008 of Banco Popolare di Verona e Novara and Banca Popolare Italiana created Banco Popolare, the fourth-largest banking group in terms of size, while 2007 saw the creation of UBI Banca – Unione di Banche Italiane, by the merger of BPU – Banche Popolari Unite – and Banca Lombarda e Piemontese.

At the end of 2010, the two largest banking groups (UniCredit and Intesa Sanpaolo) held a 32.9 per cent share (in terms of total assets) of the Italian banking market, while the other three medium-large banks (Banca Monte dei Paschi di Siena, Banco Popolare, and Unione di Banche Italiane) held 18.9 per cent of the market's assets (Banca d'Italia 2011a). Concentration measurements based on the Gini index support the evidence that the consolidation processes reinforced the banking group size distribution queues. Alongside this greater concentration in the large group band, Cerasi and Crosato (2009) report new intermediaries in the smaller size categories, with probable positive effects in terms of competition on the local markets.

The market share comparison of banking groups between 2001 and 2010 (see Table 4.2) demonstrates that the consolidation process within the Italian system was led mainly by the two largest banking groups, which succeeded in establishing themselves as major European players in the course of a single decade. The sharp increase in their combined share of the domestic market (from 24.7 per cent in 2001 to 32.9 per cent in 2010) resulted in increased geographical coverage of the loans and savings market, in line with a strategy that aimed to reap the benefits of size while continuing to occupy the role of bank of reference on the local markets.

Several studies[1] have analysed the effects of banking sector merger and acquisition (M&A) operations on the loans granted to the small and medium-sized enterprises typical of the local markets. The weight of evidence indicates that credit rationing did occur as a result of the consolidation, although in the medium term the reduction in lending proves to be temporary and to be compensated through substitution by competitor banks.

The two largest Italian banking groups stand out even on the international scene for their efficacy in fulfilling the role of commercial bank; they are well placed on the credit circuits and have a good balance between loans and funds raised from customers. Considering the ratio between loans and funds raised from customers as of June 2011, both UniCredit and Intesa Sanpaolo achieve levels amongst the highest recorded by the top 20 European banks, with values of 95 per cent and 90.4 per cent, respectively, compared to an average for the other main European banks of 77.8 per cent (Table 4.3).

These are characteristics of large banking groups, formed through the gradual consolidation of institutions with strong geographical roots, which explain the Italian banking system's ability to absorb the repercussions of the financial crisis of 2008 through 2011. Italian banks' recourse to public capital and guarantees has been particularly low

Table 4.2 Market shares of Italian banking groups and banks (% of total assets)

	2001	2010
Two largest groups	24.7	32.9
Three medium-large groups	21.8	18.9
Medium-small groups and banks	40.6	36.9
Small groups and banks	12.9	11.3

Source: Processing of Banca d'Italia, Annual Report, various issues.

Table 4.3 Indicators for the main European banks, (%)

Bank	Loans/funding from clientele June 2011	Trading earnings/Total earnings, 2010	Bad loans/ earnings, 2010	Doubtful loans/loans June 2011
Credit Suisse	54.1	32.8	0.3	0.3
UBS	58.8	23.7	-0.2	0.6
Barclays	73.0	26.5	-18.4	2.1
HSBC	62.9	8.3	-19.6	1.7
Lloyds	78.7	11.7	-44.0	6.1
RBS	72.0	17.7	-35.9	4.0
BNP	78.7	11.6	-10.9	0.9
Crédit Agricole	85.8	11.3	-21.3	1.2
Soc. Générale	72.8	20.2	-15.7	2.3
Dexia	73.6	-2.0	12.8	0.6
ING	98.1	6.6	-10.4	1.3
Rabobank	88.9	1.8	-9.8	1.2
Commerzbank	80.0	-0.9	-30.1	1.1
Deutsche Bank	59.5	14.4	-9.7	0.7
Danske Bank	94.5	15.5	-19.8	3.8
Nordea	93.8	12.0	-4.6	1.4
Banco Santander	84.9	6.2	-24.4	1.8
BBVA	91.0	5.4	-22.7	1.3
Intesa Sanpaolo	90.4	1.4	-16.7	4.7
UniCredit	95.7	1.3	-25.9	5.7

Source: Processing of Mediobanca R&S (2011c), IMF World Economic Outlook Data Base, September 2011.

compared with that of their European and American competitors (see Figure 4.1). The explanation for the small scale of government intervention is to be sought in Italian banks' lower level of exposure to the performance of the financial markets, arising from the banks' lack of diversification into investment banking. The low percentage of earnings from trading on total financial earnings proves this hypothesis (Table 4.3). Although the Italian banking model of operation, that focusses the activity on supporting the national savings and loans circuit, delivers more constant economic results, it leaves UniCredit and Intesa Sanpaolo vulnerable to the worsening economic crisis and its effects on the balance sheets

The consolidation processes involving the large banking groups did not produce significant changes in their ownership. At the end of 2010, all holdings of more than 2 per cent in the ordinary shares of the two largest groups were in the hands of financial intermediaries, banking foundations, insurance companies, and non-financial corporations.

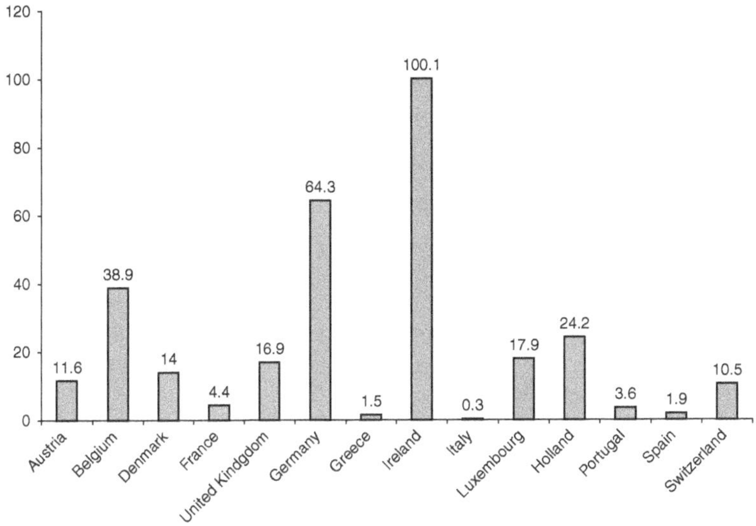

Figure 4.1 Public intervention in support of banks, 2008–10, per cent of GDP
Source: Processing of Mediobanca R&S (2011a).

4.3 The role of the foundations in banks' ownership structures

The foundations bring stability to banks' ownership structures and are seen as long-term Italian investors capable of fighting off growing foreign penetration.

Italian Law no. 218 of 30 July 1990 (the Amato law) and the implementing decrees split off the publicly owned banks' credit operations and assigned them to private limited companies, regulated by the Italian Civil Code and banking legislation, like other banks working in the credit sector. At the same time the non-profit operations that public banks carried out alongside their credit activities and that, it is important to remember, were the *raison d'être* of the savings banks (Casse di Risparmio and Banche del Monte), were assigned to new entities, the foundations.

The banking foundations are private non-profit institutions that obtain the resources for their projects of social utility from the management of assets, which consisted, at the time of their creation, of holdings in the capital of the main Italian banks. Although they have diversified the financial assets under their management – prompted by a regulatory framework that encourages an attenuation of their degree of control[2] – they are still major shareholders in the Italian banks and continue to play a key role in the banking system's strategic decisions.

The changes in the bank equity holdings of the 88 foundations during the last two decades have brought about the situation depicted in Table 4.4, as of December 2010.

As the table reveals, the system of foundations continues to play an important role in banks' ownership structures, since the majority of them (49 out of 88) hold more than 5 per cent of the equity of their banks of origin. It should also be remembered that even holdings of less than 5 per cent are of considerable weight in banks' governance when their owners operate as members of coalitions with other shareholders. This is particularly clear in the case of the two largest banking groups, since the cumulative holdings of the most important banking foundations are of a size capable of significantly affecting the governance of the banks concerned (see Table 4.5).

Table 4.4 Foundations' holdings in the capital of their banks of origin, 2010

Foundations with holding in their banks of origin >50%	15
Foundations without holdings	18
Foundations with holdings of less than 50%	55
Of which	
Holdings below 5%	21
Holdings between 5% and 20%	14
Holdings between 20% and 50%	20
Total foundations	88

Source: Processing of ACRI (2011) XVI Annual Report.

4.4 The cooperative and mutual banks

As in other financial systems, in Italy the cooperative credit sector has retained an important role in the provision of financial services, traditionally targeting a customer base of retail investors and small and medium-sized enterprises. These intermediaries' strong roots in their local markets have not prevented a gradual trend towards the formation of larger-sized banking groups, capable of competing at the national level with the main non-mutual banks, however.

This sector subdivides into two main categories, which have gradually increased their level of differentiation over time, especially with regard to the extent of services to shareholders: banche popolari (cooperative banks) and mutual banks.

Table 4.5 Foundation shareholders of the three largest Italian banking groups, 2010

Banking group	holding (%)
UniCredit	
FCR Verona	4.43
FCR Torino	3.49
Carimonte	3.15
7 other foundations	3.71
Intesa Sanpaolo	
Compagnia di San Paolo	9.72
Cariplo	4.95
FCR Padova e Rovigo	4.84
Ente CR Firenze	3.32
FCR Bologna	2.02
Monte dei Paschi di Siena	
Fondazione MPS	45.68

[a]Holdings of largest shareholders, % in excess of 2%.

Source: Processing of financial statement data of individual banks.

Banche popolari are cooperatives incorporated as limited companies. From the legal point of view, their characteristics are:[3]

- They share capital that is variable and can therefore be increased as a routine measure through the issue of new shares.
- There is just one vote per shareholder, regardless of the number of shares owned.
- No single shareholder is permitted to own more than 0.5 per cent of the share capital and the bank's approval is required for all new shareholders.[4]

From the operational point of view, during the period studied these banks' concentration on mutual credit activities, originally intended to provide their shareholders with financial support, has gradually diminished. Nowadays, the banche popolari are similar in all respects to the private banks with regard to their management of their intermediation business, targeting a wide, diversified clientele of households and firms, mainly medium and small-sized enterprises, regardless of whether or not they hold shares in the bank.

Therefore, the specific connotations of cooperative legal status have not prevented them from expanding the scale of their intermediation activities and increasing their weight within the banking system.

Tarantola (2009) notes that the banche popolari segment has contributed to consolidation within the banking system, with a number of banks in this category undertaking major expansion plans and acquiring banks, former savings banks, cooperative banks, and specialised intermediaries. At present, of the 16 groups headed by banche popolari, two are amongst Italy's five largest by total assets and eight are listed or have at least one listed member. At the end of 2010, the loans and deposits handled by the banche popolari amounted to 8.7 per cent and 9.5 per cent of the Italian total figures, respectively. These values underestimate the category's true weight, since they do not include the business of the non-mutual banks belonging to banking groups headed by a banca popolare. If all the banks within the relevant banking groups are considered, the loans provided and funds collected by the banche popolari increase to 21.6 per cent and 25.2 per cent, respectively.[5]

Mutual banks (Banche di Credito Cooperativo), the second category of the Italian cooperative credit sector, have many legal and operational features in common with the banche popolari, but contrast with them in retaining strong mutual connotations. This implies that they are obliged to comply with tighter operating constraints, since most of their lending is required to be to their shareholders. Moreover, the relevant legislation[6] underlines their local character and requires the shareholders to be continually resident in the geographical area where the bank operates, empowering the Bank of Italy to define the relevant districts, which must be specified in the banks' articles of association.

The mutual banks also differ from the banche popolari in their membership in a network comprising 15 local federations and in the national federation, which supports the local banks by providing a number of centralised services, ranging from assistance in liquidity management, internal audits, and compliance through to aspects of governance and strategy.

At the end of 2010, there were 425 mutual banks operating in Italy, most small organisations with an average of 11 branches and 76 employees, serving markets mainly limited to the individual province or to just a few municipal areas, where in many cases they are still the only banks capable of delivering services to a clientele of households and small family concerns. Their market share, expressed in terms of loans and deposits, amounts to 7 per cent and 6.6 per cent, respectively. However, their share of the market of small enterprises employing fewer than 20 people is much higher, at 19 per cent, demonstrating the strength of their local roots and their capacity for assisting what are financially the weakest members of the business world.

One feature of mutual banks' operations that has received particular attention in studies of competition in banking markets is their tendency to replace other categories of bank in the provision of credit to businesses. Their role in supporting the economy is reflected by the expansion of their lending activity, with figures systematically higher than that of the banking system as a whole in recent years. Between 1995 and 2010 the mutual banks' share of the market of loans to medium-large enterprises rose from 2 to 7 per cent.[7] This increase continued even in the most recent years, when the financial and economic crisis made risk levels on the credit market more problematical.

4.5 Conclusions

The Italian banking system has undergone a profound transformation during the last 20 years. Until the privatisations of the early 1990s, the system had remained basically unchanged since the 1930s, and the reforms introduced by the 1936 banking law, with a structure based around publicly owned banks (public banks and savings banks) that operated within narrow geographical areas and with traditional financial management models. The Amato law, and the implementation of the main European Commission directives by the "Testo Unico Bancario" marked the start of major consolidation processes, which have led to the formation of a number of large banking groups; their size and international outlook, achieved through numerous merger and acquisition operations, mean that they are now amongst Europe's main players.

The large Italian groups derive their specific operational features from this "bottom-up" consolidation process, which originated in a succession of M&A operations amongst mainly local banks. They still operate mainly on a traditional commercial banking model, in which earnings are generated to a large extent by the loans and deposits circuit, which helps, through improved efficiency in the management of risks and financial and liquidity flows, to improve the allocation of resources within the economic system. This characteristic partly explains the large Italian banks' resilience during the period of financial crisis that began in 2008.

Various features of the banks' governance are also closely linked to the type of consolidation procedure by which they were created. We have underlined the way in which the birth of the banking foundations helped to transform the banks and enabled them to combine larger size geographical links and relative stability in their ownership structures and governance. During the most recent years, the financial and economic crisis has been putting the corporate governance of the large Italian banks to the test, as they attempt major recapitalisation operations without recourse to public aid. It is probable that in the future the weight of the core of historic shareholders, first and foremost among them the foundations, will decrease, as institutional investors and sovereign funds acquire larger holdings in the banks' capital. This would complete the transformation of the banking system, creating banks with a more varied ownership structure, capable of attracting investment on the capital markets, thanks to efficient management and their ability to generate value for their shareholders.

When reconstructing the changes that have taken place during the last 20 years, it is important not to overlook the role of the cooperative banks and their success in adapting to the new competitive environment. The banche popolari category most clearly reflects the tension between local origins and the need to achieve larger size and more efficient levels of service. The greater contact with the capital markets arising from the listing of a number of large banks in this segment undoubtedly poses the problem of how to adapt their mutual-style governance to the need to reward and represent investors. A number of recent white papers and the opinions expressed by the supervisory authorities tend towards a slackening of the constraints deriving from these banks' mutual origins, adapting their cooperative legal status to the needs of their current operational models (Tarantola 2009, 2011).

For the mutual banks, links to specific geographical markets are expected to continue to be central to their business, especially in view of the difficulties encountered during the last few years in reconciling growth in size, achieved mainly by serving new types of customers, with the maintenance of satisfactory returns and capitalisation.

Notes

1. See Focarelli, Panetta, and Salleo (2002) ; Sapienza (2002); Beretta and Del Prete (2007); Bonaccorsi di Patti and Gobbi (2007).
2. The provisions of the "Ciampi" law, introduced in 1998, included an obligation on the foundations to dispose of their majority holdings in the banks' capital. Subsequently, a waiver of this obligation was introduced for foundations with assets of less than €200 million and those based in autonomous regions with special statute only.
3. For the legal and regulatory characteristics of the banche popolari, including a European comparison, see De Angeli (2010).
4. See Decreto legislativo 385/1993 Testo Unico Bancario (Consolidation Law on Banking), pp. 47–9.
5. The figures, provided by Tarantola (2009), refer to the end of 2008. At that date, the market shares for loans and deposits for banche popolari alone (not including their subsidiary non-mutual banks) were 7 per cent and 7.7 per cent respectively.
6. See Decreto legislativo 385/1993 Testo Unico Bancario (Consolidated Law on Banking) 1983, pp. 49–51.
7. See Tarantola (2011).

5
Performance and Efficiency of the Italian Banking System

Riccardo Ferretti, Marzia Torresetti, and Paola Vezzani

5.1 Introduction

This chapter describes the Italian banking system's main performance figures between 1999 and 2010. This was a period of several international crises, which also had domestic impacts. The first crisis, in the late 1990s, was due to the market collapse in a number of Asian countries and Russia, followed by the failure of a leading investment fund, Long-Term Capital Management (LTCM). The second crisis, during 2000–01, was triggered by the bursting of the dot.com bubble. Finally, the current financial crisis began in mid-2007 and caused a general recession across the economy, which is still struggling to recover even as of this writing, at the end of 2011, although conditions vary from country to country.

In all these crises, the banking systems of the industrialised countries acted and reacted in different ways. An analysis of the performance of the Italian banking system, comparing it, where possible, with those of other countries, may therefore yield interesting results.

During the last few years, the Italian banking system has been undergoing significant changes with regard to its ownership structures, organisational models, scale of operation, risk management techniques, efficiency, and more. These changes, also occurring in many other advanced economies, considerably affect the evolution of banks' performance.

This chapter is organised as follows. Section 5.2 describes the economic and financial performance of the Italian banking system, providing a short international comparison for the five largest banking groups and then, in greater detail, examining trends (in terms of profitability, efficiency, risk level, and solvency) from a strictly domestic viewpoint.

The latter analysis also examines the main features of banks within the Italian system with regard to size and legal form. We then move on in Section 5.3 to illustrate the Italian banking system's stock market performance, again by means of an international comparison and by focusing on the main national figures. Both parts study the period from 1999 to 2010. The chapter concludes with a final comparison (Section 5.4), which attempts to link market performance with economic and financial results.

5.2 Economic and financial performance

The economic and financial crisis has had deep repercussions on the entire international banking system, some only temporary, but others generating structural changes.

From the onset of the crisis, the major differences in its impact on the different banking systems were immediately clear. These can be attributed to differences in size and degree of internationalisation. The difference in impact of the crisis can be explained in more general terms on the basis of the wide variation in the main intrinsic characteristics of the different banking systems and of the leading banks operating within them. For example, in the early stages of the crisis, when many of the largest international banks were suffering huge losses due to write-downs of financial assets, the adverse effects on the Italian groups were much lighter. The reasons for these and other factors that distinguish the Italian banking groups from the other European groups can be understood more clearly if we identify the effects of the different business models on balance sheet structures, and thus on the breakdown of banks' sources of earnings.

A comparison between Italy's largest groups and their European counterparts

Before taking a detailed look at the trend in Italian banking industry performance over the last decade, we will first briefly highlight the differences that are emerging between the country's five largest banking groups—UniCredit (UNIC), Intesa Sanpaolo (BISP), Banca Monte dei Paschi di Siena (MPAS), Unione Banche Italiane (BUBI), and Banco Popolare (BPOP)—and the leading European groups, Banco Santander (SANT), Banco Bilbao Vizcaya Argentaria (BBVA), BNP Paribas (BNP), Crédit Agricole (CA), Barclays (BARC), Hongkong & Shanghai Banking Corporation (HSBC), Lloyds Banking Group (LLOY), Royal Bank of Scotland (RBS), Deutsche Bank (DEUT), Commerzbank (COMM), Société Générale (SOGEN) and

Kredietbank ABB Insurance CERA Bank (KBC). This comparison is made by offering a survey of the situation at the end of 2010. A short comparison across time will be provided for earnings only.

The first aim is to investigate the extent to which the largest Italian banking groups are comparable in size to their biggest European competitors, by looking at their total assets and loans to customer volumes: only UniCredit and Intesa Sanpaolo can really be compared with other European groups, and this is more with regard to volume of loans to customers than to total assets, a value where there is still a considerable difference from most of Europe's largest groups (Figure 5.1).

The reason that Italian groups have total balance sheet assets sharply below those of many European competitors is partly from their smaller size and partly from their more strictly commercial nature, with loans to customers exceeding financial investments. It is worth noting that loans to customers absorb much higher levels of capital than investments.

Amongst the European banks, the Spanish banks Banco Santander and BBVA are similar in size and types of business at least to the largest Italian groups UniCredit and Intesa Sanpaolo in terms of volumes handled and, above all, asset structure. The largest differences are with banks such as Deutsche Bank, Barclays, and Société Générale, which are more oriented towards financial investments, which absorb much less capital, and thus permit a higher degree of financial leverage in the bank's business.

To be specific, for Italian banks, retail lending amounted to more than 60 per cent of total assets, rising to 70 per cent for UBI and Banco

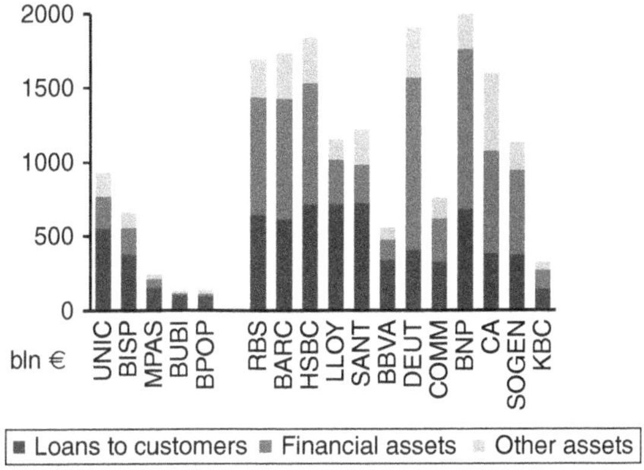

Figure 5.1 Total assets in billions of euros for main Italian and European banks, 2010: end-of-year values

Popolare, and financial investments did not exceed 25 per cent, falling to just 10 per cent for UBI and Banco Popolare. As already mentioned, similar values to those of the three biggest Italian banks (UNIC, BISP and MPAS) applied to the Spanish Banco Santander and BBVA groups, as well as to the United Kingdom's Lloyds Group. Conversely, among European competitors Deutsche Bank and Crédit Agricole had the lowest levels of loans to customers (20–25 per cent of the total), but the figure did not exceed 45 per cent for the other European groups. For BNP, Crédit Agricole, Barclays, HSBC, Royal Bank of Scotland, Deutsche Bank, Commerzbank, Société Générale and KBC the proportion invested in financial assets (including the value of trading derivatives) accounted for half total assets, or was well above that figure, as in the case of Deutsche Bank, where it was 61 per cent in 2010 (Figure 5.2).

This specific structure of Italian banks' balance sheets during the time period studied involved risks that should not be underestimated, especially when the borrower customers were companies. In spite of the current improvements, companies are continuing to feel the effects of the crisis, and the strains that emerged during 2010 have spread throughout the production system, due to the drastic lengthening of loans payment times on business deals.

The second focus of the international comparison, is to analyse some figures regarding profitability among the same European

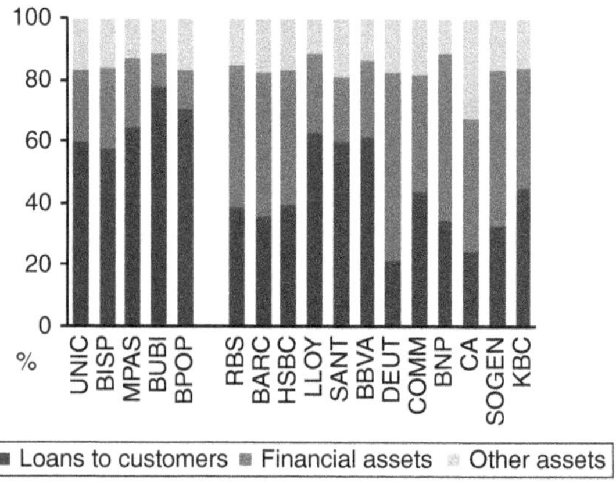

Figure 5.2 Total assets in billions of euros for main Italian and European banks, 2010: end-of-year values

Source: Processing of Prometeia analysis on annual reports data.

banking groups (Figures 5.3 and 5.4). The differences in balance sheet asset (and liability) structures lead to variations in the sources of earnings in banks' profit-and-loss accounts in different ways. In the case of the most retail-oriented groups, such as those in Italy and Spain, interest and commissions on services to customers predominated, together comprising more than 80 per cent of total earnings (Figure 5.3).

On the other hand, in groups where balance sheet assets consist mainly of securities, such as Barclays and Deutsche Bank, the lion's share of earnings derives from trading and fair value valuation of financial assets and liabilities. This is a highly volatile form of earnings, which may turn negative in the event of huge drops in the market value of securities, as occurred in 2008 for most of Europe's largest banking groups, while earnings from financial trading soar when the financial markets are growing strongly.

The Italian groups' performance

To build up a suitable sample for the long-term interpretation of banking performance, we decided to analyse the data (consolidated financial statements) of a sample of banking groups as follows:

- an open sample, to allow for the many company deletions and registrations during the period of time studied (1999–2010) as a result of merger and acquisition processes

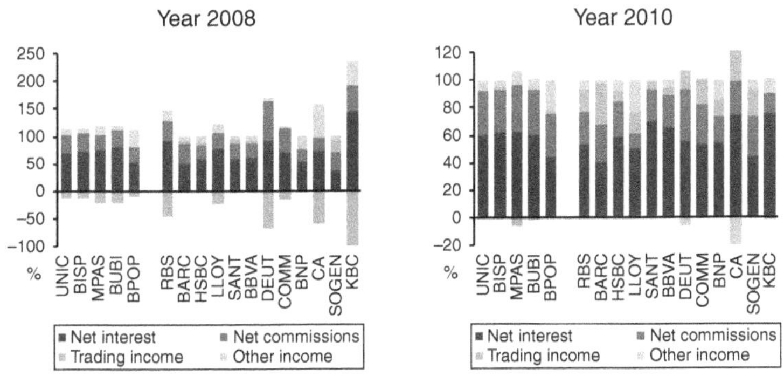

Figure 5.3 Gross operating income of main Italian and European banks: composition, 2008 and 2010

Source: Processing of Prometeia analysis on annual reports data.

- a highly representative sample in terms of size in relation to the system overall (more than 90 per cent of Italian banking groups' total assets);
- a homogeneous sample with regard to type of business, since Italian banking groups considered engage mainly in commercial banking.

Where this is considered relevant, the analysis will include reference to the banks' characterisation by size[1] (banks' data organised into big, medium and small groups) and by legal form (commercial Ltd. or cooperative).

Profitability analysis

During 1999–2010 the average return on equity of Italian banks was 7.3 per cent, with a minimum value of 3.4 per cent recorded in 2010, when profit levels dropped to levels much lower than at the beginning of the period (Figure 5.4). The slump in returns during the last three years (2008–2010) was not due only to the deterioration in trading results and the sharp increase in depreciations and write-downs necessary because of the crisis, but also to direct capital reinforcement operations, which increased the denominator of our ratio (return on equity). In general, the profitability of the banking sector mirrors the performance of the real economy fairly closely, achieving the highest returns at times of strongest economic growth. It is therefore no surprise that in 2005–06 profits were much higher, at 10.6 per cent. However, the average values concealed the spread of the sample data, which was actually very wide.

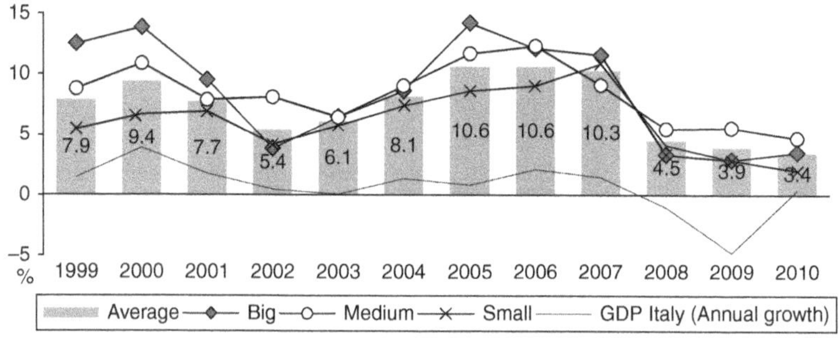

Figure 5.4 Return on equity: average value (by banking peer size group) and gross domestic product annual growth, banks in Italy 1999–2010

Source: Processing of Prometeia analysis on annual reports data.

Although it confirms the general finding, the breakdown of levels of return by banking group size shows a number of differences.

Big banking groups (henceforth "big groups") achieve their best performances at times of economic growth, when the diversification of their retail and institutional customers generates additional returns due, to a large extent, to business units within the group's consolidation perimeter operating in finance, investment banking, and investment funds. Big groups recorded maximum return on equity (ROE) levels of around 14 per cent in 2005 and 2006, but they are also more seriously affected by economic downturns; the slowdown in 2001–02 was proportionally much more pronounced for big groups, since it mainly arose from a crisis in the investment fund sector and the large number of write-downs the banking system had to make as many companies faced financial difficulties.

Medium-sized banking groups have the greatest stability in returns and therefore on average they produce the best performance, without the increase in risk levels found in big and small groups. Small groups show the lowest performance over the medium and long term, since they benefit less than other banks during periods of growth while they are badly hit during downturns.

Switching from considering banking group size to legal form, it clearly emerges that the best performances were recorded by the listed banking groups, with the sole exception of 2009, when the two categories (listed and not listed banking groups) were more or less aligned. Moreover, except for the last two years, commercial Ltd. banks showed a higher return on equity than cooperative banks showed (Figure 5.5).

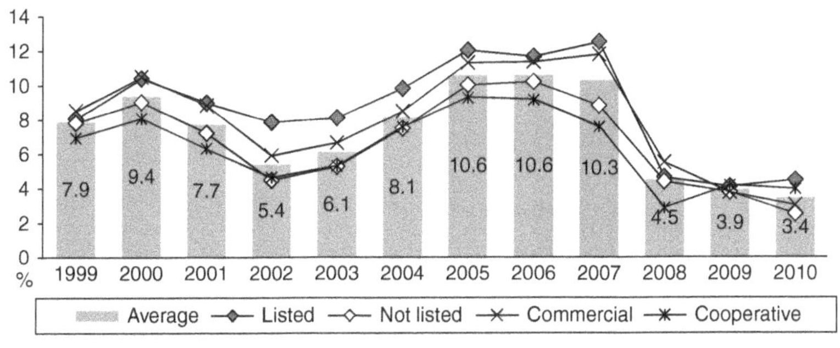

Figure 5.5 Return on equity: average value (listed v. not listed, commercial v. cooperative banks, banks in Italy 1999–2010)

Source: Processing of Prometeia analysis on annual reports data.

Analysis of earnings

The analysis of operating income in relation to total assets reveals the standard breakdown of earnings between interest on lending operations, commissions, and brokerage fees, and the revenue generated by securities trading and other income (Figure 5.6). From 1999–2010, a high proportion of earnings derived from the net interest margin, supported only in some years by an expansion in loans to customers and customer deposits, which more than compensated for the reduction in the spreads applied to interest rates during the period.

For the whole sample operating income as a proportion of total assets fell during the period analysed from 5.6 per cent in 2000 to 3.6 per cent at the end of 2010, with a trend of constant decline. The total reduction in bank earnings as a proportion of total assets, certainly affected by the growth in size arising from intensive M&A activity, is seen in all the main revenue areas. In 2010 the net interest margin fell to the lowest level of the entire historic series, held down by the still poor growth in bank lending and by unusual conditions with regard to the rise in the cost of funding. Commissions were highest at the start of the period, with values of about 1.7–1.9 per cent, falling to about half that level ten years later. Other revenues also decreased sharply as a percentage of total assets over the time period considered.

An analysis of the spread in mark-up and mark-down reveals that small banking groups enjoyed an advantage in terms of mark-up compared to their big and medium-sized competitors until the late 1990s and then again from 2005 to 2011; in terms of mark-down, small groups are virtually always in line with medium-sized groups and always at

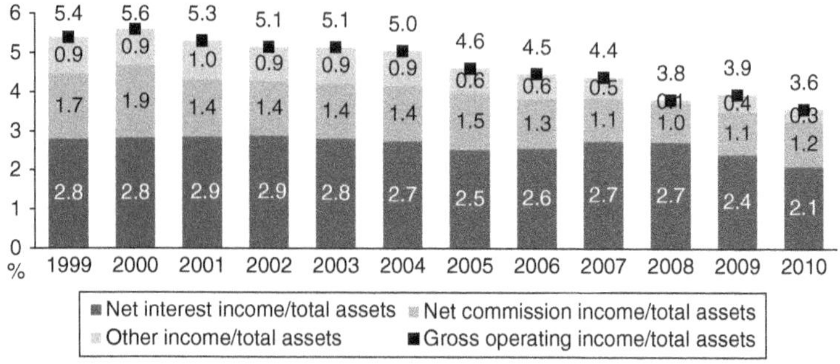

Figure 5.6 Gross operating income/total assets: composition, banks in Italy 1999–2010

Source: Processing of Prometeia analysis on annual reports data.

higher levels than big groups, which constantly have a lower spread, derived above all from the higher cost of funding (Figures 5.7 and 5.8).

If we switch from the aggregate data on commissions to their breakdown, a number of underlying trends emerge (Figure 5.9). Commissions on management and related activities predominated until 2008, even though they fell constantly throughout the decade; they were followed, as a percentage of total assets, by other commissions. During 2009–10, traditional commissions (mainly commissions on guarantees issued and commissions on collections/payments) as a percentage of total assets

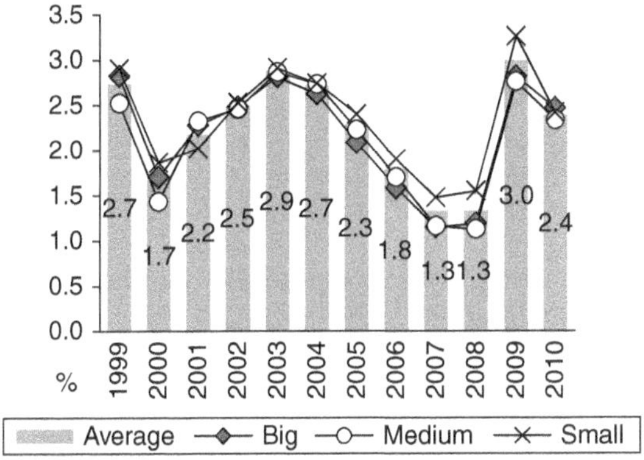

Figure 5.7 Customer mark-up, average value (peer size banking group), Italy 1999–2010

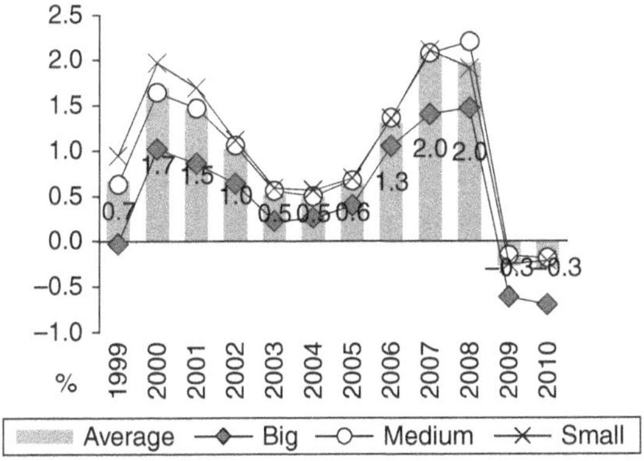

Figure 5.8 Customer mark-down, average value (peer size banking group), Italy 1999–2010

Source: Processing of Prometeia analysis on annual reports data.

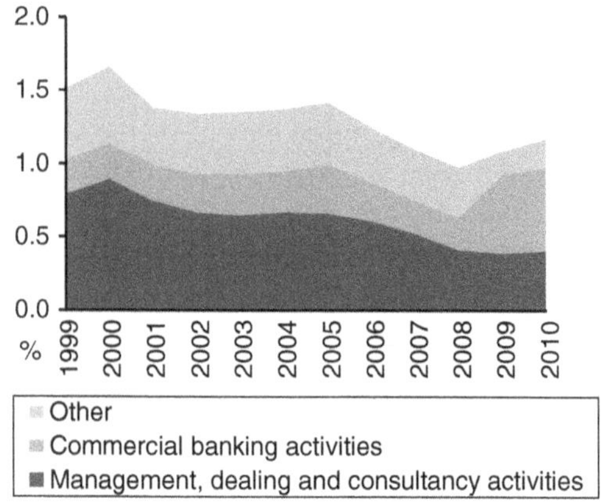

Figure 5.9 Composition of net commissions/total assets, banks in Italy 1999–2010

rose strongly, due to the introduction of the "commission for provision of funds," which replaced the "maximum overdraft commission" previously included in the interest margin.

The average figures for earnings from net commissions for peer banking groups by size reveal relatively little difference between the group averages at either end of the period, except for 2010. However, from 2000 to 2006, a period when earnings from commissions remained stable, a difference does emerge, with small groups having lower income levels and medium and big groups having a higher level of returns arising from commissions (Figure 5.10).

Efficiency analysis

Efficiency and the effective, profitable management of the production resources available has always been a crucial, essential factor for bank management, which has been forced to redefine the strategies and solutions needed to compete in increasingly complex, dynamic markets; moreover, these aspects are closely linked to the question of how to assess management performance.

The awareness that the weight of operating costs on value-added, and on earnings in general, will be central in establishing banks' earnings performance leads us to look at the structure of operating costs, the causes of their formation, and the relationships between profitability, productivity, and efficiency. After all, one way of ensuring a good return on equity is to reduce and control costs.

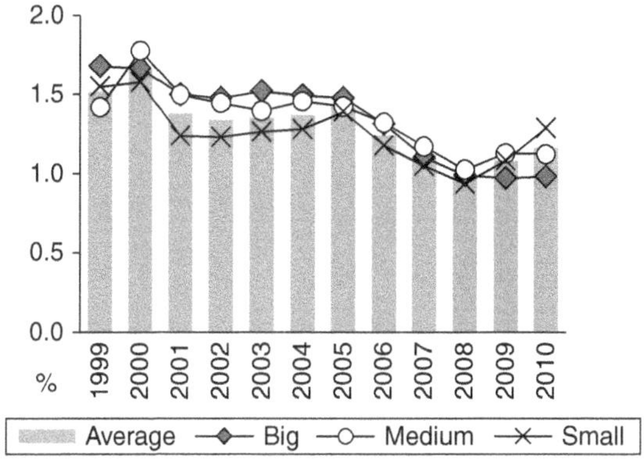

Figure 5.10 Net commissions/total assets, average value (peer size banking group), Italy 1999–2010

Source: Processing of Prometeia analysis on annual reports data.

Various factors have contributed to an improvement in banking efficiency since the late 1990s, especially the reorganisation of banking operations and the expansion in sources of earnings. In general, the sample's cost/income ratio (Figure 5.11) shows a downward trend over the long term from 1999 to 2007. It varies from a minimum of 63 per cent, achieved in the periods when business and thus earnings were growing most strongly, to a maximum of 70 per cent, in the late 1990s and 2008.

An analysis of the average values for the different peer banking groups by size reveals that:

- Small groups suffered the most and for a longer period (from 1999 to 2007 if 2005 is excluded); these organisations' efforts to improve efficiency during 2008–09 were particularly impressive.
- During the period 2006-2010, the medium-size group has shown the best levels of efficiency.
- Big groups were most efficient from 1999 to 2005, but during the more recent crisis years they have seen their efficiency index fall more than those of the other categories of bank.

Another figure of importance for efficiency, which was not included in the figures, is the average branch size, which fell constantly from 13 employees per branch in 1999 to 10 per branch in 2010, partially due to the development of alternative banking channels during the period.

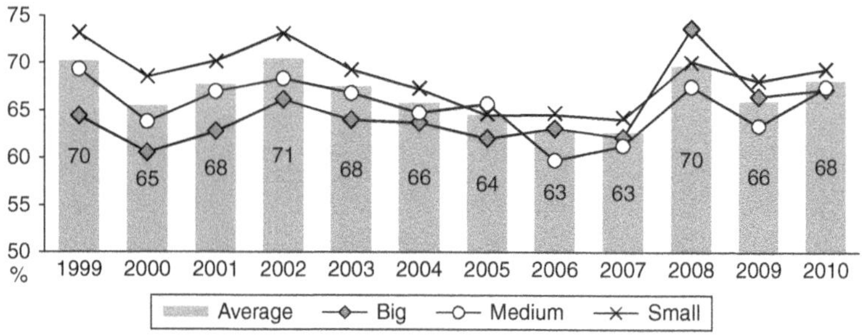

Figure 5.11 Cost/income ratio, average value (peer size banking group), Italy 1999–2010

Source: Processing of Prometeia analysis on annual reports data.

Volume of business per employee (in terms of loans to customers and customer deposits only) gradually increased, doubling over the time period considered from €4.2 million to €8.4 million per staff member.

Moreover, the improvement in network operating costs was generated both by savings on labour costs and, to an even greater extent, by reductions in administrative costs, which show gradual, constant improvement from 2002 to 2007. Big groups achieved the most sizeable reduction in staff costs, partly due to two big groups' expansion into Central and Eastern European countries, while small groups made larger savings in other administrative expenses.

Credit risk analysis

From the late 1990s to 2007, the year before the onset of the financial crisis, the quality of the lending portfolios of the banking groups in the sample steadily improved (Figure 5.12). The world financial crisis and the consequent recession led to a sharp deterioration in the finances of households and companies, triggering a growth in impaired loans and large-scale write-downs.

During the first year of the crisis, the impact on the Italian banking system was relatively mild compared to that seen in other countries. Banks' smaller holdings of the types of assets most seriously hit by the crisis, their lower level of dependency on wholesale markets, their specialisation in traditional banking operations, and a prudent regulatory and supervisory framework were the key factors underlying Italian banks' soundness. However, they were affected by the international credit squeeze and the increased perception of the riskiness of the banking business. During 2009 and 2010 in spite of an improvement in liquidity, the financial statements of banks, especially in Italy, have been adversely affected by a sharp deterioration in the quality of loans, a consequence of the recession that began in 2008. Figure 5.12 illustrates the trend in one primary risk-level indicator; we realise that many different indicators would be of use to provide a fuller picture, but they are not included for reasons of space.

In 1999 the amount of doubtful and non-performing loans as a proportion of total loans was very high at 8.6 per cent in Italy. In the years that followed, until 2002, the situation improved constantly, due to positive changes in firms' financial structures and above all due to securitisation on a huge scale.

In 2003 there was a slight deterioration in the quality of loans, reflecting the ongoing weakness of the economy and the financial difficulties of the Parmalat group companies. During 2004, the overall value of impaired loans in relation to total loans remained stable at the level of the year before (4.4 per cent); in 2005, doubtful loans (in relation to customers in temporary difficulty in repayment of loans) were largely unchanged. The year 2006 saw the continuation of the general improvement in the quality of Italian bank loans, which benefited both from the improvements in risk management and selection techniques and from firms' better financial standing.

The index (total non-impaired loans/total loans) reached its lowest point in 2007, due above all to the reduction in total non-performing loans as a percentage of total loans, which dropped from 3.8 per cent to 3.1 per cent; the level of doubtful loans remained the same, but there was a decided increase in other impaired loans. In 2008, the first

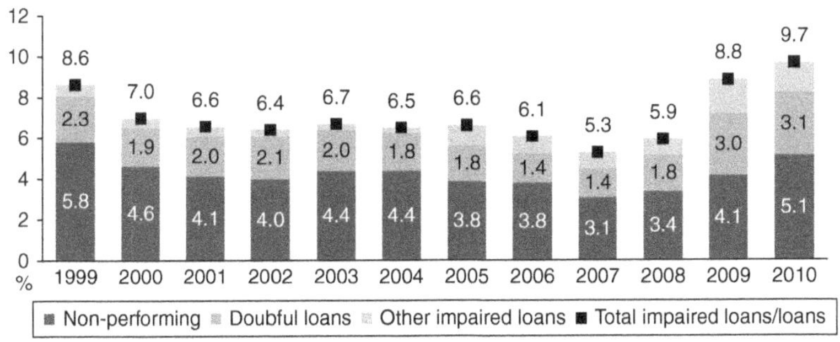

Figure 5.12 Composition of total impaired loans/total loans, banks in Italy 1999–2010

Source: Processing of Prometeia analysis on annual reports data.

repercussions of the recession on loan quality started to be felt in Italy, and the rate of doubtful loans rose from 1.4 per cent to 1.8 per cent. In 2009 the rise in the proportion of doubtful and past-due loans shows that assets were deteriorating at an increasing pace, with an increase to 3 per cent of total loans. In the same year the proportion of total impaired loans rose by almost 3 percentage points, from 5.9 per cent to 8.8 of total loans. The deterioration continued in 2010, as all the categories considered reached the highest levels of any time in the period considered.

Capital adequacy analysis

Figure 5.13 shows the Tier 1 ratio trend of the sample groups. This indicator has now acquired fundamental importance.[2] The trend over time of the overall average Tier 1 ratio shows a relatively stable situation (at around 8 per cent) from 2001 to 2007, while the figures for the late 1990s reveal higher core capital, especially for small banking groups.

From its peak in 1999, the Tier 1 ratio started to fall in the years that followed for various reasons, not least the high growth rate of loans to customers, which constantly absorbed the highest amounts of capital. In 2000, in spite of the increases in capital, the issue of subordinated liabilities and the flow of self-financing funds, the strong growth in risk-weighted assets led to a reduction in capital adequacy.

During 2005–07 the value of the Tier 1 ratio remained more or less stable, although it rose slightly during the last of these years.

In 2008, the year when the crisis was at its peak, for the groups overall, capital resources were well above the regulatory minimum levels,

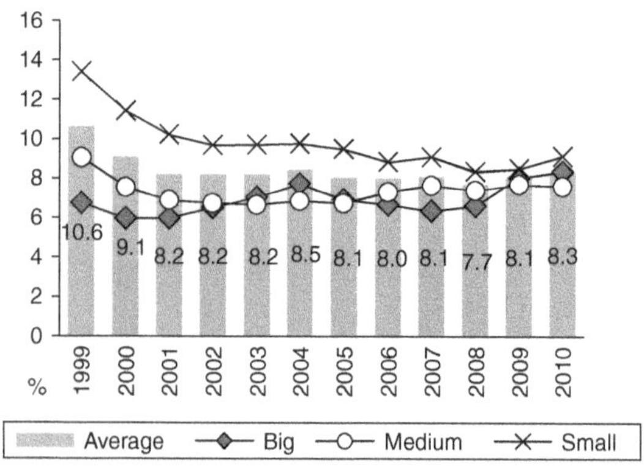

Figure 5.13 Tier 1 ratio, average value (peer size banking group), Italy 1999–2010

although for some big groups the Tier 1 ratio was below the 6 per cent target. In 2009, the capital position of the Italian banking system strengthened, especially for those banks best able to absorb losses. The forecast of tighter capital regulation and market pressures therefore led the main banks to increase their capital. The capital increases undertaken by a number of big groups, the capitalisation of a considerable proportion of profits and, for four banks, the issue of securities underwritten by the Ministry of the Economy and Finance, generated an increase in Tier 1 capital. Risk-weighted assets fell due to the reduction in loans to customers, the disposal of non-strategic assets and, to a lesser extent, the remodelling of portfolios towards assets with lower weightings. In 2010, Italian banking groups paid a great deal of attention to capital soundness, and the Tier 1 ratio increased for almost all size categories. Capital increases also continued during 2011.

Figure 5.14 shows an additional indicator that has received a growing amount of attention from regulators. The ratio between total assets and net equity measures the degree of financial leverage and thus provides an indication of banks' degree of dependency on external funding, and therefore is a very approximate assessment of their liquidity risk. Italian banks' degree of financial leverage has always been fairly low, especially compared to that of their foreign competitors, and one indicator of Italian groups' sound capitalisation is this lower level of financial leverage compared to European groups[3] (which have an average level of 24x).

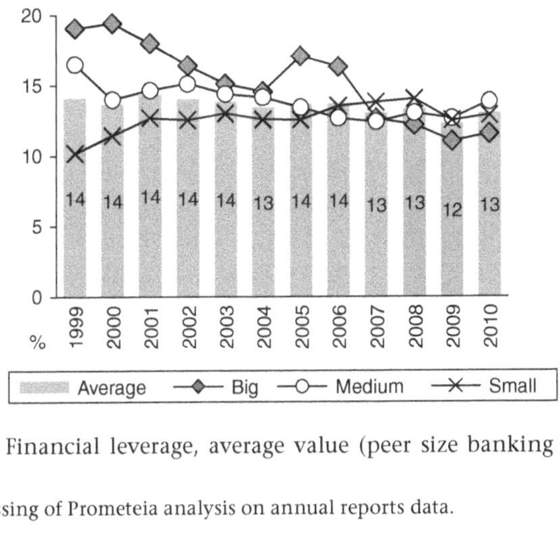

Figure 5.14 Financial leverage, average value (peer size banking group), Italy 1999–2010

Source: Processing of Prometeia analysis on annual reports data.

On average, the financial leverage of our sample varies from a minimum of 12x to 14x. The average financial leverage of small groups is 13x, and this value was very stable, especially during the period from 2001 onwards. The financial leverage of medium-sized groups has gradually decreased. Big groups have constantly worked with a level of financial leverage that in the past was significantly higher than that of the other size categories of bank group, but it has gradually moved into line with them. In 2005, further to the introduction of the International Accounting Standards/International Financial Reporting Standards (IAS/IFRS), their leverage increased more than that of the other categories, probably because their balance sheets contained a high proportion of financial assets at fair value.

5.3 The stock market performance of Italian banks

This paragraph describes the stock market performance of Italian banks. After a short introduction that discusses the weight of the banking sector within the Italian stock market, we present the risk-return profile of listed Italian banks compared to their European counterparts and analyse them in greater detail to reveal the role played by differences in size, business, and legal form.

The weight of the banking sector in the Italian stock market

The banking sector accounts for a large slice of the Italian stock market. It has continually been the largest sector in terms of capitalisation since 2005; before this, it often came second behind the utilities sector. Figure 5.15 shows the stock market performance of the banking sector in terms of relative capitalisation and number of listed firms from 1999 to 2010. On the first factor, banks constantly represented 20 to 25 per cent of total capitalisation, except for 2005–07, when this figure climbed to and exceeded 30 per cent. With regard to the second parameter, Figure 5.15 clearly shows the steady reduction in the number of listed banks, which fell from 40 at the start of the period considered to 20 in 2010; these delistings were due to the many mergers and acquisitions within the Italian banking system.

The risk-return profile of the Italian banking sector: a European comparison

In general, European banking shares did not perform well for their investors from the introduction of the euro until 2010. With the exceptions of France and Austria, the mean annual compound growth rate

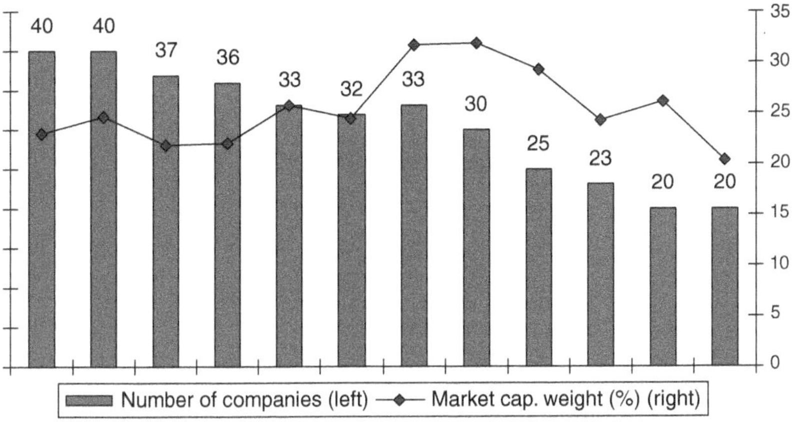

Figure 5.15 Italian listed banks: number and market capitalisation weight, 1999–2010 (end-of-year values)

Source: Italian Stock Exchange – Bit Stat (various issues).

(not including dividends) of banking sector stocks in the ten European countries included in Table 5.1 was negative. Moreover, the unsatisfactory performance in the period 1999–2010 came after four years (1995–98) of widespread growth, which tended to be more marked in the southern European countries, the United Kingdom, and Belgium. The average annual performance of Italian banking sector stocks was in third place in the four years prior to the advent of the European currency, with +32.3 per cent, behind Greece and Spain but ahead of the United Kingdom, while it was in sixth place during 1999–2010, with –6.9 per cent, directly behind Germany and ahead of Greece. Therefore, banking sector stocks in the peripheral countries, including Italy, overperformed when monetary union was still in the future and underperformed once it had actually taken place. The exceptions to this trend are Spain amongst the peripheral states and Belgium amongst the core countries, which overperformed during both phases. The only country outside the European Monetary Union (EMU) considered here, the United Kingdom, recorded performances that were similar to that of the peripheral states during the run-up to the single currency and similar to that of the core countries in the subsequent period.

The two crises, at the beginning of the millennium and more recently, can be clearly identified in the figures for the individual years from 1999 to 2010. During 2001–02, the fall in values was greater in the peripheral states, apart from Ireland, than in the core countries, except Germany.

Table 5.1 Banking sectors: stock market returns (no dividends), compound annual growth rate (CAGR) 1995–2010, and annual growth rate, 1999–2010 (percentage values)

	CAGR 1995–98	CAGR 1999–2010	1999	2000	2001	2002	2003	2004	2005	2006	2007	2008	2009	2010
Italy	32.3	−6.9	7.3	9.5	−32.6	−25.9	31.9	10.9	30.5	23.3	−13.5	−59.7	27.8	−31.3
Austria	0.6	11.8	17.9	6.1	17.6	7.5	58.8	61.4	26.6	40.7	−14.1	−71.4	70.5	26.7
Belgium	27.3	−10.1	−15.9	1.6	−15.4	−21.2	18.2	40.0	26.3	12.7	−5.6	−78.7	34.9	−22.8
France	12.6	2.7	49.1	3.6	2.5	−11.7	26.1	8.3	30.7	23.2	−18.6	−61.2	69.5	−16.5
Germany	13.2	−5.9	39.9	−5.7	−23.9	−47.0	54.2	0.8	36.0	20.0	−10.8	−71.0	56.8	−11.5
Ireland	7.9	−28.6	175.8	−84.1	3.4	0.7	12.8	21.6	19.1	26.3	−34.4	−92.3	−4.4	−61.6
Greece	51.6	−9.8	73.7	−34.2	−36.5	−42.5	65.0	38.1	31.6	21.4	19.8	−71.9	36.9	−58.3
Portugal	25.1	−11.9	11.6	4.1	−16.3	−41.3	−7.0	5.0	19.3	27.8	3.5	−65.3	7.8	−33.7
Spain	34.7	−1.8	15.8	5.5	−13.7	−29.2	30.8	7.2	18.9	26.7	−2.4	−48.7	52.2	−33.2
UK	30.1	−4.1	8.8	14.2	−2.9	−22.6	18.2	7.1	7.5	10.0	−21.3	−56.4	26.9	−0.5

Source: Processing of Thomson Financial (DJTM Price Index).

Losses during 2007–08 were heavier than in the previous crisis in all countries and were relatively more uniform; the only main differences from the mean occur in Ireland, downwards (annual average –77.5 per cent) and Spain, upwards (annual average –29.2 per cent). The trends in the peripheral and core countries started to diverge again during the following two years, with quotations bouncing back in 2009 and plunging again in 2010. While during 2009–10 Austria, France, Germany, the United Kingdom, and Belgium, in that order, achieved a positive compound annual average return (in double figures in four out of the five cases), Spain, Italy, Portugal, Greece, and Ireland, in that order, give no return or a loss in double figures in three of the five cases. During the transition from the financial crisis to the crisis involving the real economy and sovereign debt, the stock exchange performance of the Italian banking sector was the best among the peripheral countries after Spain, but it was well below the levels achieved by the core countries and the United Kingdom.

Although listed Italian banks did not perform particularly well in terms of growth in share prices, the results were much better with regard to both overall and systematic risk.

As the overall risk data illustrated in Table 5.2 reveal, Italy had one of the lowest risk levels during 1999–2010, with a standard deviation (SD) of monthly returns of 7.8 per cent; only the United Kingdom and Portugal did better, with 7.4 per cent. The risk profile of Italian banking stocks during the post-euro years was lower than that of the previous four years (9.0 per cent), as was true in most of the other peripheral states except for Ireland.

The annual data show that the volatility of Italian banking stocks was similar to that of the other countries, with the lowest levels during 2003–07 and the highest in 2002 and from 2008 to 2010, with a peak of 13.9 per cent in 2009.[4] During both phases of high volatility, the standard deviation of monthly returns of Italian banks was highly satisfactory in relative terms, placing the country in eighth position together with the United Kingdom in 2002, in last place in 2008 and eighth again in 2009. The country was mid-table in 2010 with a SD (10.4 per cent) very close to those of Germany (10.3 per cent) and Spain (10.2 per cent).

However, as we are all aware, in portfolio theory the significant risk is not the overall risk but only the systematic component. For the investors of the countries that adopted the common currency, the risk levels of the various national banking sectors are the same as their contribution to the risk level of the EMU area market portfolio. Therefore, Table 5.3 illustrates the beta index of the market model estimated by performing

Table 5.2 Banking sectors: standard deviation of monthly average returns, 1995–2010 (percentage values)

	1995–98	1999–2010	1999	2000	2001	2002	2003	2004	2005	2006	2007	2008	2009	2010
Italy	9.0	7.8	6.3	7.4	6.7	9.5	5.3	4.2	3.2	3.0	3.6	8.6	13.9	10.4
Austria	9.3	10.8	9.6	7.3	8.0	9.9	4.3	3.4	4.9	6.0	4.7	16.3	23.8	9.9
Belgium	6.3	10.2	4.9	6.1	4.5	11.0	8.3	3.8	3.1	3.7	4.7	13.8	24.4	7.0
France	8.7	8.4	6.7	6.1	6.6	12.1	6.2	2.1	4.1	3.8	5.7	11.3	13.4	10.9
Germany	8.1	10.7	9.6	6.9	10.2	13.1	11.3	4.7	3.5	4.3	5.9	13.2	19.9	10.3
Ireland	12.7	28.2	71.2	25.6	9.0	8.7	3.9	4.5	3.8	4.4	3.9	18.0	50.1	23.4
Greece	14.5	10.9	6.0	10.7	10.5	6.0	12.4	5.0	5.6	6.9	5.1	11.2	17.8	15.9
Portugal	8.0	7.4	4.2	3.0	3.4	10.1	7.3	4.4	4.0	4.6	8.8	10.4	10.4	8.1
Spain	8.4	8.0	4.5	5.6	7.3	12.0	7.6	3.4	3.7	3.8	4.0	8.9	14.1	10.2
UK	6.2	7.4	6.8	7.7	5.6	9.4	6.2	2.6	3.1	3.4	3.3	9.2	14.9	5.6

Source: Processing of Thomson Financial (DJTM Price Index).

Table 5.3 Banking sectors: EMU systematic risk, 1999–2010, market model beta on monthly returns

	1999–2001		2002–04		2005–07		2008–10	
	beta	adjR^2 (%)	beta	adjR^2 (%)	beta	adjR^2 (%)	beta	adjR^2 (%)
Italy	0.924	53.6	0.897	67.8	0.814	40.4	1.549	84.2
Austria	0.433	5.9	0.284	4.3	1.332	47.4	2.164	65.0
Belgium	0.285	6.7	1.017	59.2	1.171	70.5	1.958	57.5
France	0.641	27.7	1.083	75.5	1.310	58.1	1.514	66.7
Germany	1.225	54.7	1.397	66.9	1.301	58.7	1.809	61.0
Ireland	Ns	–	0.698	53.8	1.165	49.2	3.167	37.5
Greece	0.721	13.9	0.926	38.6	1.339	41.7	1.752	56.2
Portugal	Ns	–	0.791	40.9	1.243	31.9	1.232	69.1
Spain	0.761	50.4	1.244	85.3	0.977	50.7	1.442	71.0

Source: Processing of Thomson Financial (DJTM Price Index and MSCI EMU Price Index).

a regression analysis of the monthly returns of the national banking sector indices on the monthly returns of a stock index representing the EMU area (MSCI EMU Price Index); a fit measurement of the model is also provided (adjusted R^2). The 1999–2010 period was subdivided into four non-overlapping three-year periods, to observe the trend in non-diversifiable risk over time.

During the first three years (1999–2001), Italian banking shares showed a level of systematic risk (0.924) close to unity, and thus basically were in line with the market average. The Italian beta is only exceeded by the beta of the German banks (1.225) and shows a statistically significant difference from the values of Austria and Belgium. Italian, German and Spanish banks area also those most closely linked to the overall market trend, with an adjusted R^2 of over 50 per cent.

The situation changes during the second three years (2002–04). The Italian banking sector index continues to have a systematic risk level not statistically different from the market average; its level is in line with that of many other countries, both peripheral and core. Although Austria's systematic risk level continues to be statistically lower than that of Italy, Germany and Spain show a higher risk. Apart from Austria, there is a growth in the correlation between banking sector indices and the general index, and the Italian figure (67.8 per cent) is in line with that of Germany but behind that of France and Spain.

During the third three-year period (2005–07), the systematic risk of banking sector shares increases in all countries except Italy and Spain. The Italian figure (0.814) is actually the lowest of all, although statistically it is only lower than France, Germany, and Greece. This is the only period during which the correlation between the Italian banking sector index and the general index falls below 50 per cent (40.4 per cent).

In the last three years we considered (2008–10), banking sector betas felt the effects of the financial crisis, with a sharp rise to which only Portuguese banks were immune. The increase in the systematic risk of Italian banks (+90.4 per cent) is second only to that of Irish banks (which was +171.8 per cent), even though no Italian banks required government bail-outs, unlike those in Ireland and several other countries. Italy was also second in terms of the rate of increase in the link to the general EMU index (+108.4 per cent), behind Portugal (+116.7 per cent). For the first time, the beta of the Italian banking system was statistically above the market average; moreover, during this period, the level of systematic risk of banking stocks was above unit in all countries. Statistically, Italian banks show a non-diversifiable risk level similar to that of French, German, Belgian, Greek, Portuguese, and Spanish banks, but lower than that of Austrian and Irish banks.

Inside the risk-return profile of the Italian listed banks

The transition from the banking sector share price index to individual figures allows a closer analysis of Italian banks' stock market performance, determining above all whether differences in size, business, and legal form are reflected in different return and risk profiles. The sample consists of all 23 banks listed at the end of 2010, with a total of 22 common and 5 non-voting stocks (saving shares).[5] Table 5.4 illustrates the compound annual growth rate (CAGR; no dividends), the standard deviation of monthly growth rates and the share turnover (monthly averages) of the sample banks subdivided by size (big v. small), type of banking business (commercial banks v. other banks), legal form (Ltd. v. Coop) and stock category (common shares v. saving shares) during 1999–2010 and in the sub-periods 1999–2007 and 2008–10. The values for each subdivision are simple averages of the individual data.

The sample comprises eight commercial Ltd. banks, of which three are big and five small; eight commercial cooperative banks, of which four are big and four small; and six other Ltd. banks, of which four specialise in private banking, one in investment banking, and one in factoring (one of them is only present during 2008–10). Banks with market value of over €2 billion as of 1999 are considered "big."

First and foremost, the figures (Table 5.4) reveal the clear superiority of the specialised banks over the commercial banks in terms of the rate of growth in share price, both over the entire time period and during each of the two sub-periods. Before the subprime crisis, the specialist banks provided their shareholders with an average compound annual return three times higher than that of the commercial banks (+17.3 per cent for Other Ltd. banks v. +5.7 and +4.6 per cent for Commercial Ltd. and Commercial Coop banks, respectively), and this more or less continued to be the case during 2008–10 due to lower losses (–8.7 per cent for Other Ltd. banks v. –22.0 and –26.7 per cent for Commercial Ltd. and Commercial Coop banks, respectively). Alongside this over-performance in terms of returns, these banks' stocks showed greater volatility (see columns SD in Table 5.4), especially during the pre-crisis period 1999–2007 (13.8 per cent for Other Ltd. banks v. 6.6 and 5.8 per cent for Commercial Ltd. and Commercial Coop banks,) and a lower share turnover, especially during 2008–10 (3.2 per cent for Other banks v. 7.3 and 6.2 per cent for Commercial Ltd. and Commercial Coop banks, respectively); all data in Table 5.4.

Amongst the commercial banks, the Commercial Cooperatives show a certain degree of underperformance in returns, with a CAGR of –4.3 per cent across the entire time period 1999–2010 compared to –2.0 per cent for the Commercial Ltd. banks, due to smaller increases in

Table 5.4 Italian listed banks: stock market performance, 1999–2010 (percentage values)

	1999–2010			1999–2007			2008–10		
	CAGR	SD	Turn	CAGR	SD	Turn	CAGR	SD	Turn
Commercial Ltd.	–2.0	7.8	3.9	5.7	6.6	2.8	–22.0	10.0	7.3
Commercial Ltd. S[a]	1.5	8.9	5.9	9.7	7.7	6.2	–19.7	10.9	3.8
Commercial Coop	–4.3	7.1	3.8	4.6	5.8	3.0	–26.7	9.8	6.2
Other Ltd. banks	10.2	13.0	3.0	17.3	13.8	3.0	–8.7	11.2	3.2
Big[b] Comm. Ltd.	–7.9	9.2	8.4	0.8	7.5	5.4	–29.8	12.2	17.3
Small Comm. Ltd.	1.0	6.9	1.2	8.2	6.1	1.2	–17.8	8.6	1.2
Big Comm. Coop	–5.3	8.0	6.1	4.3	6.1	4.7	–29.0	11.8	10.3
Small Comm. Coop	–3.6	6.2	1.6	4.8	5.4	1.4	–24.8	7.9	3.1

Notes: CAGR = compound annual growth rate (no dividends); SD = standard deviation of monthly growth rates; Turn = share turnover (monthly averages).

[a]Non-voting shares (S). All other stocks are common shares.

[b]Big: banks with market value over €2 billion as of 1999.

Source: Processing of Thomson Financial.

the pre-crisis years and sharper falls from the onset of the crisis to 2010. Their volatility and turnover are more similar, although during 2008–10 the Commercial Cooperative banks recorded a liquidity level (Turn) slightly below that of the Ltd. banks (6.2 per cent v. 7.3 per cent). Larger differences emerge with regard to the banks' size factor, especially between big and small Ltd. banks. In general, small banks show lower levels of share value volatility, and especially of lower levels of turnover than big banks (see Table 5.4). The gap between small and big widened during the recent crisis period, arriving at 3.6 points in volatility for Commercial Ltd. banks (8.6 per cent for small banks v. 12.2 per cent for big banks in 2008–10) and 3.9 points for Cooperatives (7.9 per cent for small Commercial Coop banks v. 11.8 per cent for big Commercial Coop banks) and 16.1 points in turnover (Turn) for Ltd. banks (1.2 per cent for small Commercial banks v. 17.3 per cent for big Commercial banks) and a difference of 7.2 points in turnover for Cooperatives (3.1 per cent v. 10.3 per cent). Small banks also show a better return in both periods considered, striking in the case of the Ltd. banks. One reason for this may be that big banks were involved in a large number of costly mergers and acquisitions which pushed stock prices down, while the prices of small banks rose on improved expectations after changes in ownership. Naturally, this reasoning applies more to Commercial Ltd. banks than to Cooperatives (where the principle of per capita voting hinders takeovers) and this probably explains why the difference in returns between small and big banks is much greater for Ltd. banks than for Cooperatives: 8.9 percentage points (CAGR of +1 per cent for small Commercial Ltd. banks v. –7.9 per cent for big Commercial Ltd. banks) compared to 1.7 percentage points (–3.6 per cent for small Commercial Coop banks v. –5.3 per cent for big Commercial Coop banks). The better performance of Ltd. banks compared to Cooperatives, discussed above, is actually due only to the small Ltds, since the big Ltd. banks are the category with the worst overall CAGR (all data from Table 5.4).

These differences in price trends profoundly modified the relative valuations of the listed banks. Figure 5.16 illustrates the trend in the price-to-book value (PBV) in 1999–2010 for the various categories of banks. The large drop in relative prices across the board is immediately obvious (Figure 5.16 left): Ltd. Commercial banks (Commercial SpA) PBV dropped from 2.09x to 0.69x; Cooperative Commercial banks (Commercial Coop) from 1.62x to 0.55x; Other Ltd. banks (Other SpA) dropped from 2.17x to 1.81x. From 2000 onwards, the Other Ltd. banks

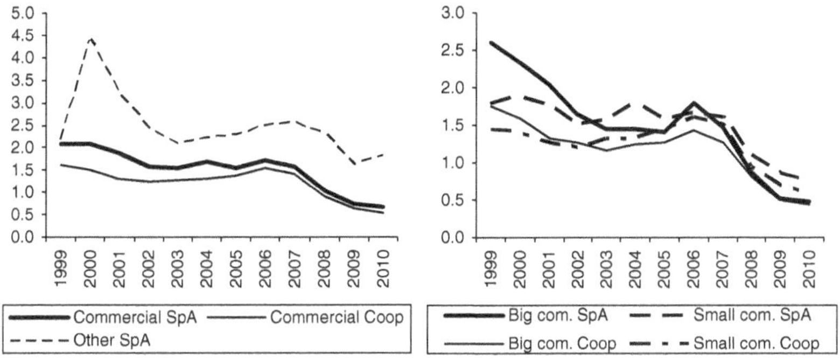

Figure 5.16 Italian listed banks: price-to-book values, 1999–2010 (monthly averages). Left: data by legal form (Ltd. v. Coop) and type of banking business (Commercial banks v. Other banks). Right: data by legal form (Ltd. v. Coop) and size (big v. small)

Source: Processing of Thomson Financial.

were valued at a premium over the commercial banks, with a gap that decreased until 2003 and then started to expand again. The positive PBV gap of Ltd. over Commercial Cooperative banks tended to fall throughout the period.

As we see in Fig. 5.16 right, at the beginning of the period stocks in big commercial banks (Big. com) were sold at higher prices than those of small commercial banks (Small com.) in both the Ltd. and the Cooperative categories, and the big Ltd. banks had the highest PBV (2.59x). In 2010, the small Ltd. banks topped the PBV ranking with 0.79x, with the small Cooperatives second with 0.63x; the big Ltd. banks were third with PBV 0.51x and the big Cooperatives brought up the rear with a PBV of 0.47x.

Concluding with a look at the type of share, the return on savings shares exceeds that on common shares (the differential would be even greater if dividends were considered, since by law the dividend assigned to savings shares must always be higher than that assigned to common shares), especially during the pre-crisis period. However, savings shares show slightly more volatility and a high degree of liquidity during the pre-crisis period, significantly lower from 2008 to 2010. It should be noted that the overperformance of non-voting stocks is due at least in part to the considerable reduction in the price differential between savings shares and the corresponding common shares, which fell from about 50 per cent in 1999 (average weighted by capitalisation) to about 5 per cent in 2010.

Since this price gap is interpreted in the literature as the value of the voting rights and thus as an indicator of the private benefits of control, the reduction in its size would appear to reflect an improvement in the protection of minority shareholders due to changes in the law.

For the same categories of banks as are shown in Table 5.4, Table 5.5 illustrates the beta and fit (adjR^2) of the market model estimated by performing a regression analysis of the monthly returns of individual shares on the monthly returns of a stock index representing the EMU area (MSCI EMU Price Index) during 1999–2001, 2002–04, 2005–07, and 2008–10. As before, the values for each subdivision are simple averages of the individual data.

As we found for other performance measures, bank size and type of business seem to be the most significant factors with regard to systematic risk. The lowest beta values are those of the small Commercial Cooperative banks, with the sole exception of the small commercial cooperative banks during 2005–07. (The data in this paragraph are from Table 5.5.) The incidence of size is greater amongst the Ltd. banks and during the two periods when quotations were most volatile: 2002–04 and 2008–10. The beta of the specialised banks exceeds that of the commercial banks (common shares) in all the periods examined, but during 2002–04 and 2008–10 referred to it is overtaken by the beta of the big Commercial banks. The role of legal form is less clear-cut: if size is not considered, the beta values of Commercial Ltd. and Commercial Cooperative banks were fairly similar, except during 2002–04, even though the systematic risk of big Cooperatives tended to be lower than that of the big Ltd. banks, especially during the two most volatile three-year periods, 2002–04 and 2008–10 (it should also be borne in mind

Table 5.5 Italian listed banks: EMU systematic risk, 1999–2010, market model beta on monthly returns

	1999–2001		2002–04		2005–07		2008–10	
	beta	**adjR^2 (%)**	**beta**	**adjR^2 (%)**	**beta**	**adjR^2 (%)**	**beta**	**adjR^2 (%)**
Commercial Ltd.	0.489	11.1	0.545	26.6	0.758	17.2	0.982	43.2
Commercial Ltd. S	0.474	11.2	0.619	20.2	0.995	15.1	1.028	39.4
Commercial Coop	0.445	15.4	0.289	11.8	0.804	14.1	0.946	42.5
Other Ltd. Banks	1.346	11.1	0.685	26.6	1.039	23.3	1.006	36.0
Big Comm. Ltd	0.598	15.2	1.013	48.1	0.797	19.5	1.486	68.2
Small Comm. Ltd	0.424	8.7	0.265	13.8	0.735	15.7	0.680	28.1
Big Comm. Coop	0.518	16.1	0.464	23.4	0.755	13.6	1.250	54.0
Small Comm. Coop	0.371	14.7	Ns	–	0.854	14.6	0.641	31.1

Source: Processing of Thomson Financial (MSCI EMU Price Index).

that the average size of the big Ltd. banks is considerably larger than that of the big Coops). This finding is confirmed by the savings shares (Commercial Ltd S), which often have a slightly higher systematic risk level than the common shares, as for other forms of risk. Last but not least, the expected positive relationship between bank size and model fit emerges (see columns adjR^2).

To conclude, the banks in which international investors are most likely to trade (i.e. the big Commercial Ltd. banks), whose shares therefore undergo comparative assessment at least at the European level, returned the worst average performance over the time period considered: low returns and high risks.

5.4 A final comparison

With regard to listed banks, we give only a few comments concerning the relationship between the trend in market values and economic-financial performance as revealed by the most representative balance sheet ratios. The comparison is not easy, since the samples of banks examined in the two sections discussed so far differ in part, but we attempted as far as possible to create a specimen set of banks which, although not very large, would be highly representative of Italian listed banks overall.[6]

In an attempt to detect any possible relationship between stock market value and balance sheet performance, the analysis considers two parameters: profitability, measured by means of the CAGR for stock market value and measured by the return on equity for economic performance, and the risk level, expressed by the beta of the listed stocks and the cost of risk ("loan loss provisions/loans").

At the national level, distinguishing the biggest from the medium-sized and small banks and breaking the total time period from 1999 to 2010 into two separate sub-periods for a clearer understanding of the situations pre-crisis (1999–2007) and post crisis (2008–10), there is a clear direct link between stock market value and fundamentals, in terms of both earnings and risk levels.

Before the onset of the financial crisis, meaning until 2007, in terms of profitability the big groups returned the best combination of the two separate performance indicators, since they recorded a very high average ROE level (average annual value of 11.3 per cent) and an upward trend in stock market values (annual average of +3.5 per cent). (Data in this paragraph from Figure 5.17.) Small and medium-sized groups also achieved excellent results in economic and financial performance, with

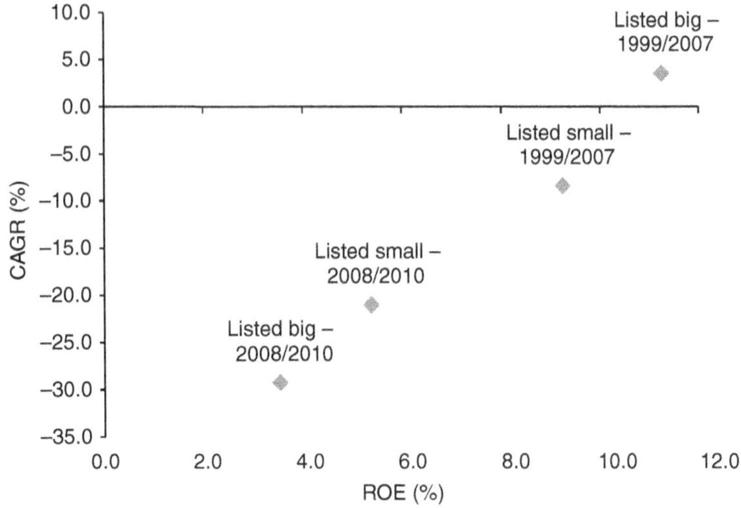

Figure 5.17 National comparison: market and economic-financial profitability (CAGR v. ROE)

an average ROE of 9.2 per cent, but these figures received little response from the stock market since the annual average CAGR was negative at –8.4 per cent.

During the years after 2007 the situation was reversed. Small groups recorded lower stock market "losses" than the big players (average CAGR –21.0 per cent for the former compared to – 29.3 per cent for the big groups; see Figure 5.17 vertical axis) and their average profitability was also greater (average ROE of 5.4 per cent compared to 3.5 per cent; see Figure 5.17 horizontal axis). Therefore, the extreme volatility was detrimental in all senses to the big groups, which certainly have greater cross-border risks and are intrinsically more vulnerable to international contagion, while the banks with closer local ties and with fewer financial assets other than customer loans in their balance sheets were less affected.

In terms of risk level, the situation deteriorated for both size classes, although once again the big groups suffered more. The average level of cost of risk of the big banks rose from 0.57 pre-crisis (1999–2007) to 0.86 in 2008–10, while for the small groups it did increase, but at a lower rate, from 0.51 to 0.68 (see Figure 5.18 horizontal axis). The average beta of the big groups more than doubled (from 0.67 to 1.35), while that of the medium-sized and small groups rose, but to a lesser extent, from 0.50 to 0.77 (see Figure 5.18 vertical axis).

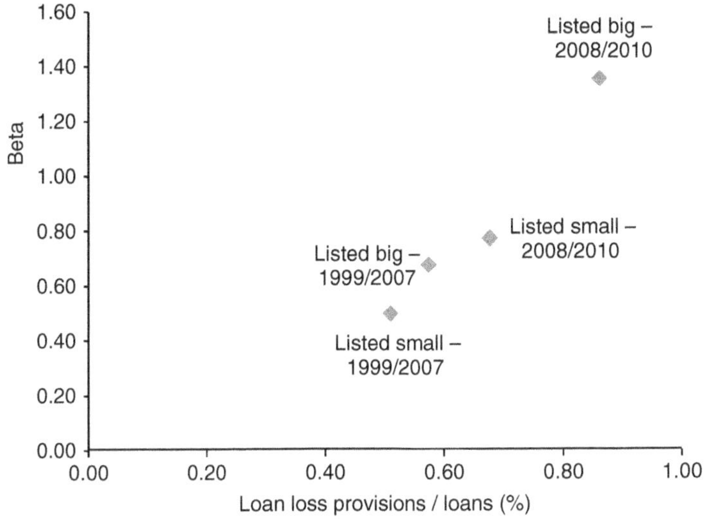

Figure 5.18 National Comparison: Market and economic-financial risk (beta v. Loan Loss Provisions/Loans)

Source: Processing of Prometeia from balance sheet and Thomson Financial.

Acknowledgements

The authors wish to thank Chiara Fornasari for her valuable comments and suggestions on an early draft.

Notes

1. The size classification criterion used in Section 5.2 is the value of the total assets as published in the financial statements. Small banking groups report values of €10–15 billion or below, big groups exceed €80–100 billion.
2. With its significance acknowledged at the international level. For several years now, The Banker has drawn up its annual rankings of the world's top 1000 banks on the basis not of their total assets but of the monetary value, in $US, of their Tier 1 capital.
3. Average value for the 12 European groups discussed at the start of the chapter.
4. In the United States, the financial crisis in late 2008 was associated with historically high levels of stock market volatility, particularly among financial sector stocks. See Schwert (2011).
5. The number of banks in the sample is higher than the 20 included in Figure 5.15 because the Italian Stock Exchange classifies some of them in the financial services and not the banking sector (Banca Ifis, Banca Profilo, Banca

Intermobiliare). Only saving stocks in Banco di Sardegna are listed. For Intesa Sanpaolo, UniCredit, Banco di Desio and Carige, listings include both common and saving stocks.

6. The group considered comprises 13 banks. Compared to the Section on stock market performance, "specialist" banks (other banks) and three small banks not featured and available in the economic-financial performance sample are left out.

6
Organisational and Business Models of Italian Banks

Stefano Cosma and Paola Vezzani

6.1 Introduction

Since 1990, the Italian banking system has undergone major changes involving ownership structures, scale of operations, risk management techniques, efficiency incentives and, above all, organisational and business models. Changes in legislation and deregulation begun by the 1990 Amato-Carli Law have increased banks' operational independence and their range of activities and services, leading to a corresponding growth in the complexity of the banking environment and market.

The shift in the legal and regulatory framework towards the universal bank institutional model, moving away from the specialist bank model that had been adopted in Italy since 1936, has made it essential for banks to acquire organisational models capable of managing their consequent greater variety of products, markets, and customers and, above all, the increasing variability of the external environment, which has become much more competitive than in the past.

Since 1994, Italian banks have been engaged in a rapid diversification and expansion both of the range of services delivered and of the product-customer-channel combinations in their chosen market mixes. At the same time, the greater complexity of their operations has obliged them to adopt organisational models capable of recognising and managing the many interdependent relationships created and the higher degree of market uncertainty.

This expansion of the range of services has been accompanied by a large-scale consolidation of ownership within the banking system, resulting in a high level of polarisation, with a few large and some medium-sized banking groups operating alongside a large number of small banks.

The organisational models specialised by function that were typical of Italian banks until the 1990s have been replaced by divisional models and by "multifunctional" groups for the largest banks, which presumably cover all areas of business.

Smaller banks, operating on a more limited scale in terms of services, customer segments, and financial needs, have basically continued to employ a simple, functional organisational model, although one capable of accommodating and coordinating the many partnerships arising from the outsourcing of the most complex types of business to larger intermediaries.

Amongst the smaller banks, the mutual banks (MBs) form a separate category. Instead of individual partnerships with larger financial intermediaries, they have created a single confederation, including both the individual MBs with their simple organisational models and a joint-venture financial intermediary, which produces most banking and financial services for all MBs.

The aim of this chapter is to describe the organisational models that banks adopt for their operations in the banking market and in the various areas of business. The analysis of organisational models discusses large banks; medium-sized banks; andsmaller independent banks organised into consortia and networks.

The chapter consists of three main parts. The Part 6.2 introduces and describes Italian banks' organisational models from a theoretical point of view, with the aim of outlining the main strategic options available (diversification vs. specialisation) and the models adopted by large, medium-sized, and small banks. We then move on (Section 6.3) to illustrate the organisational models implemented by Italian banks to cover the principal strategic areas of business (retail, corporate, investment, and private). The final part of the chapter analyses the network organisational model used by the mutual banks, which increases the scope and efficacy of the operations of Italy's more than 400 banks in this category and makes them, as a body, a major player within the Italian banking system.

6.2 Italian banks' organisational models

Ownership structures, business models, size, and the importance of ties to a specific territorial area are all currently hot topics for discussion in the Italian banking industry after almost 20 years of change, generated basically by deregulation and financial and technological innovation.

The 2008 crisis gave a further boost to a complex process of change that had already been under way in the Italian banking system for a considerable period of time.

The factors referred to above have modified production processes and have made a significant increase in the size of financial institutions necessary. Investments in new technologies, their continual upgrading, and the higher level of management skills required have raised the optimal size thresholds for the various sectors of operation, for the business areas and, last but not least, for the different phases of the production and distribution process.

Strategies involving an expansion of sectors of operation and customer segments have inevitably implied organisational restructuring to ensure effective management of the various customer-product-channel segments. Although the trend towards diversification has been obvious throughout the system, a distinction must be made between large and small banks. The former have opted for a high degree of diversification of services and customers, combined with considerable growth in size, pursued through external expansion. Small banks have chosen selective diversification, concentrating on the financial needs of their own clientele and on local areas, and on their already existing areas of professional expertise. This has all led to greater organisational complexity, both horizontally (business areas) and vertically (corporate governance).

The rapid growth in areas of business and the swift succession of merger and acquisition (M&A) operations by which banks have increased their size have generated problems for the creation of an organisational model[1] capable of managing this complexity: amongst the largest Italian banks, some have adopted the divisional or universal bank model, while others have taken the form of banking groups. These models become less clear-cut in the transition from theory to the situation on the ground, which does not offer any pure archetypes of either category.

The organisational strategies of the largest banks, with diversified activities and clientele, can be analysed with regard to the main general areas of business (retail banking, corporate banking, private banking, investment banking, and institutional banking) and oscillate range between divisional and group models.

In divisional models, the units that handle the main general areas of business are all included in a single legal entity; in the group model, these units become separate firms.

Small banks that have selectively expanded their operations have tended to maintain a simple, functional organisational model, creating specialist organisational units within the various function areas, with some organisational differentiation, especially in the distribution phase.

Small banks and the functional organisational model

All the most highly developed financial systems include banks that have decided to specialise in a specific product/market/customer combination. In this case, specialisation is therefore the outcome of voluntary strategic decisions relating to product range, clientele segments, geographical markets, and distribution channels, and specialization does not necessarily apply to all areas of business; it may refer to just one.

In Italy, the banks that have chosen to specialise fall mainly into two categories:

- those with voluntary strategic specialisation, which has led to the creation of intermediaries operating in private banking, consumer credit, and other sectors of the financial services market;
- those with strategic specialisation by force of circumstances, where limited internal resources and size factors have forced the bank to concentrate on its core activities and small customer and market segments.

For these banks, the adoption of a complex organisation model is neither appropriate nor economically viable.

Operational specialisation and the focus on a clearly defined clientele and market do not require a high degree of organisational differentiation, so in specialized banks of this kind operations are traditionally organised by functions and activities. In the functional model, management responsibilities are allocated on the basis of phases or functions within the production process, and strategic control and coordination are firmly concentrated in the hands of the general management. In structures of this type, the offices in charge of the different functions, which may be structured in a variety of ways, are often all classified as first-level and are under the direct control of the chief executive officer (CEO).

In some cases, thee small size specialized banks extend their expertise and business models through membership in networks for the joint performance of phases in the production process, or for the more favourable acquisition of products and services for distribution to their customers. Agreements under which the smaller banks distribute the products and services of larger banks are also very common.

The networks take different forms, varying from contractual networks based on reciprocal operating commitments to more structured consortia, in which the member banks invest, acquiring holdings in the joint ventures created. These forms enable small banks to benefit from a number of centrally produced services while still retaining their specialised nature. To ensure the stability and efficacy of the cooperation agreement and allow its smooth operation, the member banks must be of more or less the same size and their geographical territories must not overlap. As we will see below, in Italy this optionhas been adopted by the mutual banks.

Large banks and the divisional organisational model

For regulatory and other reasons, the "pure" form of the universal bank[2] rarely occurs in practice, and we therefore focus our attention here on the organisation of the core processes relating to the areas of business listed above. In the divisional model, these processes are combined within a single legal entity, managed by means of hierarchical coordination and decision-making mechanisms and channelled towards the various customer segments in a coordinated manner. The operational management of each strategic business area is in the hands of a specific division, responsible for the economic returns achieved. Divisions are independent within their own areas of operation, which may be defined by specific markets or products, market segments served, and/or a mixture of these.

The divisional organisational model's unified governance and strong decision-making chain, involving broader systems for the delegation of powers and suitable control mechanisms that allow managerial roles to be created throughout the organisational structure, deliver undoubted benefits in terms of information in risk management and other management, and provide better coordination in the management of customer relations by reducing the distance between the customer and the point where decisions are made. They also facilitate the achievement of economies of scope, in view of the close links between the technical production and distribution aspects of the banking industry. In this regard, the wider opportunities for re-engineering banking operations have enabled banks operating under divisional models to centralise a large number of activities common to the difference areas of business, by increasing the separation between production and distribution and by reinforcing the subdivision of organisational units with specific duties in production, services, coordination, and market coverage (Mottura 2011).

It goes without saying that, compared to the functional model, the division model involves a higher risk of conflict of interest in the bank-customer relationship and increases the difficulties and costs of integration because of the model's greater operational complexity. Opportunistic behaviours on the part of subsidiaries become less probable, since their activities are continually monitored and observed both by the division heads and by the parent company. Operationally, a universal bank is much more complex than a specialist firm, and this makes the achievement of operating efficiency more problematical, also because the adoption of a *true* universal bank model involves not only an expansion of the areas of operation, but also a transformation of production and distribution processes, which increases organisational differentiation.

Large banks and the group organisational model

A banking group is a combination of operating units, including banks, financial intermediaries, financial firms, and specialist financial product companies, linked together by major similarities in ownership and coordinated by the business plan of the parent company (bank, holding bank, or holding company). A banking group must therefore have the following features: a) a number of legally independent, economically separate firms; b) a single economic entity providing unified strategic management; c) effective control by the parent company; and d) responsibility for external relations assigned to the parent company.

Within this business model, the individual companies aim to maximise the synergies and interrelations that will optimise the achievements of the objectives of the group as a whole. The parent company provides the group with strategic management and coordination, not on the hierarchical principle typical of the divisional model, but by means of direct and indirect control. From this point of view, the group model creates a large number of agency relationships between the central parent company and the management of the various subsidiaries.

Control is exercised in the forms envisaged by corporate law but is also backed up by other, more effective, continuous control mechanisms intended to align the interests and objectives of the principal and agent, such as the appointment of a member of the main bank's management as CEO of the subsidiary, the centralisation within the parent company of important management functions to ensure coordination (finance and treasury, planning, risk management, etc.), and the issue of group regulations.

In many cases, the creation of companies to contain business units is chosen as an alternative to the divisional model with the aim of benefiting from the various firms' specialisation and reducing the organisational complexity typical of divisional models in cases where the various organisational units are required to provide their services to the market as well as to the other divisions.

In Italy, the popularity of the group model is also explained by history, since the regulatory approach in force until the 1990s encouraged the fragmentation and specialisation of financial intermediaries. The reorganisation and growth of Italian banks has inevitably involved the external acquisition of specialised intermediaries, and in many cases it has been less complex and costly to place them under the control of a holding company than to merge them in a single organisational structure, with all the relative expenses and integration problems.

Large banks and the federal group organisational model

In some cases, the banking sector consolidation process has created a "federal" organisational model, which strikes a compromise between the centralisation of production and coordination functions capable of generating cost economies and the operational and decision-making autonomy of the banks within the "confederation".

This model enables smaller-sized banks to reap the benefits of diversification and specialisation while retaining the distribution and relational advantages generated by their traditional links to their local areas. Equally important, they are placed in a better position to defend themselves from external acquisition attempts, thanks to the improved efficiency and competitiveness achieved.

The federal group model also produces advantages for larger banks, since it gives them greater opportunities to enter new, traditionally well-protected markets (which have informational and relational barriers), without the difficulties and costs of an external acquisition, and it allows them to benefit from the relationships and image of the federal bank by simply reaching agreement with regard to production and mandates.

In the federal group model, the parent company guarantees strong central guidance and is capable of effectively handling strategic planning, coordination, and control with a high degree of separation of the governance, production, and distribution areas. In all cases, the upstream coordination has a more consensual character than in the "pure" group model. Downstream of the parent company, as the empirical section of this chapter illustrates, are the business units (production companies), which provide the member banks and companies with quality services at prices not above the market prices (optimal internal transfer rates), achieved above all through economies of scale and specialisation. At the end of the chain are the federation's member banks, which are independent and have their own specific territories (or areas of business); they act basically as distributors, although within their traditional credit operations they may be involved in the production and decision-making process. The parent company in the federal model is owned and therefore controlled by the banks and companies within the federation, with control exerted in an upward direction, not downward, as in the banking group model discussed previously.

There are no pure federal groups in the Italian system (Mottura 2011). In many cases, the federal group is a sort of hybrid organisational model, often adopted by banks that have decided or have been compelled to implement growth policies for reasons of competitiveness and efficiency but are reluctant to embark on full-scale organisational and corporate integration. The banks involved may be similar in outlook (e.g., the mutual banks) or may be complementary, covering interlocking business and geographical areas; the federal model offers them a means of transition towards the establishment of a single, integrated banking group.

The fact that the single brands are maintained, which may also be the case in non-federal banking groups, fits the strategy of promoting the images and reputations of the member banks in their markets of reference and ensuring that customers still perceive the bank as local, with decision-making centres close to the needs of the clientele and to the socioeconomic communities of reference.

In some cases, banking groups describe themselves as federal simply because the bank includes legally independent banks with their own brands. The use of the term in these cases is not really justified, because the parent company has controlling interests in all the banks in the group (which are sometimes wholly owned); federal often reflects "soft" acquisition strategies, in which the target banks retain their own operating structures, even if they are strictly supervised by the parent company and aligned with its policies.

Due to the hybrid nature described above, federal groups tend to be unstable. The model has to reconcile the centripetal forces deriving from operational needs, which might lead to excessive planning, shifting the balance amongst the member banks' interests, and frustrating their plans for independence, and the centrifugal thrusts arising from the individual member banks' tendency to maintain their separate behaviours and decision-making procedures.

On the ground, pure divisional, group, or federal organisational models virtually never occur; banks have created a wide assortment of hybrid models, which involve varying combinations of the different features of the original theoretical models, which will be described in the empirical part of this chapter.

6.3 Empirical analysis

An examination of Italian banks' organisational structures, subdivided by size category, provides important information concerning the strategies and business models adopted by Italian banks and groups and current trends.

This empirical study aims to describe the organisational models and the main organisational solutions banks have adopted for their principal business areas (retail, corporate and private banking and asset management). Other business areas are also examined where they are of interest; it must be borne in mind that it is difficult to allocate banks' organisational models to one or the other of the theoretical categories in the strict sense, since each intermediary designs its own business areas and chooses the appropriate organisational solutions in response to highly subjective criteria linked to the cultural and competitive context.

The empirical study discussed next considers the following categories of bank:

- large: i.e., the five largest Italian banking groups
- medium-sized, i.e., a sample of banks with total assets between €20 and €60 billion;
- small: banks that do not belong to either of the first two categories, especially mutual banks and the network model created amongst them.

The large banks

The fundamental characteristics of the evolution of the organisational and business models of the five largest Italian groups are

- prevalence of strategies of diversification rather than specialisation, due to imitative behaviours and in response to dimensional requirements and competition for positioning

- natural tendency to grow in size through consolidation operations, undertaken partly as a defensive measure against hostile takeovers by international competition and by the activism of the institutional investors
- different business areas/customer segments served both through separate, dedicated divisions and through more federal organisational structures

The choice of organisational model for the large Italian banking groups has been influenced, over time, by at least a couple of factors. First, changes in groups' perimeters through acquisition of control that was not followed by merger operations gave them the opportunity for a period of strategic experimentation, with the option of changing their minds at a later date with fewer damaging consequences. Second, the maintenance of the corporate identities of the banks that were taken over enabled the controlling entity/parent company to analyse and understand their diversity as the basis for appropriate planning of their integration into the group. Table 6.1 contains the main findings for the various business areas.

The two largest Italian groups – UniCredit and Intesa Sanpaolo – serve all clientele segments with an extremely diversified range of products and services. Unlike the other groups, they have a significant presence in the international markets.

UniCredit

The UniCredit group comprises five divisions, covering the various business areas: retail, corporate, private, asset management, and foreign. The divisions, especially those serving the retail and corporate segments, are subdivided in turn into business units. The business units are structured by product lines for the delivery of specialised services within the corporate divisions, which also handles the investment banking business, while in the retail division business units are structured by geographical area.

The UniCredit model can be described as follows:

- It is a mixed model, in group form but with a strong tendency to involve independent economic players and adopt the divisional model. It still contains a large number of legally separate companies, although over time the process of mergers amongst the different domestic banks has been intensive, and has led towards the divisionalised universal bank model.

Table 6.1 Organisation model and management of business areas in large banking groups)

Name	Organisational model	Retail Division	Private banking	Corporate	Asset management	Institutional	Foreign business
UniCredit	Combined divisional/group model	Division with internal separate business units to manage the main geographical areas	Division	Division, also including investment banking	Division with own brand		Division for the group's business in the various countries where it operates
Intesa Sanpaolo	Combined divisional/group model	Division	Retail division companies	Division, also including investment banking	Division with own brand and network of financial advisers	Division	Division for the group's business in the various countries where it operates
Banca Monte dei Paschi	Combined divisional/ group model	Division	Retail division	Division			Activities carried out by corporate management
Banco Popolare	Combined divisional-federal model	Division/ Management	Investment and private banking and asset management division	Business handled by the retail banks	Investment and private banking and asset management division		Group staff area
UBI Banca	Federal model	Federation member banks	Business handled by asset management companies	Federation member banks	Group companies with financial advisor and asset management network		Group staff area

Source: Our processing of corporate consolidated financial statements for year ending 2010 and consolidated half-year reports at end of June 2011.

- It is a divisional model with subdivision by customer segment, with specific evidence of a large number of product and service lines centralised at the group level.
- It has a "multilocal" business approach, through the creation of geographical areas with considerable decisional autonomy.

UniCredit has gradually moved beyond the federal phase typical of the formation of most Italian banking groups, through an intensive process of mergers amongst the member companies, which first created three large banks (UniCredit Retail Banking, UniCredit Corporate Banking, and UniCredit Private Banking), before leading on to the establishment of a single bank handling business on the Italian market.

The Intesa Sanpaolo group comprises five divisions (called business units): retail, corporate and investment banking, asset management, institutional, and foreign, which report directly to the CEO.

Intesa Sanpaolo has adopted a very different solution from that of UniCredit for the management of its retail clientele. The retail division consists of a large number of subsidiary banks and financial companies, with a geographical structure that allows the maintenance and promotion of the regional brands. This division also includes the private banking business area and bank assurance, handled by specific financial product production companies. The commercial banking operations of the group's foreign banks are placed in a different division.

The corporate and investment banking division handles all services for corporate customers as well as M&A, structured finance, capital markets, and merchant banking business. This is a very large division, which takes care of all the operations in these areas in all the many countries where the group is active.

Last but not least, in an arrangement unique to Italy, Intesa Sanpaolo has an institutional division serving public and institutional bodies, supplying financial backing for their operations, and financing for public services and infrastructures.

The Monte Paschi di Siena group mainly serves an Italian clientele through what is basically a divisional organisational model, with some aspects of group form, since the various divisions include subsidiary companies. The parent company coordinates operating activities on behalf of the distribution networks. There are two separate divisions defined by clientele segment: household and corporate. The non-corporate clientele are served, together with retail customers, by the household customer management. Distribution is in the hands of the network of group banks, which retain strong territorial roots.

There are dedicated production structures for the development of specialist financial instruments to be offered to the market, and service structures comprising companies formed to handle IT services and the property sector, as well as a number of companies providing support services to all the business areas.

The organisation of the Banco Popolare group has some federal group features. It has two large sectors, subdivided by customer segment and business area, handling retail and corporate banking in one part and private and investment banking and asset management in the other.

The main retail and corporate banking sector includes seven local banks, which serve all retail, small business and corporate customers in their geographical areas. However, an integration process now underway will involve mergers between the local banks, forming divisions integrated into the parent company's organisation, which will correspond to the geographical areas of the original banks involved, in order to eliminate territorial overlaps.

The private banking market is served by a specific bank within the group, which is included in the investment banking and asset management sector, together with other subsidiaries.

The UBI Banca group has the typical characteristics of the federal group: an operational parent company, a network of independent banks, and specialist financial product production companies and service companies serving the entire group. In this case, the retail segment is served in a more traditional way, by the individual brands of the independent banks within the network, which also handle corporate customers, whose more specific needs are covered by production companies also operating in other business areas such as asset management and the bank assurance. There is also a network of financial advisers for private banking clientele.

This survey of the main Italian banking groups confirms that the federal group model tends to be transitional and unstable. Although it allows the local banks within the confederation to maintain stronger territorial roots and also reduces the organisational costs of integration, the federal model has no effective solution to the problems of the coordination and control of governance, which are a threat to efficiency, strategy, and competitiveness in the long term. This organisational model has definitely played a major role within the consolidation processes that led to the formation of the large Italian groups, but after the initial phase it has tended to be gradually abandoned in favour of greater integration.

The medium-sized banks

There is greater variety in the strategies of the medium-sized banking groups than in those of the large banking groups, partly because the smaller size of their business and the specific needs of the communities served require different, stricter criteria to be applied when deciding on diversification and market positioning strategies. Organisational structures vary from models that are a combination of the divisional and federal group through to functional models.

The large number of groups[3] we examined makes an analysis of organisational solutions by business area/customer segment appropriate.

Retail operations are mainly handled by the parent bank (in medium-sized groups, the parent company is very often a bank and not a holding company) and by any network banks. These banks manage the household and small business operations area, and in some cases also the private banking clientele.

There is not always a separate organisation for private banking, although specialist staff are almost always involved at the distribution level. However, compared to the larger groups, fewer of the medium-sized players allocate specific resources, business units, or divisions to the private bankng customer segment, since they are not the group's core business, in dimensional or other terms. In some cases, organisational strategies have combined this business area with asset management, treasury, investment banking and/or insurance services, outside the retail area.

Although there are some differences among banks, in general corporate banking services are managed and provided by the parent bank and by all the other banks, with separate organisational units and distribution channels within the banks concerned only in some cases. More specialised activities such as leasing, factoring, and, if present, private equity and investment banking, are more often allocated to controlled companies or associated companies.

Asset Management services are almost always provided and delivered by the group's specialist financial product companies and by external companies, which sometimes serve the entire category of intermediary (e.g., Arca in the case of the mutual banks). There are various solutions for the insurance business, which is sometimes handled separately and sometimes combined with activities such as investment and private banking.

Medium-sized groups often feature a parent bank that holds controlling interests in most of the group's banks and companies. The parent bank and the other banks manage distribution and the most traditional business areas, while specialised products and services are in the hands of internal specialist financial product companies, in virtually all the groups examined.

6.4 The mutual bank network organisational model

The mutual banks are generally small, local cooperative companies, which provide banking and financial services on a mutual basis, with a mission of solidarity and subsidiarity in relation to the communities from which their shareholders are drawn. In 2011, there were 414 mutual banks, about 54 per cent of Italy's banks, and they had 4406 branches, about 13.1 per cent of total branches (Banca d'Italia 2011a), covering 2,682 municipalities, in 20.4 per cent of which they were the only bank present. However, over time the mutual banks have increased their presence in the larger municipalities and big urban areas (Tarantola 2011).

The mutual banks play their role as local banks above all by serving micro and small family enterprises, tradesmen, and households, often in small geographical areas with a specific cultural identity.

One feature of the mutual banks is their ability to bring banking to areas or villages whose small size or low output for the markets would not justify the cost of a branch for the larger banks, and their ability to maintain and reinvest the funds raised within the specific areas concerned.

Nevertheless, the mutual banks are also found in towns, where they benefit from the favourable conditions governing their establishment and from access to the market,[4] and they provide provide an alternative to the large banks and banks based in other areas, which are less able to provide a flexible response to the credit needs of some customer segments.

Although retaining their independence, Italian mutual banks have formed a network to enable themselves to compete more effectively. The mutual banks have therefore adopted an organisational model that focuses on consortium-style groupings, benefiting from their legal and corporate characteristics and the absence of problems of competition and/or conflicts of interest.

The network functions at two separate levels: from the political and institutional point of view, the banks belong to the national federation (Federcasse) and the regional federations; the production and operational network is based around the Istituto Centrale delle Casse rurali e Artgiane (ICCREA) banking group, which belongs to the mutual banks and to the federation and controls a large number of financial companies for the centralised production of the services delivered by the individual banks.

Institutional and strategic unity has been pursued by creating a national federation (Federcasse) to which all the mutual banks, the local federations, and the other cooperating banking consortia all belong. The federation brings the banks together at the sociopolitical level, planning and coordinating the development of the mutual banking system, promoting its image, representing the sector, and protecting its interests, and managing its external relations. As in all associations, the national federation consists of local (regional) federations, which provide the linkage to the specific needs of the various areas where the mutual banks operate and the channel through which central polices are adapted to local requirements.

From the operational point of view, the nerve centre of the mutual banks is the ICCREA holding company. ICCREA takes the form of a banking group containing a large number of financial companies that specialise in the production of the main financial and credit services delivered by the mutual banks in the context of their business.

The ICCREA group subdivides into three large business areas – institutional, corporate, and retail – to which the group companies are allocated on the basis of their type of business and the recipients of their services.

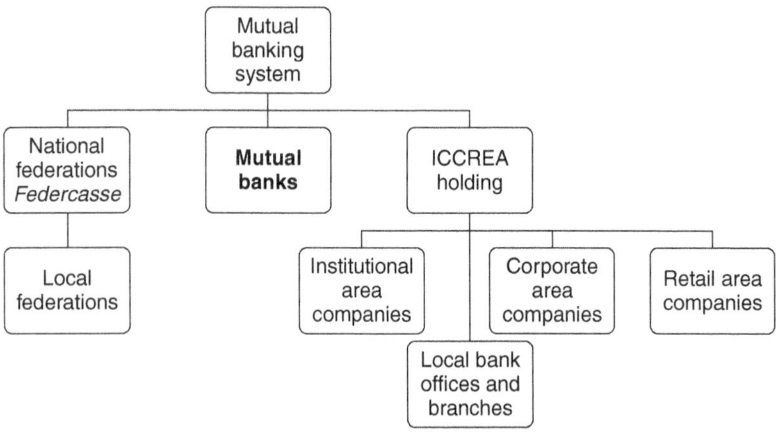

Figure 6.1 The mutual bank network model

Source: Processing of ICCREA Annual Report 2010 and official website data.

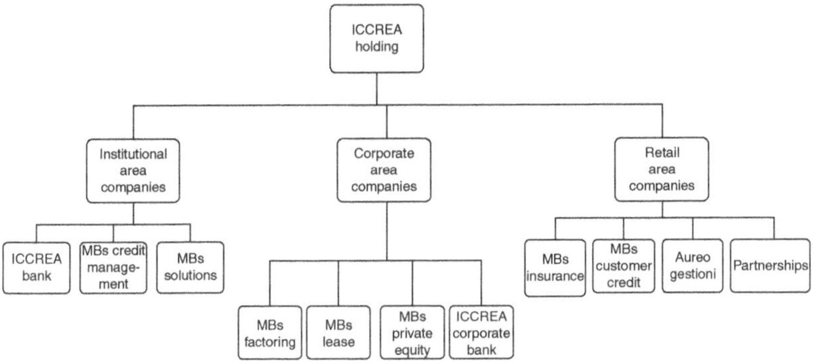

Figure 6.2 The structure of the ICCREA group
Source: Processing of ICCREA Annual Report 2010.

The institutional area of ICCREA contains all the companies that produce services intended to support mutual banks' own financial management and business strategies relating to channels other than their branches. The main areas covered relate to securitisation, institutional insurance products, payment services, securities administration, management of doubtful loans, credit recovery services, and Web and call-centre services. ICCREA Banca falls within this area; it is one of the group's two banks, and supports the mutual banks in payment services, assists in management of the payments system and, above all, handles the acquisition of mutual banks' credit and debit cards. It also serves as a kind of group financial centre and offers the mutual banks trading, funding, settlement, and securities administration services, where it plays the role of Depository Bank.

The corporate area of ICCREA includes all the companies that specialise in services for the mutual banks' small and medium-sized enterprise (SME) customers other than routine current account operations. As in many banking groups, the main centralised activities involve corporate finance services, medium and long-term credit, complex loans, foreign exchange services, leasing and factoring, and advisory services in many other contexts relating to the customer companies' individual, specific needs. ICCREA enables the mutual banks to meet the needs of a large number of SMEs' in critical stages of their life cycles by providing them with the capacity to intervene in internationalisation processes, in the most critical growth phases, and in risk management and coverage.

The corporate banking segment is served by ICCREA BancaImpresa, the group's second bank, which delivers credit services in the strict sense (leasing, factoring, secured credit, and foreign services) together with extraordinary finance and risk management services.

The retail area of ICCREA includes all the companies specialising in the production of household banking services, including home loans and consumer credit and investment, asset management, insurance, and pension requirements. In this area, the ICCREA group has established a joint venture with Agos Ducato, the consumer credit industry leader. The company's products of joint veture are offered under the Crediper brand, but ICCREA benefits from the production efficiency and innovation of Agos Ducato, which has a 40 per cent holding in BCC Credito Consumo SpA. In the business areas where the ICCREA group is unable to reach the economic-financial sustainability thresholds to justify the creation of a specialised financial product company, it has entered into partnerships with specialist external financial intermediaries.

In addition to the production centralisation achieved by means of ICCREA, the mutual banks have established a territorial network of 15 organisational offices, ensuring effective interaction with the individual banks and greater expertise in the definition of services for SMEs and in meeting some mutuals banks' specific needs.

The mutual bank network organisational model differs from the federal groups of larger banks in the greater number of member banks involved and in the use of the consortium structure. The distinctive features of the mutual bank network model can be summarised as follows:

- It is single system, based on federation membership.
- individual banks retain decisional and operational independence.
- There is mutuality within the system, based on relationships of collaboration between the mutual banks, which rarely operate in the same geographical area.
- There is solidarity and subsidiarity within federations, which contain coordinated, complementary functions.
- There is transparency and reciprocity in commitments and contributions to joint activities.

The mutual banks' internal organisational model reflects the existence of the network described above, the high degree of externalisation of some activities, small size, local character, and minimal distribution networks (some banks operate from their registered office alone). Mutual banks' considerable specialisation in traditional credit activities and in the retail segment (savings and loans) encourages the adoption of functional organisational models with very few hierarchical levels (Albareto et al. 2008).[5]

Notes

1. Actually, in textbooks this is often referred to as "institutional form." Institutional form refers to the distinction between banks organised as one single legal entity and those that are aggregations of separate companies. See Mottura (2011), *Banche. Strategie, organizzazioni e concentrazioni*, Milano: Egea, p. 313.
2. The "pure" form of the universal bank is rarely found in practice because for regulatory reasons various types of business have to be located in and undertaken by separate firms. For example, asset management and insurance operations must be carried out by legally separate companies, subject to different regulations. Therefore, the concept of the universal bank as discussed here becomes one more of substance than of form, adopted to identify those banks that have decided to combine most of their strategic business areas in one main corporation. See Mottura (2011), *Banche. Strategie*, p. 315.
3. The following medium-sized banking groups were examined: Banca Popolare di Milano, Banca Popolare dell'Emilia Romagna, Credito Emiliano, Gruppo Carige, Banca delle Marche, Credito Valtellinese, Banca Popolare di Vicenza, Banca Popolare di Sondrio, Veneto Banca. Although of comparable size, the Cariparma, Banca Nazionale del Lavoro and Deutsche Bank groups were not considered since they belong to foreign banking groups (Crédit Agricole, BNP Paribas, and Deutsche Bank Group).
4. Cooperatives must deliver their services mainly to their members, of whom each bank must have at least 200. Each member is entitled to just one vote, regardless of holding size, which must not exceed a nominal value of €50,000. This principle of prevalence is complied with when more than 50% of funds invested are allocated to loans to members and/or to risk-free assets, according to the criteria laid down by the Supervisory Authority.
5. Albareto, Benvenuti, Mocetti, Pagnini, Rossi, L'organizzazione dell'attività creditizia e l'utilizzo di tecniche di scoring nel sistema bancario italiano: risultati di un'indagine campionaria, Questioni di Economia e Finanza, Banca d'Italia, 2008, n. 12.

7
Retail Banking for Households in Italy

Stefano Cosma

7.1 Introduction

As we have seen in the previous chapters, the Italian banking system consists of banks that operate as commercial banks with a strong orientation towards retail banking. This chapter focuses on the role of the household sector and the retail banking services provided to this market. Retail banking is defined as: "the cluster of products and services that banks provide to consumers and small businesses through branches, the Internet, and other channels." On the basis of this definition, Italian banking for households can be defined as the cluster of investment, payment, and lending services offered to households as depositors or consumers, through direct distribution channels (branches), virtual channels (telephone, Internet, call centres, and ATMs), and indirect channels (agents, credit brokers, commercial dealers, etc.).

Our analysis of retail banking for households concentrates on a number of fundamental services. On the asset side of the balance sheet, the key retail (household) banking products are consumer credit (credit cards, auto loans, and other personal loans) and loans for house purchase. On the liability side, the core retail (household) banking products are transaction deposits, savings deposits, and bank bonds.

The aim of the analysis is to identify the role and contribution of banking for households in improving stability and mitigating the effects of the financial crisis.

Retail banking is the traditional credit intermediation model under which funding is received from households in the form of deposits and is used to finance lending to households and small and medium-sized enterprises (SMEs), especially by direct channels. It is founded on a broad customer portfolio and normally on lasting relationships with customers, which respond to and satisfy the various financial needs typical of a household's life cycle over the long term (Clark et al. 2007). From a more corporate point of view, the large number of customers tends to stabilise the banking business's volumes and margins by providing naturally diversified, granular loan and deposit portfolios. Within a bank's operations, retail banking brings stability to profit margins, since it tends to compensate the trend in income from services (non-interest income and fees) against the trend in the net interest margin (Stiroh 2004). Traditional commercial banks (with relatively high core deposit ratios), in particular, tend to show lower profitability levels than other banks do (DeYoung and Rice 2004).

From the capitalisation point of view, it should be remembered that retail banking absorbs smaller than corporate lending amounts of regulatory capital, since consumer credit and lending to SMEs in general are classified as part of the retail portfolio, where the natural granularity of the loans portfolio has the benefit of lower capital adequacy requirements. The regulatory framework (Basel II) sets a very low capital requirement for mortgage loans and loans for house purchases.

Traditionally, Italian commercial banks' level of financialisation of their capital is low, and their credit intermediation operations are based mainly on a deposit-funded model (Mottura and Paci 2009) in which, on the assets side, loans predominate over the other areas of business, while on the liabilities side, retail funding (sight deposits, term deposits, and bonds) plays a larger role than wholesale funding and liquidity generated by the securitisation of assets. Together with a low funding gap (measured by the proportion of loans not financed by retail funding), in general this bank financial equilibrium and operating model mitigated the consequences of the 2007 financial crisis, leading to fewer liquidity and credit rationing problems, especially amongst the smallest banks (Mussari 2010).

On the assets side, loans to households and companies account for the majority of the lending portfolio. This assets make-up helped to reduce the fall in the banks' economic value arising from the slump in the market value of financial assets as a result of the crisis, although it left them exposed to the credit risk generated by the resulting recession. All this also helped to increase Italian banks' solidity after the rise in the weight of the credit risk, which augmented Italian banks' capitalisation both from the point of view of financial leverage and with regard to their ratio of capital to risk-weighted assets (Draghi 2011b).

On the liabilities side, the importance and role of retail funding contributed to Italian banks' stability and helped to reduce their liquidity constraints. In 2008, wholesale funding accounted for about 29 per cent of the total funding of the Italian banking system, compared to a European average of 41 per cent (Banca d'Italia 2010a).

The contribution of savings by retail customers (households) to banks, and the high incidence of transactional and precautionary savings in Italian households' current accounts, were vital in financing banks in the most critical periods of the financial crisis (2007–09), and they are also mitigating the economic and financial effects of the current fresh difficulties on the financial markets for Italian banks.

The stability report (Banca d'Italia 2011b) defines Italian banks' short-term liquidity position as balanced; the high weight of retail funding provides stability in fund raising, and the funding gap continues to be favourable. The level of wholesale funding has remained low compared to the Euro Area average, although in 2011 the related strains generated by the risk associated with the sovereign debt of some Euro Area member states led to major difficulties in terms of cost and the sensitivity of demand. From this point of view, in spite of the importance of retail funding, the spread that has arisen between the yields of Italian and German government securities has triggered a rapid increase in banks' funding costs, forcing them to issue shorter-term securities to mitigate interest rate risk and the impact on their profit-and-loss accounts.

Section 7.2 of the chapter examines the characteristics of Italian banks' loan portfolios and the importance of loans to households, with international comparisons. Section 7.3 takes a more in-depth look at the composition and evolution of household credit in Italy. Section 7.4 concentrates on banks' role on the home loans market, while Section 7.5 examines their role on the consumer credit market. To conclude, Section 7.6 investigates Italian banks' fund-raising characteristics and especially the role of retail funding, with special reference to the household sector.

7.2 The role of Italian banks in lending to households

Italian banks' assets consist mainly of loans to customers and, within this category, of loans to SMEs and to households in particular.

As we saw in Chapter 2, Italy is a bank-based economy. In 2007, the year in which the financial crisis occurred, loans accounted for 68 per cent of total assets in the Italian banking system, well above the Euro Area average of 57 per cent. Italian banks play a key role in financing businesses and, as we will see, in financing households' property investments; their role in consumer credit is smaller.

One major factor is the low level of financialisation of the Italian banking system; when the crisis began, it had only 20 per cent of its financial assets invested in securities other than loans to residents in the Euro Area,[1] making it the country with the lowest exposure to securities in the entire Euro Area (Table 7.1). This situation helped to reduce the negative effects triggered by the write-down of financial assets further to the crisis in securitised subprime mortgage loans and the consequent uncertainty.

The years since 2007 have seen a gradual increase in investments in securities, alongside a reduction in the loan portfolio, due to the financial and capital stresses that reduced the supply of credit, especially on the part of the large banking groups, and also due to the drop in domestic and export demand and the recession with regard to lending to companies (whose demand for loans decreased as a result of the slowdown in investments). Other factors were the property market crisis and the drop in consumption, especially of durables, which triggered a shrinkage in lending to households. The data appear to indicate that the reduction in loans is due mainly to a drop in demand, rather than rationing and/or a credit crunch (Panetta and Signoretti 2010).

There has also been a reduction in loans to monetary financial institutions (MFIs), due in part to the system-wide liquidity provided by the monetary authorities' actions during the crisis and partly to the uncertainty arising from the sovereign debt situation, since most of the government bonds concerned are held by the leading European banks.

The evolution of banks' loan portfolios in the years since 2007 has been shaped, above all, by the effects of the recession that hit the real economy and the increase in risk of the corporate and households segment (Table 7.2). In Italy the rates of growth in bank lending have slowed and there has been a shift in loan portfolio composition in favour of household customers, who by June 2011 represented 25 per cent of total assets, driven by the growth in demand for home loans.

In spite of the crisis and the uncertainty of the economic context, Italian households' demand for credit has been above the Euro Area average (Table 7.3). The higher growth rates can be explained by Italian households' lower levels of indebtedness: the household debt/GDP ratio was 41 in 2010, compared to the Euro average of 59 and the United Kingdom figure of 103 (see European Credit Research Institute Statistical Package 2011). However, the growth in the home loans segment reveals that Italian families express financial demands that cannot be attributed to need and/or poverty, but rather show them allocating their wealth in a way that helps to shape the trend in lending within the

Table 7.1 Total loans and financial assets of banks: an international comparison (2006–10)

	Total loans to Euro Area residents/ Total assets[a] %						Financial assets/Total assets[b] %				
Country	2006	2007	2008	2009	2010	Country	2006	2007	2008	2009	2010
ES	75	73	69	66	66	PT	21	21	23	28	33
PT	71	72	69	65	60	ES	19	21	23	27	26
IT	68	68	67	67	64	GR	33	32	31	33	27
GR	59	61	59	58	66	FI	34	33	26	29	31
DE	60	59	60	61	56	**Euro Area**	**35**	**35**	**34**	**34**	**33**
AT	58	57	59	60	59	FR	37	35	32	32	32
Euro Area	**57**	**57**	**57**	**57**	**55**	DE	38	37	36	35	30
FI	55	55	48	49	45	AT	38	38	36	36	36
NL	58	54	54	56	53	BE	41	39	38	40	38
FR	50	52	51	52	51	NL	36	39	36	36	37
BE	49	51	46	47	48	IE	55	55	56	58	57
LU	39	41	41	39	41	LU	58	56	56	59	56
IE	39	38	39	38	40	IT	21	20	20	23	25

[a]The item considered includes: Loans to Euro Area residents.

[b]The item includes: Holdings of securities other than shares issued by Euro Area residents, money market fund shares/units, holdings of shares and other equities issued by Euro Area residents and external assets (non-Euro Area residents).

Source: Processing of Bank of Italy Eurosystem statistics: Euro Area aggregates and national contributions.

Table 7.2 Incidence of loans to firms and households on total assets (TA), (2006–10)

	Loans to NFCs/TA (%)							Loans to households/TA (%)					
Country	2006	2007	2008	2009	2010	2011	Country	2006	2007	2008	2009	2010	2011
SI	54	57	57	54	54	54	FI	53	52	49	50	48	49
MT	44	42	45	46	35	33	PT	41	40	40	41	42	43
ES	40	42	41	41	40	39	GR	42	40	35	34	40	40
GR	39	37	37	32	35	35	ES	40	39	38	38	39	38
IT	37	35	35	35	36	37	NL	39	36	35	34	34	35
SK	33	34	33	42	41	42	DE	34	31	30	31	31	32
PT	33	33	36	36	35	36	CY	32	31	29	28	30	30
FI	30	31	32	29	27	28	**Euro Area**	**30**	**28**	**27**	**28**	**29**	**29**
CY	28	31	34	31	32	32	Malta	29	28	28	30	24	25
AT	28	27	25	25	27	27	SK	24	25	26	39	42	43
Euro Area	**26**	**26**	**27**	**27**	**26**	**26**	AT	27	25	21	22	24	24
IE	25	28	27	27	17	18	IE	24	25	22	23	22	24
NL	24	25	27	28	29	29	FR	25	24	23	24	25	25
FR	22	21	21	21	21	21	SI	22	22	22	22	24	24
DE	19	19	20	20	19	20	BE	25	22	19	19	20	22
BE	18	17	21	21	20	22	IT	22	20	19	20	24	25
LU	10	11	13	14	13	13	LU	6	6	5	7	7	7

Source: Eurosystem Statistics: Euro-Area aggregates and national contributions, various years.

Table 7.3 Compound annual growth rate (CAGR) of total credit to households, loans for house purchase, and consumer credit (in order of period 2005–10)

	Total credit to households				Loans for house purchase				Consumer credit		
Country	2005–10	2005–08	2008–10	Country	2005–10	2005–08	2008–10	Country	2005–10	2005–08	2008–10
SI	14	18	6	SI	25	30	15	GR	9	7	13
GR	13	11	17	GR	11	12	8	PT	9	14	–2
IT	8	6	11	LU	11	13	7	LU	7	4	13
FI	8	9	4	IT[a]	9	7	14	IT	6	7	5
FR	7	8	5	FI	9	10	5	SI	6	10	–2
PT	6	9	1	FR	8	10	6	FI	5	7	1
ES	6	9	0	AT	7	8	6	**Euro Area**	**2**	**3**	**0**
LU	5	5	4	ES	7	10	0	NL	2	0	5
Euro Area	**4**	**4**	3	PT	6	9	2	FR	2	2	1
AT	4	4	4	**Euro Area**	**5**	**5**	**3**	BE	1	1	1
IE	2	5	–4	NL	2	1	3	DE	1	1	1
NL	2	1	3	IE	1	4	–5	IE	1	8	–14
BE	0	–3	5	DE	0	0	0	ES	0	5	–10
DE	0	0	0	BE	0	–3	7	AT	–3	–4	–1

[a]The rate of growth of loans for house purchases was affected by the discontinuity introduced in the survey statistics. The rate corrected by that effect is 8.5 (Assofin, CRIF, Prometeia 2011).

Source: Eurosystem Statistics: Euro-Area aggregates and national contributors, various years.

banking system, and helps the stability of its operations, in a countercyclic fashion. This behaviour also coincides with a stiffening of selection and creditworthiness assessment criteria (ESBC, Bank Lending Survey, various years).

As we have already mentioned, Italian households have lower levels of debt than those in other countries, in Europe and beyond (Figure 7.1).

At the start of the crisis, Italian households had the lowest level of debt of all the main European countries and the United States, a significant factor, especially in the area of real estate, where the importance of property holdings and the intergenerational transfer of real estate and financial assets explain the lower level of recourse to borrowing. With regard to consumer credit, Italian households have gradually brought their behaviour into line with that of other countries, thanks to the rise in the availability of consumer credit and forms of lending more linked to households' financial needs than the financing of purchases at points of sale.

It is interesting to note the trend in credit to households in the United Kingdom and the United States, where households' post-crisis deleveraging is ongoing with regard to consumer credit and loans for house purchase, the latter with a greater time lag, due to their long duration and large amounts, which mean that the current drop in new loans has relatively little effect on the overall picture. In the Euro Area countries, on the other hand, the process is less accentuated in the use of consumer credit, while the use of loans for house purchases is on the increase, although the trends vary from country to country, depending on the performance of their respective property markets. In Italy, the demand for loans to purchase houses has been particularly high, and

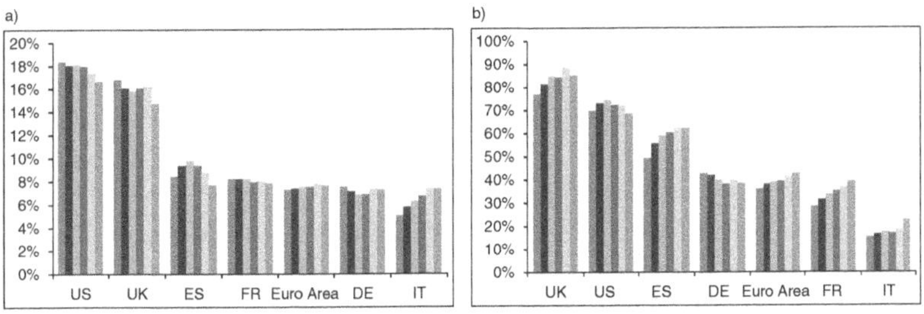

Figure 7.1 The evolution of credit to Italian household sector ,as a percentage of GDP, 2005–10. (a) Consumer credit as a percentage of GDP; (b) Housing loans as a percentage of GDP

Source: Processing of European Credit Research Institute Statistical Package 2011.

households' home loan debts as a percentage of GDP have risen from 13.3 per cent at the start of 2006 to 22.7 per cent in 2010.

7.3 Credit to households in Italy

As we have said, Italy is a bank-based country when it comes to the financing of businesses, with a rate of corporate bank lending much higher than the Euro Area average. However, the role of banks in household credit is traditionally much lower, due to both the lower level of demand and to the large number of specialist firms covering almost half the consumer credit market.

During the last decade, the extent of lending to consumer households has increased, due in particular to the strong growth in loans for house purchases and other purposes related to real estate. In 1998, households accounted for about 18 per cent of the portfolio of loans to customers resident in Italy, but in 2011 this figure had risen to about 30 per cent (Table 7.4).

The growth in loans to households has led to a gradual reduction in the weight within the loans portfolio of lending to government in general and to financial firms, while the proportion of loans to corporations and producer households remained more or less stable until 2009. During 2010–11, the recession that followed on from the financial crisis adversely affected corporate lending but encouraged loans to households, and in particular mortgage loans used to purchase houses, in view of the low interest rates and the drop in property prices. On the supply side, this trend is explained by the lower risk level of loans to households, which have a lower loan to value (LTV) than in previous years and very good security, obviously making them an attractive alternative to the risks involved in loans to companies.

The risk level of consumer households is lower than that of companies and producer households, especially in the area of loans for real estate purchases. The financial and economic crisis led to a worsening of families' creditworthiness, leading to a growth in the proportion of non-performing loans amongst banks' assets. Figure 7.2, which plots the level of total bad debts, fails to reflect the gradual improvement from 2010 onwards, which further encouraged the offering of new loans to households.

The supply of home loan and consumer credit products to households by Italian banks has grown over time, but at different rates, reflecting the different sizes of the potential markets and the intensity of the competition from other financial intermediaries. The effects of these

Table 7.4 Breakdown of percentage of total loans to customers resident in Italy, by debtor type, 1998–2011

Debtor	1998	1999	2000	2001	2002	2003	2004	2005	2006	2007	2008	2009	2010	2011[a]
General government	8	8	6	6	5	5	4	4	4	4	4	4	3	3
Non-financial corporations	54	52	53	53	53	53	53	52	53	54	55	54	51	52
Producer households	7	7	7	6	6	7	7	6	6	6	6	6	6	6
MFIs	13	13	14	15	15	13	12	12	12	11	11	11	11	10
Consumer households	18	20	20	20	21	22	24	25	25	25	24	26	29	29
Totale	100	100	100	100	100	100	100	100	100	100	100	100	100	100

[a]Values as of 30 June 2011.

Source: Processing of Banca d'Italia (BIP online statistical database) (www.bancaditalia.it).

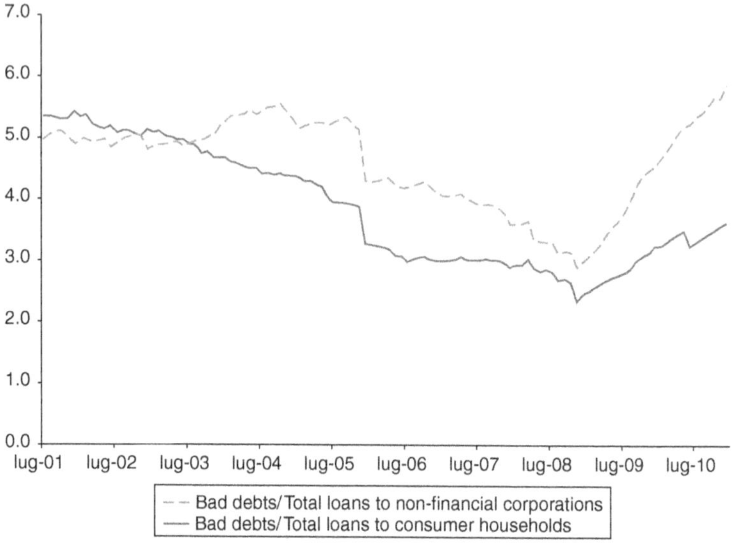

Figure 7.2 Bad debts to non-financial corporations and consumer households, banks in Italy 2001–10

Source: Processing of Bank of Italy (BIP online statistical database).

different trends can be perceived in the composition of banks' loan portfolios; they consist mainly of mortgage loans, which accounted for about 84.8 per cent of lending to households in 2010 (Table 7.5).

This situation derives from banks' long-established focus on households' property investments, mainly the purchase of their main home, as against a lower degree of interest in consumer credit. The outcome of banks' strategies is clear in the striking difference between their roles on the two different markets: the mortgage loans market is almost all in the hands of the banks, while they share the consumer credit market with specialist firms and financial intermediaries, through the creation of specialist firms within their groups, as we will see below.

7.4 Italian banks and mortgage loans for house purchases

Italian households' borrowing behaviour varies considerably between the areas of mortgage loans for house purchases and consumer credit.

Taking out a home purchase mortgage is a stressful event for households; the procedure involves considerable costs and a complex,

Table 7.5 Mortgage loans for house purchases and consumer credit by banks only, Italy 2003–10

	Loans to consumer households		Outstanding (billions of €)	
	Mortgage loans for house purchases	Consumer credit	Mortgage loans for house purchases	Consumer credit
2010	84.8	15.2	321	58
2009	82.6	17.4	255	54
2008	82.3	17.7	241	52
2007	82.0	18.0	226	50
2006	81.6	18.4	208	47
2005	81.5	18.5	184	42
2004	81.3	18.7	155	36
2003	80.5	19.5	126	31

Source: Processing of Banca d'Italia (BIP online statistical database).

carefully considered purchase process, which includes consideration of alternative proposals and may even cause a household to change banks. In response, in the early years of this century Italian banks placed mortgages at the centre of their clientele acquisition strategies, undertaking a large-scale product innovation process and modifying creditworthiness requirements to increase demand for these products and make them affordable for more potential customers.

During these years, many banks expanded their range of products in response to competition in the mortgage market, to attract new clientele or, much more often, to defend their own customer base from competitor banks.

The traditional mortgage loan, a mature product, was revitalised by means of new mechanisms to make it more responsive to households' needs for greater flexibility of use and less uncertainty. The range of mortgages available was extended with the addition of products capable of stabilising repayment installments by means of flexible duration, mitigating interest rate risk by means of caps on financial charges and forms of supplementary cover, and transferring the household's risks (death, injury, unemployment, and various adverse events) by means of a variety of different insurance policies (Assofin, CRIF, Prometeia, various years).

From the credit point of view, at the same time the banks reduced the requirements of mortgage loan operations with regard to duration, the type of interest rate, amounts, loan to value and, last but not least, the debtor's characteristics. However, it must be underlined that although Italian banks expanded the amounts, duration, and LTV of their home loans, their policy in selling mortgages to households continued to be, on average, more prudent than that of the banks of other countries. Moreover, from the risk management point of view, this expansion of the offering coincided with wider use of credit scoring techniques in the screening of operations and borrowers (Rossi 2008).

Although a greater awareness of risk and a more prudent approach are noticeable in the period after the Lehman Brothers collapse, banks' strategies and the increased offering of home loans continued largely as before (Figure 7.3).

The trend in the mortgage loan market during 2007–08 was shaped more by uncertainty and weakness in demand and in the housing market than it was shaped by a credit squeeze due to funding costs or constraints. Italian banks revised some characteristics of their products in response to the changes in economic conditions and in households' disposable incomes, increasing margins on riskier mortgages and reducing the LTV on long-term home loans (Del Giovane et al. 2010).

The crisis did not cause a break in the rising demand for mortgages and neither did it significantly change the characteristics of the mortgages granted in terms of amount and duration, except for a small reduction in mortgages with repayment times of over 25 years, which in 2010 were still 38 per cent of the mortgages agreed upon.

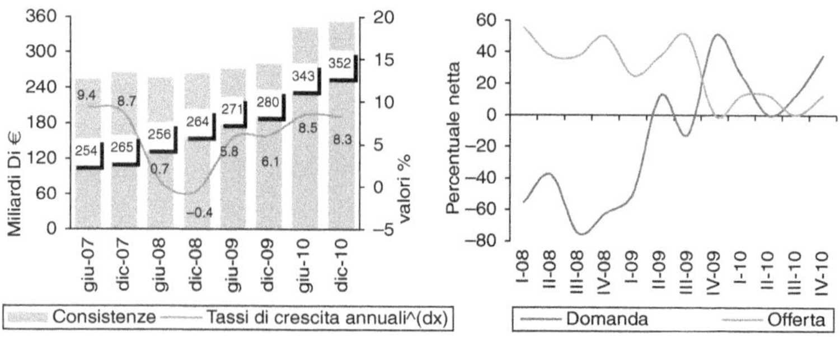

Figure 7.3 (Left) Market of Mortgage loans for house purchases. (Right) Index on the supply and demand conditions for house purchase loans

Note: ^2010 growth rates corrected for the discontinuity effect introduced by the banks' statistics.

Source: Processing of Assofin, CRIF, Prometeia, Ossservatori sul credito al dettaglio, various years.

The effects on mortgage interest rate choices, influenced by the trend in interest rates and the Euribor (European Interbank Offered Rate), were more significant (Figure 7.4). During the economic crisis, Italian households mainly chose fixed-rate mortgages, which in 2008 accounted for 72 per cent of the total, due above all to the higher degree of certainty. During the next two years, households again turned their attention to variable interest rate mortgages, although the widespread, growing use of formulas providing protection against interest rate rises and the setting of a rate cap is noticeable. Households were also encouraged to take this approach by a number of inefficiencies in the Italian banking system with regard to the pricing of fixed-rate mortgages, the costs of which are higher than the Euro Area average (Rinaldi 2009), which might be the outcome of a policy of transferring interest rate risk to households.

The analysis of the level of risk of mortgage loans for house purchases clearly reveals that they are the most stable, least risky form of loans to households. The effects of the financial crisis and the recession are clearly visible in the trend in impaired loans, in spite of the action taken by the government and the Associazione Bancaria Italiana (ABI) with the "moratoria" (measures to support mortgage borrowers – ABI Agreement, 2009), which helped to stabilise the trend in bad debts and allow households in difficulty to set their finances in order, and which were applied to almost 2 per cent of mortgage loans for house purchases during 2009–11.

From the organisational point of view, the processes for the granting of home loans are less standardised and require more staff involvement

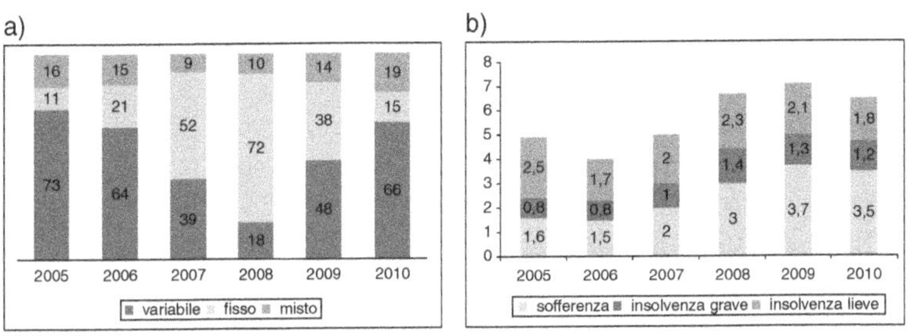

Figure 7.4 Features of mortgage loans for house purchases. (a) Interest rates by type; (b) Bad debts

Source: Processing of Assofin, CRIF, Prometeia, Osservatori sul credito al dettaglio, various years.

than consumer credit decisions, during interaction and negotiation with the customer and the gathering of the necessary information, in view of the complexity of the assessment of the borrower's creditworthiness and the duration of the operation. Creditworthiness assessment and lending decisions are being increasingly handled by means of credit scoring systems, which, however, are still not widely used during the loan pricing process (Rossi 2008). The need for a phase of direct interaction and the importance of the advisory service the bank is able to offer households, as well as the regulatory requirements for contracts, increase the importance of the direct distribution channels, the branches, and reinforce banks' ability to dominate the mortgage loan market, where there are no alternative competitors except for a few banks that use different business models, based to a greater extent on "virtual" channels (Internet, call centres, or online brokers) and indirect channels (agents, brokers, and financial advisers) and on cost leadership strategies.

In 2010 almost 71 per cent of mortgage loans were provided through direct distribution channels, while 24 per cent passed through longer distribution channels with the involvement of a third party. The proportion of mortgage loans managed by means of direct or indirect online channels is rising, accounting for 5 per cent of mortgages granted in 2010 (Assofin, CRIF, Prometeia, Retail Credit Observatory 2011).

7.5 Banks and consumer credit

Italian households' use of credit has been gradually increasing in recent years. The change in households' behaviour and their greater willingness to borrow is due not only to a large number of economic, demographic, social, cultural, psychological, and institutional factors, but also to the policies implemented on the supply side. From the cultural point of view, the negative connotations traditionally associated with borrowing to finance personal consumption are evolving towards a more ordinary concept of consumer credit as a way of managing needs and purchases of varying importance. Use of consumer credit has also risen as a result of changes in social organisation and household composition – greater mobility within the country, decline of the patriarchal and/or extended family, reduction in the financial importance of family groups, and a decrease in forms of informal lending (Table 7.6).

The overall market for consumer credit delivered by banks and specialist financial firms, calculated before securitisation, amounted to

Table 7.6 Evolution of consumer credit in Italian households

	2005	2006	2007	2008	2009	2010
Outstanding (billions of €)	78	91	102	111	121	123
Growth rate (stock) (%)	18.5	17.5	14.1	8.7	8.8	–1.8
Growth rate (new business; %)	n.a.	n.a.	9.6	1.3	–11.2	–5.2

Source: Processing of Assofin, CRIF, Prometeia, Osservatorio sul credito, various years.

€123 billion in 2010, which maintained the upward trend of previous years, although rising at a slower rate than in 2009. It is only during 2010, due to the financial crisis and recession and regulatory changes, that demand has shrunk for the first time.

In fact, the effects of the crisis are clear if we observe the new loans; they affect the trend in loan sizes, with some delay due to the compensation between new loans and annual repayments of existing loans.

During the period after the Lehman Brothers collapse (2008–10), the growth in the consumer credit market in Italy came to an abrupt halt after 15 years of continual, rapid growth. During the second half of 2008 and the first six months of 2009, on the supply side, the reduction in the amount of consumer credit provided derived from the liquidity squeeze affecting a large number of specialist financial firms due to the stop in securitisations and the reduction in the parent banking groups' funding capacity.

On the demand side, the reduction was due to the shrinkage in consumption, especially consumer durables and car purchases, and the rationalisation or postponement of household purchases in a climate of great uncertainty and falling disposable income.

Although the trend in demand has suffered from the economic situation of the last two years (2009–10), households are showing considerable financial maturity in their use of consumer credit, also reflected in the growing use of direct forms of credit (personal loans), which are not related to the purchase of a specific asset and which require households to go through a specific research and decision-making process. (Figure 7.5)

With regard to demand and households' financial behaviour, the recomposition of the market in favour of non-purpose loans (personal loans, credit cards and loans backed by the assignment of one-fifth of the borrower's salary) reflects a less improvised, ad hoc use of credit on the part of households, with borrowing increasingly occurring outside

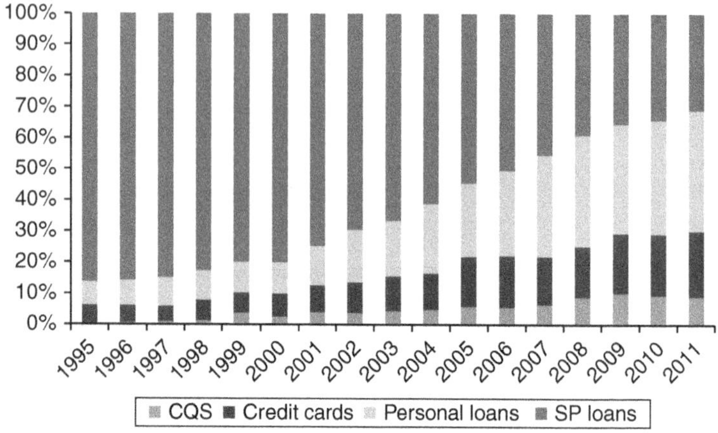

Figure 7.5 Consumer credit by type: Personal loans, credit cards, SP (special purpose loans: loans with special purpose to pay a good or a service, they are alloted by the lender to the seller directly), and CQS (loans backed by the assignment of one-fifth of the borrower's salary)

Source: Processing of Assofin, CRIF, Prometeia, Osservatori sul credito al dettaglio, various years.

the retail stores. However, this change is also due to a major shift in banks' role in the supply of consumer credit.

During the last few years, households' preferred form of consumer credit has been non-purpose loans, obtained through direct channels (branches of banks and specialised financial institutions); they are loans of increasing amount and duration. Although influenced by policies on the supply side, households have shown a preference for more traditional channels, a factor beneficial to banks that are capable of making good use of their distribution networks, reputations, and clientele relations.

During the last decade, in Italy Italian banks have significantly modified their role and importance in consumer credit. Traditionally, their level of interest in consumer credit has been low. Until the early years of this century, they left this business to specialist firms, foreign banks, and the large automotive groups' captive firms.

It is only during the last decade that Italian banks have turned their attention to this business segment, in response to three main factors: moves on the part of companies that supplied consumer credit to add payment and investment services to their offering, which increased the competition for household clientele; the drop in the profitability of corporate banking and asset management compared to consumer credit;

and the growth and development in demand for consumer credit from households, who were starting to assign consumer credit a complementary role in the management of family budgets, moving from specific-purpose loan products to personal finance services.

Italian banks, and the largest banking groups in particular, adopted external growth strategies, taking over specialist firms that operated in the market to create a culture and to develop the skills typical of an activity that required different lending processes from those traditionally applied by banks (Table 7.7).

Unlike mortgage loans for house purchases, consumer credit requires processes that deliver credit quickly and efficiently. From this point of view, the market and competition mechanisms have gradually rewarded the specialisation and industrialisation (meaning above all standardisation and automation) of consumer credit production processes.

The acquisition and incorporation of specific companies within banking groups (Table 7.7) in the Italian banking system have enabled banks to redefine and revitalise their role in consumer credit market, redrawing the structure of the market offering and the overall organisation of the consumer credit industry.

The growing integration of specialist firms and banks has helped to improve banking groups' ability to deliver consumer credit (Cosma 2009). This has brought the following factors to the fore:

- There has been differentiation and organisational independence of those companies whose specialisation in terms of production-distribution and the standardisation of processes enables them to optimise costs and improve selection and credit-allocation procedures.

Table 7.7 Italian banking groups with consumer credit specialised financial institutions (SFIs)

	2003	2004	2005	2006	2007	2008	2009	2010	2011
Banking groups with specialised financial institutions (units)	3	7	8	11	16	16	17	19	19
Specialised financial institutions (units)	3	8	9	12	24	22	23	24	25

Source: Processing of Banca d'Italia banking group register and supervisory lists. Specialised financial institutions ranked by Bank of Italy as consumer credit specialised financial institutions.

- Banks have made use of their access to information, their relational capital, and their territorial networks, which are capable of understanding the clientele's needs, and they have used established relationships to distribute their credit products.

In 2010, almost all the main Italian banking groups included a consumer credit specialised financial institution (SFI), operating in relation to strategic targets, both as a supplier of products for addition to retail banks' offerings to improve relationships with the clientele of reference and as an independent firm with its own distribution channels, working to acquire new clientele and develop volume and margins (Cosma 2009). In the early 2000s, the consumer credit market was characterised by a high degree of segmentation by product, with the banks playing a marginal role in the market, merely delivering personal loans, while the specialist intermediaries provided the lion's share of loans for specific purchases. A decade later, the consumer credit market is still highly segmented, but by function: specialist financial firms dominate production, and banks handle most of the distribution.

Specialist firms whose operations integrate with and complement those of the banking groups have clearly played a key role in maintaining and revitalising the role of the banks in the area of consumer credit (Figure 7.6). At the end of 2010, the retail banks (which deliver consumer credit under the traditional model, without specialist processes) had a market share of 11 per cent, which had gradually fallen over the previous years. Although it is not possible to reconstruct the historic series for the years before 2005, it is clear that the combination of banks-specialist firms within banking groups has proved successful, capable of giving new vigour to banks' role. If we bear in mind the acquisitions of two major specialist banking companies by two independent SFIs in 2008, the banks' total market share in 2010 becomes 52 per cent rather than 46 per cent.

The right-hand side of the Figure 7.6 reveals the banks' growing role in the distribution of consumer credit, partly through partnerships between small banks and specialist firms, which provide both production and service.

7.6 Retail funding and the role of the household sector

Italian banks have a deposit-funded lending model, predominantly using financial resources generated by deposits and bonds, in contrast to other systems where funding is obtained from major securitisation of assets, typical of a market-funded model (Mottura and Paci 2009).

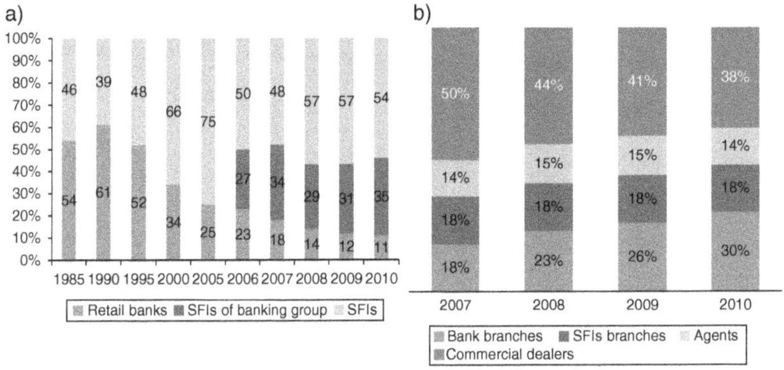

Figure 7.6 Consumer credit by lenders: the role of retail banks and banking groups. (a) Market of Mortgage loans for house purchases; (b) Consumer credit by distributive channels

Source: Processing of Assofin, CRIF, Prometeia, Osservatori sul credito al dettaglio, various years.

An analysis of Italian banks' liabilities (Table 7.8) reveals a number of important features of the banking business and the funding models used by the Italian banking system. A sort of polarisation emerges in Italian banks' funding sources, between other euro resident deposits (overnight) and debt securities (bond).

Both before and after the crisis, sight deposits account for about one-fifth of Italian banks' total funding, a level almost double the Euro Area average. A survey performed over a longer time-span than 2007 reveals the striking stability of sight deposit levels and their contribution to the system's economic-financial equilibrium, due to a considerable extent to their lower cost compared to time and notice deposits.

Provided the payments circuit functions effectively, sight deposits are a stable source of bank funding. From this point of view, Italian households' payment habits and the trend in their transactions and precautionary savings also play an important role. Another reason for the high proportion of sight deposits compared to time or notice deposits is the Italian tax system, which does not provide incentives for longer-term deposits (except for bonds).

Bank bonds are another important source of funding for Italian banks. They accounted for a proportion of funding above the Euro Area average before the crisis, and after the Lehman Brothers collapse, this percentage increased, until by the end of 2010 bonds represented about 21.2 per cent of Italian banks' entire balance sheets.

Last but not least, the low level of funding obtained from residents in countries outside the Euro Zone should be underlined. This is due

Table 7.8 Aggregated balance sheets of MFIs

	2007					2010				
	Euro Area	DE	ES	FR	IT	**Euro Area**	DE	ES	FR	IT
Deposits of Euro Area residents	**51.4**	58.5	65.1	42.8	53.2	**51.2**	54.3	64.2	43.6	54.8
MFIs	**20.6**	23.4	15.5	22.5	22.0	**17.9**	18.0	13.0	21.0	16.7
Central government	**0.4**	0.5	0.9	0.3	0.4	**0.6**	0.5	1.3	0.5	0.4
Other general government/other Euro Area residents	**30.3**	34.5	48.7	20.0	30.8	**32.7**	35.8	49.8	22.1	37.6
Overnight	**10.7**	10.4	16.1	6.4	19.1	**11.9**	13.3	14.7	6.7	20.1
With agreed maturity	**13.1**	16.4	29.6	6.7	1.8	**13.2**	14.0	32.8	7.9	5.9
Redeemable at notice	**5.5**	7.3	0.0	6.2	6.7	**6.2**	7.5	0.0	6.6	7.3
Repos	**1.0**	0.4	2.9	0.7	3.2	**1.3**	1.0	2.3	1.0	4.2
Money market fund shares/units	**2.6**	0.4	0.0	5.9	2.1	**1.9**	0.1	0.2	5.0	1.0
Debt securities issued	**15.7**	21.6	14.1	13.8	18.0	**15.0**	17.0	12.4	14.1	21.2
Capital and reserves	**5.7**	4.6	6.9	5.5	7.8	**6.4**	4.6	8.1	6.1	9.2
External liabilities	**15.4**	9.7	7.1	16.3	6.3	**13.1**	8.5	8.2	13.2	5.1
Remaining liabilities	**9.3**	5.2	6.8	15.6	12.6	**12.4**	15.5	6.8	18.0	8.7
Total	**100**	100	100	100	100	**100**	100	100	100	100

Source: Processing of Banca d'Italia – BIP online statistical database (www.bancaditalia.it).

partly to structural features of the Italian banking system and partly to a mixed bag of historic, social, reputational and naturally, economic-financial factors.

The wealth of Italian households (Figure 7.7) must be considered when assessing Italian banks' demand for financial funding. Italian households' financial wealth in relation to disposable income is above the Euro Area average. This position is further reinforced if we consider real estate investments, which account for about 60 per cent of Italian households' wealth.

From this point of view, although it has risen during the last few years, Italian households' use of credit has not reduced their overall wealth. Net wealth (real estate and financial wealth minus households' liabilities) has continued to grow at an annual rate of 1.7 per cent, in spite of the significant reductions in the value of financial assets and homes after the financial crisis and the uncertainty of the property market.

Real estate wealth consists almost entirely of homes, which account for about 83 per cent of property wealth. On the other hand, the breakdown of financial wealth confirms the importance of bank deposits, which account for about 30 per cent of Italian households' savings, with a positive trend in both sight deposits and bank bonds.

During the crisis, households shifted their financial assets into more liquid forms of investment, but without reducing their contribution to banks' funding. It was only in 2010 that families reduced their bank deposits and investments, in response to both the fiercer competition

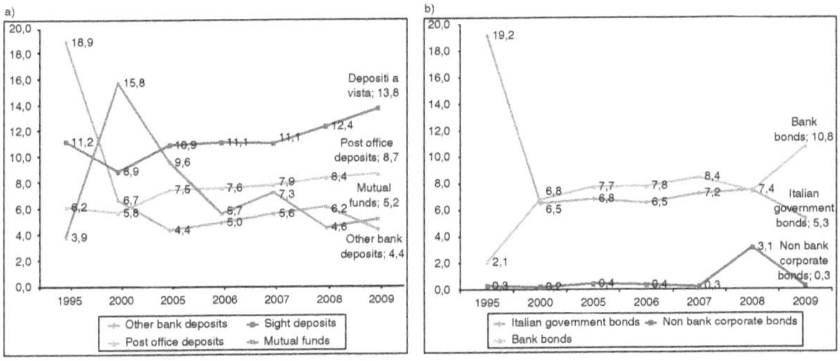

Figure 7.7 Composition of household financial wealth in Italy, 1995–2009. (a) Bank and post office deposits to total financial wealth; (b) Bank bonds, government bonds and non-bank corporate bonds to total financial wealth

Source: Processing of Banca d'Italia – Household Wealth in Italy 2010.

from post office saving products and the effects of banking strategies, which increased the offering of investment products other than direct deposits and insurance plans (Banca d'Italia 2011a).

One central factor in the assessment of Italian banks' funding capacity and financial stability, even during the credit crunch, is the role of retail funding compared to wholesale funding and, closely linked to this, the role of households in the funding of Italian banks.

This was a strong point of the Italian banking system at the peak of the financial crisis, helping to mitigate its negative effects both on banks' liquidity and on their capacity to continue to fulfil their role of financing the economy.

Retail funding is measured as the sum of bank deposits and bonds held by subjects other than banks, financial companies, institutional investors and/or common monetary funds. Consisting basically of household savings, retail funding is more stable in terms of price and volume because it is less vulnerable to market stresses and feels their effects later than wholesale funding.

In 2007, retail funding accounted for 68.7 per cent of Italian banks' total funding, more than 10 percentage points above the Euro Area average (Figure 7.8). The increase in the perceived counterparty risk on the international markets, the tensions on the wholesale markets, and the reduction in financial investments held by both Italian and foreign banks led to a significant increase in retail funding in 2008. Households retained their trust in banks and responded positively to their bond and deposit offerings, guaranteeing them continued stable funding.

It was only in 2010 that the weight of retail funding fell, although it was still above the Euro Area average; this happened due to the recovery in wholesale funding arising from the improvement in the international situation and because of the increase of deposits from non-residents, generated by the recovery in funding of foreign banks after a shrinkage in 2008.

The financial stability of Italian banks' deposit-funded model, based mainly on retail funding, was further reinforced by the level of the *funding gap* – measured as the proportion of loans not financed by retail funding – which was and has remained stable with values of around 9 per cent in 2011.

One possible point of weakness in the deposit-funded model based on retail funding from the household sector might be revealed by the current critical macroeconomic situation and the instability of the labour market, which could lead to a reduction in households' willingness and ability to save as a result of uncertainty over earnings, a drop in real

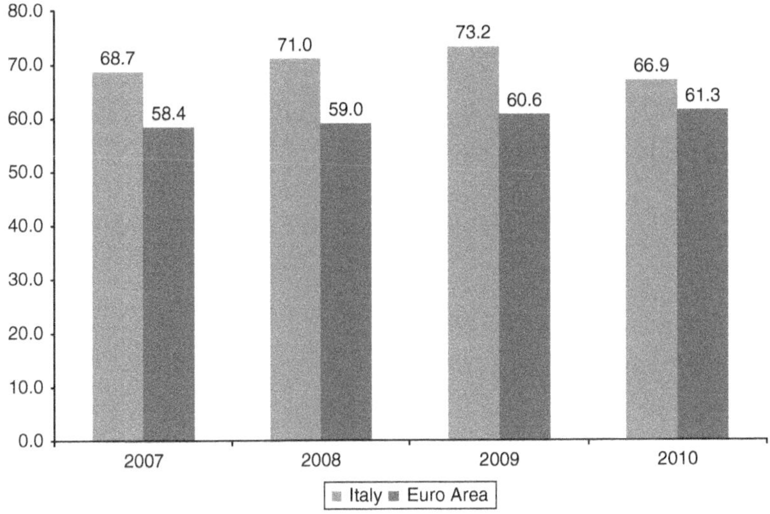

Figure 7.8 Retail funding compared to total funding in Italy and Euro Area (%)
Source: Processing of Banca d'Italia – Annual reports 2007–11.

disposable income, and a gradual increase in the pressure caused by the growing demands on households' budgets.

Note

1. Financial assets other than loans to Euro Area residents consist of: holdings of securities other than shares issued by Euro Area residents, money market fund shares/units, holdings of shares and other equities issued by Euro Area residents, and external assets (held by non-Euro Area residents).

8
Corporate and Investment Banking in Italy

Cesare Bisoni, Andrea Ferrari, and Alessandro Giovanni Grasso

8.1 Introduction

The chapter investigates the way in which the approach taken to corporate banking, and the bank-company relationship, and the strong local roots retained even by the largest groups, all helped to reduce the risk of credit rationing for firms and improved credit risk management on lending to companies in Italy.

Within the bank-company relationship, the second part of the chapter illustrates the nature of corporate and investment banking (CIB) in Italy, describing the way this sector is served by the country's largest banks and outlining possible developments in the light of the recent financial crisis.

8.2 Lending to companies

In Italy, banks have always been the main source of external financing for companies, and especially for small and medium-sized enterprises (SMEs),[1] which are constantly increasing in number due to a general failure to grow in size. The main reasons for this preference for bank finance are the low credit access threshold, the flexibility, and the speed with which loans are issued, the combination with payment services, the easier accessibility and lower cost compared to financing through securities, and the fundamentally "detached" approach of the bank, which does not interfere in the management of companies. This aspect is still very important for family-run companies, which continue to be an essential feature of the Italian industrial scene (Belli and Giordano 2007).

Small and medium-sized enterprises, with informal governance models, generally use fairly simple forms of financing and in particular are suspicious of external equity. The resulting financial structures are based largely on debt, especially short-term borrowing, often supported by the entrepreneur's personal assets, generating an undesirable confusion and a lack of transparency in creditworthiness assessment. The fragility of firms' financial structures leads to the inappropriate transfer of some of the company risk to the bank, which can only be overcome through closer links to the equity market. Italian firms' financial indebtedness in relation to gross domestic product (GDP) is growing constantly, reaching 84 per cent at the end of 2010; leverage has been over 40 per cent for some time, with a high proportion of short-term bank loans to financial debt (Banca d'Italia 2011a).

Even before the start of the financial crisis, Italian companies showed more obvious signs of weakness than the European average: less ability to generate earnings from the core business, a high level of indebtedness in relation to both sales and equity, and a high incidence of financial costs (De Socio 2010). With the latest developments in the sovereign debt crisis in the Euro Area, and in Italy above all, companies' financial fragility and vulnerability have become even more accentuated.

Table 8.1 highlights the undercapitalisation of small and medium-sized enterprises and reveals that the weight of bank lending within their financial structure is constantly around 25 per cent, even exceeding this value in some years. About three-quarters of debts to banks are short-term, although during 2009 there has been a partial shift towards medium- to long-term loans, generating improvements in financial stability.

Larger companies' lower rates of indebtedness are compensated by higher net capital.

The many studies conducted over time by the Bank of Italy, by many academics, and by various industrialists' associations have underlined the need to improve the bank–firm relationship, viewed as unsatisfactory above all because it is often "transaction" rather than "relationship" based. The relationship is therefore rather short on mutual knowledge and understanding, which partly derives from the sharp separation between bank and company introduced by the 1936 banking law.

Companies' tendency to engage in multibanking, leading to the fragmentation of their relationship with the banks, has always been considered emblematic of this situation.

Table 8.1 Financing of Italian manufacturing firms, values as percentages of total liabilities

	Small businesses (revenues lower than €10 million)			
	Bank loan			
Year	**Short term**	**Medium- to long-term**	**Total**	**Equity**
1999	17.66	6.68	24.34	25.75
2000	17.75	6.88	24.63	26.47
2001	18.02	6.71	24.73	27.45
2002	17.82	7.05	24.87	26.67
2003	18.43	7.53	25.96	25.58
2004	18.07	7.89	25.96	26.02
2005	17.86	8.38	26.24	26.65
2006	18.40	8.56	26.96	26.05
2007	18.89	8.85	27.74	26.00
2008	18.09	7.98	26.07	32.43
2009	16.02	9.32	25.34	34.19
	Medium-sized enterprises (revenues between €10–50 million)			
	Bank loan			
Year	**Short term**	**Medium- to long-term**	**Total**	**Equity**
1999	18.42	7.02	25.44	26.26
2000	18.84	6.51	25.35	26.70
2001	18.81	6.53	25.34	27.52
2002	17.73	6.70	24.43	28.13
2003	17.40	7.26	24.66	29.16
2004	17.08	7.38	24.46	29.14
2005	16.51	7.83	24.34	29.89
2006	16.69	8.04	24.73	29.29
2007	17.81	8.32	26.13	29.02
2008	17.49	7.88	25.37	33.03
2009	15.65	8.62	24.27	36.11
	Large corporate banks (revenues more than €50 million)			
	Bank loan			
Year	**Short term**	**Medium- to long-term**	**Total**	**Equity**
1999	12.38	7.19	19.57	29.84
2000	12.26	6.59	18.85	31.07
2001	12.43	7.18	19.61	30.38
2002	11.02	6.58	17.60	31.22
2003	10.24	6.86	17.10	30.92
2004	9.17	6.03	15.20	32.71
2005	8.67	6.24	14.91	32.96
2006	9.11	6.09	15.20	33.47
2007	9.17	6.68	15.85	33.37
2008	9.93	6.37	16.30	34.22
2009	8.34	6.86	15.20	34.33

Source: Processing of BACH – Bank for the Accounts of Companies Harmonized.

8.3 The practice of multibanking

Multibanking has been encouraged by wide variety of factors, including

- from the banks' side: by the lending timespan specialisation imposed by the 1936 banking law, which basically remained in force until 1993;[2] by the constraints with regard to risk concentration; by the small size of most of the banks, meaning that they were unable to completely satisfy the largest firms' financial needs; and by the low margins on loans, which led to a preference for insurance-based risk management;
- from the companies' side: by the positive attitude to indebtedness encouraged by more favourable tax law and entrepreneurs/shareholders' strong propensity for a lack of transparency in their reporting, partly for fiscal reasons.

Pelliccioni and Torluccio (2007) attempted to identify the main reasons for the popularity of multibanking. Their study reveals that the number of banking relationships increases in direct proportion to company size, leverage, and the need for financial instruments other than those traditionally offered by banks. Multibanking decreases in step with lack of clarity in investments in research & development and investment in tangible fixed assets, and when economic and financial conditions improve.

Both banks and companies considered the practice of multibanking to be beneficial. From the bank's point of view, multibanking reduces credit risk by sharing it across a large number of institutions, with a consequent limitation of the costs of information and creditworthiness assessment (often problematic due to the lack of transparency in information), and makes it possible to stop financing the company further in the event that danger signals are noted, and to cancel the credit line if necessary. Companies view favourably the fact that they can trade their supplier banks off against each other and thus save on the cost of money, avoid revealing their real economic and financial situation to any of the banks, and protect themselves against the sudden cancellation of credit lines, which may occur, especially at times of financial difficulty.

In reality, these benefits are more apparent than real. The fragmentation of credit risk due to the spread of lending across a number of banks, and the strong weight assigned to collateral as a parameter for assessing the company's solvency, discourage banks from acquiring significant information about companies, weakening their role as selectors of investment projects. The consequence may be that they lose a sense of responsibility, and tend to follow, as one author has aptly put it, a sort of "herd instinct" (Ciocca 1991). These types of inefficiency in the allocation of lending may be even more detrimental for the small and medium-sized enterprises with the best prospects for growth and profitability. Furthermore, an approach based on limited mutual knowledge leads the bank to underestimate overall credit risk and to apply a higher spread across-the-board to cover higher losses on loans, not to perform creditworthiness assessment with the necessary professionalism and expertise, and thus to require higher collateral, behaving in the way companies have always criticised; it also prevents banks from providing companies with useful advice and recommendations.

For the company, multibanking implies sacrificing the opportunity of across-the-board financial advice from a single source and losing the chance of reducing overall costs by integrating the various services used. Moreover, empirical research has demonstrated that firms are less likely to suffer credit constraints when they do business with only a few banks (Guelpa and Tirri 2004).

Therefore, in general terms, the practice of multibanking creates a weak relationship between the bank and the firm, which, as we have already seen, tends to be transaction-based (Ruozi and Zara 2001) and multibanking discourages the establishment of relationships that last over time. A respected leading figure in the Bank of Italy summed up the problem in a nutshell years ago: "*Firms rely on banks both too much and not enough*" (Padoa-Schioppa 1995).

The multibanking approach is still very widespread, although there has been a gradual reduction in its prevalence in the last few years, hand in hand with an increase in the proportion of lending provided by the company's chief bank.

Table 8.2 reveals that the average number of banks per borrower company fell between 1998 and 2010 from 2.96 to 2.51. The data by size category of the total credit line granted reveals that this reduction, which has accelerated from 2006, is particularly noticeable for companies in the largest size classes, although they still do business with a large number of banks. This is no surprise, given that even companies with total access to credit of less than €1 million, and thus of small size, work with nearly three banks from 2005. Basically, progress in the reduction of the number of banks is in the right direction but is rather slow; there is still a long way to go towards the model in which one main bank satisfies the majority of the company's financial needs.

Table 8.2 Average number of banks per borrower, by company's credit line. Manufacturing industry

<table>
<tr><th></th><th></th><th colspan="8">Total credit granted</th></tr>
<tr><th>Year</th><th>Total</th><th>From €75,000 to €125,000</th><th>From €125,000 to €250,000</th><th>From €250,000 to €500,000</th><th>From €500,000 to €1,000,000</th><th>From €1,000,000 to €2,500,000</th><th>From €2,500,000 to €5,000,000</th><th>From €5,000,000 to €25,000,000</th><th>More than €25,000,000</th></tr>
<tr><td>1998</td><td>2.96</td><td>1.01</td><td>1.39</td><td>2.18</td><td colspan="2">3.88</td><td>6.60</td><td>9.22</td><td>14.51</td></tr>
<tr><td>1999</td><td>2.91</td><td>1.01</td><td>1.37</td><td>2.13</td><td colspan="2">3.79</td><td>6.36</td><td>8.92</td><td>14.09</td></tr>
<tr><td>2000</td><td>2.86</td><td>1.01</td><td>1.36</td><td>2.12</td><td colspan="2">3.69</td><td>6.12</td><td>8.59</td><td>13.59</td></tr>
<tr><td>2001</td><td>2.76</td><td>1.01</td><td>1.35</td><td>2.07</td><td colspan="2">3.57</td><td>5.84</td><td>7.98</td><td>12.38</td></tr>
<tr><td>2002</td><td>2.70</td><td>1.01</td><td>1.32</td><td>2.01</td><td colspan="2">3.43</td><td>5.57</td><td>7.65</td><td>11.96</td></tr>
<tr><td>2003</td><td>2.67</td><td>1.00</td><td>1.30</td><td>1.98</td><td colspan="2">3.37</td><td>5.45</td><td>7.60</td><td>11.64</td></tr>
<tr><td>2004</td><td>2.67</td><td>1.00</td><td>1.30</td><td>1.96</td><td colspan="2">3.33</td><td>5.43</td><td>7.56</td><td>11.78</td></tr>
<tr><td>2005</td><td>2.67</td><td>1.00</td><td>1.29</td><td>1.94</td><td>2.77</td><td>3.90</td><td>5.38</td><td>7.53</td><td>11.81</td></tr>
<tr><td>2006</td><td>2.68</td><td>1.00</td><td>1.28</td><td>1.92</td><td>2.73</td><td>3.85</td><td>5.27</td><td>7.43</td><td>11.69</td></tr>
<tr><td>2007</td><td>2.64</td><td>1.00</td><td>1.26</td><td>1.87</td><td>2.66</td><td>3.73</td><td>5.03</td><td>7.12</td><td>11.31</td></tr>
<tr><td>2008</td><td>2.56</td><td>1.00</td><td>1.25</td><td>1.84</td><td>2.59</td><td>3.60</td><td>4.82</td><td>6.62</td><td>10.15</td></tr>
<tr><td>2009</td><td>2.39</td><td>1.29</td><td>1.64</td><td>2.16</td><td>2.82</td><td>3.68</td><td>4.85</td><td>6.56</td><td>9.99</td></tr>
<tr><td>2010</td><td>2.51</td><td>1.28</td><td>1.61</td><td>2.07</td><td>2.67</td><td>3.48</td><td>4.54</td><td>6.21</td><td>9.57</td></tr>
</table>

Source: Processing of Banca d'Italia, *Bollettino Statistico*, various years (data at end of December). Values prior to 2002 converted into euros.

Table 8.3 shows that this is already the case for the smallest firms, while for those with access to credit of more than €1 million, the chief bank covers less than 60 per cent of their borrowing needs; this figure falls to around 40 and 30 per cent for companies in the two largest size categories. In any case, predominance from the point of view of the credit line granted is not in itself symptomatic of a satisfactory preferential relationship.

Therefore, on average Italian companies maintain relations with more banks, with a smaller proportion of their lending from their chief bank, than companies in other countries.

The reduction in multibanking that has occurred cannot be imputed only to the consolidation process that has taken place in the banking industry. It is partly due to the process of branch liberalisation. The reduction in the total number of banks has been accompanied by a significant increase in the average number of banks operating in the local markets (Tarantola 2007). This increase has occurred above all in the markets where economic activity is most intense, and thus where the needs for financing to cover investment projects mainly arise. Therefore, the trend away from multibanking can also be interpreted as a growing awareness of the costs and risks of this practice (Cesarini 2003).

The weakness of bank-firm relationships based on multibanking is also confirmed by studies performed to examine its effects on credit availability in the specific context of the financial crisis. In particular, empirical findings reveal that "Firms which borrow from a larger number of banks experience lower credit growth, while firms with more concentrated credit experience higher credit growth." (De Mitri et al. 2010).

Moreover, companies that borrow from many banks are also more likely to be credit-constrained. On the other hand, more concentrated lending with the main bank, with the latter providing a high proportion of lending, reduces the probability of being asked to cut credit. The effects of the stability of the banking relationship are clear, since the relationship only becomes significant if it is of sufficiently long duration (De Mitri et al. 2010).

With the start of the crisis, there has been a great deal of discussion as to the degree of credit constraint firms may have suffered from, and this has highlighted a controversial aspect of the bank-company relationship. More rigid lending criteria and an increase in the number of firms having difficulty in accessing bank loans are typical of recessions and arise from a deterioration in the quality of loans. However, since the crisis had a number of causes, it is not possible to establish whether

Table 8.3 First bank's share of total credit granted. Manufacturing ndustry (percentages)

Year	Total credit granted							
	From €75,000 to €125,000	From €125,000 to €250,000	From €250,000 to €500,000	From €500,000 to €1,000,000	From €1,000,000 to €2,500,000	From €2,500,000 to €5,000,000	From €5,000,000 to €25,000,000	More than €25,000,000
1998	99	82	64	48		38	32	26
1999	99	83	65	48		39	33	27
2000	99	83	65	49		40	34	26
2001	99	84	66	50		41	35	29
2002	99	85	68	52		42	36	29
2003	99	85	68	52		43	36	30
2004	99	86	69	53		43	36	30
2005	99	86	69	58	50	43	35	28
2006	99	87	70	59	50	43	35	28
2007	99	87	71	60	51	45	37	28
2008	99	88	72	61	52	46	38	30
2009	88	79	69	60	53	46	39	30
2010	89	80	71	63	55	48	40	30

Source: Processing of Banca d'Italia, *Bollettino Statistico*, various years (data at end of December). Values prior to 2002 converted into euros.

and to what extent the credit squeeze that undoubtedly occurred during the period was due to demand-side factors or to a supply-side shortage. Similarly, it is not possible to state beyond doubt whether the reduction in the availability of loans was due, even partially, to decisions and constraints within the banking system. During 2011, the raising of the bar noted in the criteria for lending to companies appears to be directly linked to banks' liquidity situation and funding difficulties, as a consequence of the tensions surrounding Italy's sovereign debt.

However, with regard to the existence and extent of constraints on lending to companies, the findings of questionnaire surveys conducted regularly by Osservatorio UniCredit have been available for some time, and thus also cover periods prior to the crisis.[3] Their results provide information about small firms' perception of the degree of rationing suffered before and after the peak of the crisis. A comparison between the replies provided during the two years covered by the survey, 2008 and 2009, indicates that, while there was a clear increase (from 26.7 per cent to 44.4 per cent) in the number of firms that would have liked to obtain more loans (weak rationing), the number that would have been unable to obtain loans even if they had been prepared to pay a higher interest rate (strong rationing) was 5.0 per cent for 2008 and 7.6 per cent for 2009. The data indicate only a fairly limited rise in the level of rationing. If the comparison is extended to the pre-crisis period, the proportion of companies that feel credit-constrained, although significant,[4] is sharply below the level for 2008 and 2009.

With the onset of the crisis, there was also a marked deterioration in the quality of the loans granted. Bad debts (loans granted to borrowers who are insolvent or are in basically equivalent situations, regardless of collateral), which accounted for 3.11 per cent of the total loans granted in December 2007, had risen to 5.40 per cent in March 2012.

If measured on the basis of impaired loans, meaning not only bad debts but also loans to subjects in temporary financial difficulty,[5] the quality of loans is very low, and is constantly deteriorating. Compared to December 2008, the number of impaired loans as of March 2012 (Banca d'Italia, Bollettino statistico, various years) had doubled, from 5.11 per cent to 11.62 per cent of total loans.

8.4 The process of change within the banking system

During the last twenty years, especially due to the introduction of the Consolidated Law on Banking of 1993, the Italian banking system has undergone deep-seated change involving the main factors influencing the bank-firm relationship, which has led banks to rethink their approach in this area. The following are particularly significant:

- consolidation within the banking system, which has involved a large number of banks of all sizes and has caused major changes in market shares, also benefiting the "independent" banks, i.e., mutual banks and banks that do not belong to groups (Tarantola 2008);
- the inclusion of efficiency amongst the aims of supervisory policy, which has generated changes in banks' culture and governance;
- the despecialisation of intermediaries in terms of areas of business and lending time-scales, the introduction of the universal bank and the consequent opening-out of operating possibilities;
- the growth of competition and the increasing specialisation of the financial system, which have led banks to prioritise "relationships" and thus to introduce loyalty-creation strategies based on the delivery of customised services rather than strategies for increasing client numbers through price alone;
- the evolution of banks' organisational models, partly as a result of the many M&A operations, which has increased the capability for meeting firms' needs by means of a broad, complete product offering.

The changes outlined above have created favourable conditions for the improvement of the quality of the bank-firm relationship. In fact:

- Banks are free to target their policies, and, although with variations within the system, they have developed an entrepreneurial approach to the market, offering a full, diversified service. Therefore, the relationship with firms is able to become deeper and more complex and can be fulfilled through new operating procedures. Basically, the conventional lending function can now form part of a complete, integrated assistance and advisory service.
- Firms are showing signs of paying more and more attention to their relationships with banks and the opportunities offered by the financial markets. They tend to classify banks' offerings on the basis of their ability to satisfy specific needs that arise, and they appear to be tending to rationalise the number of their banking relationships, reducing their degree of multibanking, the supposed benefits of which now seem to be less clear. Many well-run companies have already introduced measures to restructure their relationships with the banking system and to attempt to established closer relationships with individual banks.

8.5 From the Consolidated Law on Banking to Basel II: Implications for the bank–company relationship

In Italy, there has always been a tight bond between small and medium-sized enterprises and the local banks, whose main strength lies in their local roots, which allow them to maintain close relationships with the local economy and community; the absence of geographical separation between the bank's top management and the clientele; and their greater willingness to support firms in hard economic times.

These banks have always placed their dealings with small and medium-sized enterprises on a relational footing. This is due to the characteristics of firms of this kind, in terms of both ownership structure and financial management, since their level of capitalisation is low and the processes by which they analyse and plan their financial needs tend to be rudimentary.

If this model of relationship, which includes the positive features mentioned above, is not to produce adverse effects, the bank must retain its own independent capacity to assess a firm's creditworthiness, ensuring that the personal acquaintanceship with the firm's owner that has developed and has been consolidated over time does not lead to decisions inconsistent with the degree of risk considered acceptable, especially in situations where the company's continuity and survival may depend on increased access to credit. In this area, organisational decisions and considerations with regard to the degree of mobility of branch managers are significant; keeping staff in one place for a long time aids the acquisition of soft information, but on the other it may lead to information asymmetries with the bank's central management.

The basic aim of Basel II was to foster a culture of risk awareness amongst banks and to create a direct link between levels of capitalisation and the degree of risk actually undertaken, increasing management's involvement and sense of responsibility in this area (De Laurentis and Caselli 2004). For banks capable of implementing proper, effective risk management methods, this should lead to a reduction in costs, enabling banks to charge lower prices to their best corporate customers, and in particular to those capable of providing, in a transparent, standardised form, current and budget information useful for the accurate assessment of their economic and financial stability and thus of their creditworthiness. In any case it is possible to establish a clearer link than in the past between the price of loans and the risk undertaken by the bank, also benefiting small and medium-sized enterprises, often penalised by their lack of bargaining power (Tarantola 2008).

Basel II encourages banks to introduce more structured lending processes, greater standardisation and formalisation of information, and a different sequence of phases in their creditworthiness assessment procedures.

The problems lie, on the one hand, in smaller-sized firms' inability and/or unwillingness to provide the bank with correct, transparent information in a standardised form, often due to their lack of a properly developed financial function, and on the other, in the difficulty of incorporating soft information, and subjective information above all, in models. Soft information is the type most subject to information asymmetries and is the most difficult type for the relationship's manager to assess and interpret, but it is often the most crucial form of information because it reflects the most important, distinctive aspects of the company's business.

Assessing the creditworthiness of small and medium-sized enterprises is problematical as a result of their undercapitalisation, poor returns, and consequent low investment capabilities; the use of the entrepreneur's own assets as collateral is often fundamental to the granting of a loan. In cases of this kind, qualitative information is of major importance (Mieli 2009).

Apart from causing the loss of valuable information available to the client manager (often the branch manager), the problems of giving due weight to the soft information in the evaluatuion process may result in significant changes in bank-firm relationship, including on the availability and cost of credit, something that like many representatives of the business community complain. It is worth focusing attention on this topic because it may have negative consequences for the relationship between the bank and the customer firm and its potential development; in general terms, it may delay or even prevent the transition from the transaction to the relationship banking model (Cosma 2002).

The use of soft information for the purposes of credit risk assessment is easier where the distance between the bank's decision-making centres and the firm's geographical location is small, because an appreciation of specific features of the local economic and sociocultural context is fundamental for the correct interpretation and exploitation of information of this kind (Cosma et al. 2003). This points to a potential competitive advantage for local banks over large intermediaries, especially when the organisational model chosen by the latter is divisional by areas of business, which may cause fragmentation of the relationship with the customer-enterpreneur. This may explain the strategies adopted by some large banks, and especially those created by merger processes involving local banks, which have reviewed past decisions with regard to the localisation of lending decision-making centres and shortened the decision-making process (Albareto et al. 2008), handing a major role back to outlying offices, with the added advantage of reducing information transfer costs and the length of time needed to respond to customers' requests. These decisions have also been triggered by the erosion of the shares of the small and medium-sized enterprise market segment suffered by the large banks during the last few years,[6] which might be explained by these companies' preference for the relational approach (Bonaccorsi di Patti et al. 2005).

The negative impact on relations with small and medium-sized enterprises, especially with regard to the proportion of lending allocated to them, was less in cases in which growth was achieved during acquisition processes that kept the local target bank in operation, meaning that the benefits of geographical roots, in information and other terms, were not lost (Beretta and Del Prete 2007). It should also be mentioned that thanks to the development of information technology (IT), it is now possible to process a large proportion of soft information, reducing the large banks' competitive disadvantage in relations with small and medium-sized enterprises compared to their smaller counterparts.

A sample survey conducted by the Bank of Italy and involving more than 300 banks reports an acceleration in the introduction of quantitative models for the assessment of creditworthiness, even for smaller firms, in smaller-sized banks; in 2006 about 60 per cent of these banks applied the new methods to their lending decisions and to the calculation of credit lines and collateral requirements. However, it should be underlined that only 18 per cent of the banks in the sample considered these tools of key importance, and virtually the only factors considered were financial statement data and current borrower status (Albareto et al. 2008), confirming the difficulty of completely including soft information and the amount of work still to be done before it becomes possible to assign the right weight to qualitative information which, if overlooked, could lead to the rationing of credit or unnecessary increases in the costs applied (Tarantola 2007).

Qualitative information can be acquired and used more easily and with less complexity by smaller banks in view of their nearness to the customer. Under Basel II, the clientele of small and medium-sized enterprises enjoy favourable treatment: for banks that use internal ratings, loans granted to them require capital coverage up to 50 per cent lower than those granted to large corporations, which are considered more exposed to economic cycle risks (Mieli 2009).

In spite of this, with the onset of the financial crisis firms have faced tougher lending terms, and in their perception the banks' changed behaviour is due not only to the different economic context but also to the application of the Basel II rules. Although really the outcome of the increased credit risk, difficulties in accessing credit have been attributed to the new rules.

Banks appear to make little use of the override mechanism envisaged by the regulations to ensure that rating systems are flexible and up to date, mainly because of risk managers' unwillingness to take responsibility for using it. This instrument, where the necessary conditions are met, allows the bank to make effective use of the information available to it and increase its lending efficiency (Mieli 2009).

De Angeli et al. (2007) reveal that small enterprises believe that they have not received sufficient information about the rating process and its underlying principles, and thus about the factors that affect the rating assigned; in their view, this prevents them from taking action to ensure that they are assessed more accurately. Moreover, there is still a widespread conviction that the banks assign great importance to economic and financial information in their lending decisions, and do not pay due attention to qualitative information. Last but not least, although they realise there are benefits in establishing closer relations with one or just a few banks, many small firms hesitate to reduce their number of banking relationships because they are afraid that this may lead to a reduction in the financial resources to which they have access, and they still believe it is advantageous to trade banks off against each other. This may also be due to the belief that obtaining bank loans has become more difficult as a consequence of the transition to Basel II.

8.6 Towards a new bank–firm relationship

If the bank-firm relationship is to be improved, banks need to continue resolutely with the changes implemented in the last few years, above all by extending their knowledge of the firm and the sector in which it works.

This implies making an assessment of the firm that includes an analysis of its competitive position in its sector, verification that the critical factors for success are available, forecasting the cash flows associated with investment projects, and identifying the characteristics of financial needs, essential for choosing the appropriate mix of financing.

An approach of this kind conflicts with the practice of multibanking but is compatible with the use of a single bank of reference, which knows the company and is capable of supplying a broad range of financial services, aiming to achieve a return not on the individual operation but on the relationship overall.

The bank must have suitable technologies and professional competences, together with an organisational structure that facilitates contact with the company, the acquisition of the necessary information on investment projects and on the business as a whole, and correct, swift lending decision-making. The principles on which the bank organises the division and coordination of work in this sector affects the quality of the credit-offering process and its ability to select and support deserving projects.

The degree of development and formalisation of the financial function has a major impact on firms' ability to communicate their objectives and financial needs to the bank and helps to improve the quality of the relationship (Ruozi and Zara 2001).

Another important factor is the bank's ability to support the company's growth by organising integrated financial service packages and offering professional advisory services that assist the firm in making fully informed decisions, especially with regard to harmonising the characteristics of financial needs and the instruments used to cover them, in line with strategic objectives. This aspect, which still appears to receive too little attention (Bentivogli et al. 2007; De Angeli et al. 2007), is particularly problematical for small banks, which have traditionally concentrated on lending but may lose their role of main bank if they are unable to adapt their offering to the changed needs of the core clientele. The problem can only be partially resolved through the development within groups or categories of banks of forms of collaboration with larger-sized intermediaries, from which the products required by the clientele can be purchased.

Last but not least, banks can provide a major contribution to strengthening the financial structures of even small-sized firms with growth potential, by assisting their entry onto the equity market.

Venture capital and private equity can also be useful tools for diversifying SMEs' sourcing of finance, with the aim of maintaining leverage at an acceptable level in terms of risk and the cost of finance. Moreover, these forms of investment may enable the firm to grow its management expertise, because the financing project generally involves involvement in the management of the firm, which may be particularly useful in growth phases, and may help to reduce information asymmetries in relation to the market. The underdeveloped state of these markets not only constitutes a gap in the Italian financial system, but also discourages the stock market listing of companies, already viewed with suspicion by many entrepreneurs, who are afraid of losing control of their businesses. Moreover listing is considered problematic due to the costs and the organisational and corporate structural changes required by the current regulations. Companies' failure to list on the stock exchange reduces the ability of venture capital and private equity operators to make funding available, which discourages investment.

In addition, banks' support in obtaining funds from equity markets not only assists companies' growth, but also extends the intermediary's knowledge of its client, the importance of which has already been underlined above.

However, for the banking system to make the necessary contribution to strengthening firms' financial structures, the latter must become more willing to accept the bank as a partner, interested in both the success of business and in the inclusion of new shareholders when it becomes necessary to increase its risk capital, overcoming the typical fears of Italian entrepreneurs. It is also essential for the bank not to exploit the dominant position acquired in relation to the firm solely to its own advantage, and to reinforce the relationship and the loyalty of the customer firm by its behaviour.

The above comments clearly reveal that, in spite of the progress made in recent years, there is still room for improvement in the bank-firm relationship, which must constantly adapt to changes in the factors that influence it.

First and foremost, both parties must make a great effort to change their mindsets, essential for the transition from what is often an antagonistic relationship to one of open collaboration based on mutual trust, which may allow the bank to support good business ventures even in unfavourable economic contexts. This process is definitely under way, and it has recently accelerated, but it is important to be aware that there are wide variations, especially between different parts of the country, and rapid progress is required.

An improvement of the professional competences of the people working within both banks and firms is also necessary; the lion's share of responsibility in this area lies with the banks, in view of their tradition and of the experience they have acquired over the years. What is required is progress in the direction many banks have been following for some time, with an increase of the number of people, within their organisations and above all in the points of contact with the clientele of staff, who are capable of managing highly specialised demand with a strong degree of personalisation.

Finally, firms, and especially small and medium-sized enterprises, must equip themselves to extend their knowledge of their economic and financial situation and its expected evolution. This would benefit their management and would enable them to provide the bank with the information needed for an objective reliable evaluation of their creditworthiness and for monitoring of the relationship on a regular, standardized basis. Furthermore, firms' adoption of formal governance and control models would also win them easier access to external finance, essential for the support of growth processes and for reducing their capital costs.

In conclusion, greater cooperation between the two sides is required, based on transparency; willingness on the part of firms to provide banks with the quantitative and qualitative information necessary for familiarity with their situation and characteristics; the full, correct use of this information by banks in the creditworthiness assessment procedure and in the choice of financing services and their pricing; and a durable relationship.

8.7 The development of the corporate and investment banking business

The positive development of the bank-firm relationship involves the evolution not only of corporate lending, but also of corporate and investment banking services.

The term "investment banking" normally refers to a combination of products and services designed to satisfy a wide range of complex financial needs, which are different from the ordinary financing requirements of the firm's business operations.

The corporate and investment banking services area may offer concrete solutions to a variety of requirements. Financing for growth strategies that represent a major break with the past; access to the equity market; management of generational changeovers; optimisation of debt structure; reconfiguration of the core business; and plans for ownership restructuring or the entry of new financial investors are all examples. These services satisfy needs shared by all firms, needs whose intensity and nature vary depending on the firms' size, sector of business, life cycle phase, ownership structure, and governance model.

Moreover, the complexity of the needs served means that the solutions offered by intermediaries must be equally complex in terms of know-how, production processes, technical-contractual profiles, and pricing models. Therefore, the survey of corporate and investment services gives separate consideration to the various areas of business: capital markets, corporate finance, merchant banking, project finance, asset management, and risk management. It is not necessarily the case that all these areas must or can be effectively covered within the organisation of a single financial intermediary (Capizzi 2007).

The 1990s saw the introduction of processes intended to extend the range of services offered to firms. Interest in this business sector developed mainly within the banking system and to a much lesser extent amongst specialist and specific financial service companies. This is due above all to the process of diversification of areas of business that affected banks during this period and the largely marginal role of specialist financial intermediaries in the Italian context. In contrast to the situation in the United States and the United Kingdom, banks in Italy became the focal point for the development of CIB services.

The characteristics of the financial system, focused more on intermediaries than on markets, meant that in Italy CIB was on a smaller scale than in other financial contexts such as the United States, the United Kingdom, France, and Germany. Some figures will provide a clearer understanding of the context. At the end of 2010, Italy had only 332 companies listed on the stock exchange, compared to 639 in France, 765 in Germany, and 2,603 in the United Kingdom. In terms of breakdown by industry, two-thirds of the value of the Italian stock market were represented by just 10 corporations, operating in the financial, oil and public utilities industries, and there were very few listed firms in the most high-tech, innovative sectors. Considering the 10 initial public offerings and 18 rights issues during the year, in 2010 the equity segment of the capital market attracted investments of €10 billion, 25 per cent of which referred to just one operation. The most important part of the entire Italian capital market is thus the bond segment, with €713 billion. The corporate sector accounts for just 4 per cent of this total, and here again it is extremely concentrated, with 50 per cent of the funds invested received by just four issuers. Therefore, in general the corporate segment features low volumes and very few issuers, reflecting the fact that only a small number of large-sized firms use the financial markets as a source of capital.

The nature of the entrepreneurial fabric and the financial system thus underlie the characteristics of the supply and demand for corporate finance and investment banking services in Italy. The distinctive features of Italian industry are the large number of small-sized enterprises (Eurostat 2011), the centrality of family-based capitalism (Amatori et al. 2011), and the predominance of owner-management (Brandolini and

Bugamelli 2009), which leads to a lack of distinction between the assets of the family and those of the firm, problematical when complex economic variables have to be managed.

Firms' size and governance models influence their financial strategies. Several studies of the Italian situation (Caselli 2001; Cenni 2006; Caselli and Gatti 2005; Caruso and Palmucci 2008) have demonstrated a high degree of correlation between the services requested and corporate dimensions. The range of financing services used by small firms in particular is very limited, and as the first section of this chapter makes clear, bank lending is the method of choice. In line with the pecking order theory, Italian firms' financial preferences start with the least complex and expensive option in terms of organisation and relationships, and they rarely make use of sources of financing (whether risk capital or lending) requiring greater openness to the outside in terms of information.

The demand for CIB can be clearly subdivided by firm size. SMEs are apparently largely excluded from access to the capital markets, in spite of the launch of segments specifically intended for them, such as the Alternative Investment Market (AIM), both for cultural reasons and due to volume factors. They are therefore more interested in advisory and merchant banking than in underwriting services. On the other hand, large corporations are potentially interested in the entire range of CIB products and services.

As well as demand, the supply of corporate and investment banking services is also affected by the regulatory framework, which affects operators' strategic choices. This market has developed in Italy more recently than in other contexts, and it is smaller due to the regulatory framework of the financial sector and the state's involvement in the economy, arising from the financial crisis of the 1930s. Although it did not create legal impediments to the securities industry, the inspiring principle of Italy's 1936 banking law, which remained in force for more than half a century, was to prevent commercial banks from making direct investments in corporate equity. The experience of the crisis that hit the universal banks in the 1930s led to the fear that any long-term financial support, whether in the form of lending or equity investments, might make commercial banks' solvency too closely dependent on that of its customer corporations. The consequent strict distinction in operating time-scales and types of business between banks and special credit institutions survived until the 1990s.

It was not until the implementation of European Union (EU) legislation that a number of independent investment banks and the commercial banks started to extend their operations to include the provision of financial assistance to firms. The period from the 1990s onwards has seen a number of changes with regard to investment banking and private equity on the Italian market; in particular, commercial banks have shown a decided interest in the investment banking sector. This has led to acquisitions of investment banks that originated from strategic motives regarding the cross-selling of services and the internalisation of higher-margin earnings. Acquisitions have involved both investment banks and specialist merchant banks.[7] This process was encouraged by the reduction in margins on the traditional lending business, as well as by the new regulatory approach.

Another factor that helps to explain firms' preference for lending as a source of finance derives from fiscal regulations. In Italy, this has historically not been neutral in relation to corporate finance strategies, favouring the financing of investments through indebtedness over the use of equity. The interest paid on loans can be deducted from the company's taxable income, while the financial costs of risk capital cannot; moreover, returns on risk capital are subject to higher taxation than those on capital used for lending. This fiscal favouritism has been reduced but not eliminated over the years.

8.8 The structure of the supply of corporate and investment banking services

In Italy, the corporate and investment banking services market is occupied by domestic and foreign operators, with a variety of organisational types: the investment banking units of the large banking groups, the few remaining pure investment banks,[8] and the many financial advisory firms.

The foreign operators[9] cover large geographical areas, offer a wide variety of products, and serve a large number of types of customer. Their main clientele consists of large or medium-large corporations, since the resources available for the Italian market and the budget targets set by central managements make the middle market less profitable. Some operations are handled directly by teams working in Italy, while particularly complex transactions requiring large amounts of funding are referred to central offices.[10]

Domestic operators subdivide into two categories: banking and non-banking. The banking operators include international groups: UniCredit and Intesa Sanpaolo, which at the end of 2010 held 32.9 per cent of the system's assets, (Banca d'Italia 2011a) and Mediobanca.

From the operating point of view, UniCredit and Intesa Sanpaolo can be defined as commercial banks that engage in investment banking; Mediobanca, the intermediary closest to the United States' or United Kingdom's investment bank model, is historically the most important institution on the Italian corporate and investment banking scene, and since 2003 it has followed a policy that has made it into an investment bank that engages in commercial banking business. These organisations hold large shares of the domestic market and offer a very wide variety of services that place them in direct competition with foreign banks.

There are also banking groups operating only at the domestic and local level, such as Monte dei Paschi di Siena, Banco Popolare, and UBI Banca, with 18.9 per cent of the system's assets. These three institutions offer products comparable with those of the main players; smaller banks may even not offer products in this category at all, by reason of the type of clientele served.

As well as the banks, the sector is also served by a wide variety of other organisations, such as professional firms, financial intermediaries, and securities firms, which all together produce the usual assortment of CIB services.

An examination of the business model of the top five banking groups listed above and Mediobanca highlights some significant factors: the organisational model adopted, the type of service offered, the clientele segmentation, the depth and breadth of the service, and the degree of internationalisation.

An analysis of the business model of the main Italian operators, based on the model of the multifunctional group that provides investment banking functions within its organisation, reveals a number of major differences compared to the wholesale/broker-dealer model generally found in the United States and United Kingdom. The latter model has a number of key features (Scardovi 2009): a high level of financial leverage; widespread use of maturity transformation, leading to a rise in liquidity risk if the rate of portfolio rotation slows due to unfavourable conditions on the financial markets; use of the financial markets as the main source of funding; and a cyclic trend in asset management and proprietary trading business, with an absence of profit stabilisation. As a result of the liquidity crisis associated with the recent financial crisis, the panorama of big investment banks has undergone profound changes since 2007.[11]

Most Italian operators, including the largest players, adopted an approach that integrates their lending, advisory, and capital market activities. Wholesale lending is financed with the deposits of the retail clientele, a source of funding that is less expensive and more stable for the borrower (Banca d'Italia 2011a) and thus allows the relative degree of liquidity risk to be reduced for a given level of investments. The level of leverage is generally lower than that of international players, even in the case of Mediobanca.[12]

Here it is of interest to trace the story of Mediobanca, which was founded just after the Second World War to serve the medium-term needs of industrial enterprises and to establish a direct relationship between savers and the finance needed to restore companies' production operations. It eventually became Italy's leading investment bank. Since 2003, Mediobanca has also diversified its operations towards retail banking, especially the acquisition of deposits from savers, to expand its access to "quality" sources of funding that are less expensive and considered more stable.

From the institutional point of view, the way banks choose to locate the lines of business that make up the corporate and investment areas within their organisations varies. Banks' organisational strategies favour divisional or group models, with a greater (divisional) or lesser(group) degree of centralisation of the structure respectively. UniCredit and Intesa Sanpaolo are divisionalised groups, while Monte dei Paschi di Siena, Banco Popolare, and UBI Banca have adopted federal models. Mediobanca is in a category of its own due to its origins as an investment bank. Intesa Sanpaolo and UniCredit manage their corporate and investment banking business through a special division, which includes both the interface with corporate customers and product specialists. The service model is based mainly on the synergy between the network of relationship managers, who interact with companies, and whose task it is to respond to and identify their financial needs, and the product specialists who select, design, and adapt the most suitable instruments for them. In both cases, the coverage network fulfills a number of different functions: 1) management of the complete relationship with the customer corporation under a unified, global approach; 2) provision of a contact point to which the corporation can turn with its financial needs; 3) activation of the product specialists when appropriate. Basically, the territorial network acts as originator, turning as appropriate to the various teams of specialists, who operate within external companies with a high degree of independence. Intesa Sanpaolo has placed these specialist competences in a bank dedicated totally to this area of business, while UniCredit groups its product specialists together in product lines, specific units within the division.

Monte dei Paschi di Siena, Banco Popolare, and UBI Banca have adopted a similar model but with separation between the coverage and product networks. Coverage is provided by the group's member banks, which retain independence and visibility by reason of their distribution networks. Within these banks, specific business centres are assigned to the provision of coverage for investment banking. On the other hand, product specialist functions are organised within totally dedicated banks. Differences emerge with regard to the activities undertaken by these specialist entities. In the case of Monte dei Paschi di Siena, the specialist bank delivers services to the group, while in that of UBI Banca, the specialist bank both functions as product specialist for the group and supplies coverage in relation to large corporate and institutional customers, which it handles directly. The Banco Popolare specialist organisation is different again, since it also operates in the areas of investment and private banking. This arises from the fact that the customer base consists largely of small and medium-sized enterprises, where the distinction between the entrepreneur and his business is extremely blurred; therefore, the bank has integrated its corporate and family businesses to offer entrepreneur families a single contact, for both the routine and the extraordinary needs arising within the management of their business and private affairs.

As already mentioned, Mediobanca is the Italian bank closest to the US and UK investment bank model. Over time, the frontiers of its operations have been expanded, and simultaneously its organisational model has evolved, to the point where it now comprises three business areas: corporate and investment banking, also including the wholesale banking and financial leasing businesses; principal investing, managing the portfolio of long-term investments in firms and the merchant banking and private equity portfolios; and retail and private banking, comprising consumer credit, retail banking (with the primary aim of acquiring deposits), and private banking. The organisational structure is that of a group, which does not include any specific firms in the CIB area (except for the asset management side of private equity, managed by a separate company), but rather uses teams of specialists. The retail and private banking business areas, on the other hand, are covered by specific companies directly responsible for both coverage and production.

8.9 Corporate and investment banking business areas

Exactly which services are included in the corporate and investment banking area depends on the definition of investment banking used

(Kuhn 1990; Iannotta 2010; Brigham and Ehrhardt 2011; Fleuriet 2008). There is no single, universally accepted criterion for setting the boundaries of this area of operations. Various studies have made a detailed examination of how the relevant services should be identified, but no single view emerges from the literature on the subject. At the two extremes there are one restrictive and one broad definition. The former derives from the historic model of underwriting on the primary market and trading on the secondary market and excludes all the other areas of activities, including advisory services in merger and acquisition processes. The broad definition, on the other hand, reflects the evolution of the business of banks in this sector and includes a varied array of services: as well as underwriting and trading activities, it comprises merchant banking, asset management, advisory services in merger and acquisition or restructuring operations and risk management activities, through to lending. Between these two extremes there are other definitions, which may exclude asset management, lending, risk management or merchant banking, considering them not to be intrinsic to the investment banking business.

According to a broad definition, CIB services can be subdivided into the following business areas (Liaw 2011; Capizzi 2007):

- investment banking in the strict sense
- corporate finance services
- structured finance
- merchant banking
- risk management

Investment banking in the strictest sense relates to access to capital markets through operations in the primary market. The service is based on a process comprising four phases: origination, advisory, arranging, and distribution. In view of the economies of scale that can be generated, secondary market trading is often included in this area of business, although the services are kept separate.

The corporate finance services area covers a combination of various services intended to optimise the financial strategies of customer corporations and has strong advisory connotations. Here again, the process can be subdivided, this time into three phases: origination, advisory, and fund raising. Fund raising refers to the sourcing of the funds needed to complete the operation and often involves the organisation of syndicated loans. Corporate finance services provide support for extraordinary financial operations, relating to the acquisition of other companies, or conversely, to corporate sales and restructuring processes.

Structured finance involves the organisation of operations based on cash flows derived from assets or from investment projects separate from the company's core business, handled through special purpose vehicles (SPVs). The process subdivides into four phases: origination, advisory, arranging, and fund raising. Project finance, securitisation, and leveraged finance operations fall within this category.

Merchant banking operations involve the acquisition of equity holdings in non-financial companies by the financial operator. This is not strictly speaking a corporate banking service, since the package is acquired not by a customer but by the bank itself. It can, however, be defined as an asset management service if the funds used do not belong to the bank but are managed under a specific mandate.

In the CIB services, the risk management business area is the most recent and can be subdivided into two segments: the supply of products and services for the management of the risks of corporate customers, and the research and development of risk measurement and management models.

From the operational point of view, the distinction in the above business areas is less clear, since the teams assigned to these services often operate transversely and not just vertically, depending on whether fund raising or advisory services are involved. For example, within an extraordinary financial operation, funding may be handled by the structured finance team, working alongside the team from the corporate finance area.

In terms of the services offered, the sample consists of the top five banking group and Mediobanca, appears to be more uniform. The only exception is UniCredit, which has cut back its merchant banking business to virtually nil. With regard to all the other services, the banks studied declare that they cover all corporate and investment banking services in the broad sense.

However, the importance of each individual area of business within the total volume handled, and the depth of the service offered, vary from bank to bank, depending in particular on the geographical area covered and the clientele served.

In the case of the commercial banks, it is interesting to note the size thresholds into which the business is subdivided, which indicates the orientation towards and importance of relationship banking. Table 8.4 illustrates the situation in 2011. Naturally, the levels of the thresholds and the number of segments depend on the portfolios of companies served. In general, the definition of these is still

Table 8.4 Segmentation thresholds of banks, in millions of euros, 2011

		Corporate	
Bank	**SME**	**Mid**	**Large**
Intesa Sanpaolo	€2.5–150	€150–500	>€500
UniCredit	€3–50	€50–250	>€250
Monte dei Paschi di Siena	€0–5	€5–200	>€200
Banco Popolare	€0–5	€5	
UBI Banca	€3–15	€15–250	>€250

Source: Processing of corporate data (various years).

ongoing; some banks (Intesa Sanpaolo and UniCredit) have revised their categories, while for others the revision in currently underway. Intesa Sanpaolo and UniCredit have the largest, most varied corporate customer portfolios and have proceeded in two stages. First, they excluded small firms from the market of reference by introducing a minimum threshold for access to this type of service, and they established corporate centres, branches specialising in handling relations with corporate clientele. In the second phase, they redistributed the clientele by introducing a distinction between large corporate and corporate customers, setting new quantity thresholds with a higher access threshold and assigning customers to specific coverage facilities: corporate centres and business centres. The customer bases of Monte dei Paschi di Siena, Banco Popolare, and UBI Banca consist largely of SMEs. These banks also initially set an access threshold and redistributed the companies above it, but they have only recently announced that they intend to rationalise their organisation, raising the threshold for access to corporate banking services and reallocating firms amongst the specialist facilities.

Basically, by raising the threshold for access to corporate and investment banking services, Italian banks are creating conditions that will enable them to strengthen the figure of the client manager, through the greater concentration of resources in a more uniform customer portfolio. The client manager is the key figure, since he acts as the contact for the user's needs, facilitating the relationship with the organisation, especially when the service required is complex and a large number of functions have to be involved.

Several significant differences emerge from the breadth and depth of the range of CIB services. Intesa Sanpaolo, UniCredit, and Mediobanca are revealed to be universal banks, capable of providing clientele with assistance in all phases.

In the case of merger and acquisition operations, market scouting and feasibility studies are carried out in the preliminary phase, moving on to the analytical due diligence procedure and financial structuring and optimisation, through to the negotiation and closing stage.

In structured finance operations, the teams are involved in all phases of the process, from organisation, acting as advisers and arrangers and assisting the project's promoters in the drafting of the business plan, through to the structuring and underwriting stages, with definition of the optimal mix of funding sources.

In securitisation operations, teams are specialised in the management of the entire process structuring phase, from detailed analysis of historic performances and portfolio composition through to complete management of the rating process, which involves the due diligence analysis, preparation of the rating book, selection of the portfolio, negotiation of credit enhancement levels, and the definition of structural and legal characteristics.

In both equity and debt listing operations, teams assist the issuer in all phases of the process: from the design of the structure of the offering in terms of both amount and characteristics, to coordination of the offering and investor relation services both during the process, with organisation of the road shows and, during the after-market phase, with the aim of maximising the value of the issue in the medium-long term.

These operators also cover the role of project manager, organising and coordinating the work of the entire specific desk: from auditors and legal, fiscal, and communications advisers through to professionals specialising in management problems.

With regard to breadth of service, Monte dei Paschi di Siena is in an intermediate position, since it has the know-how necessary to supply a high degree of breadth and depth of service but its relational network is currently less broad and it therefore mainly operates at the domestic level, and rarely as the leader of a syndicate. Banco Popolare and UBI Banca, on the other hand, offer less depth of service, since they have more focused operating capabilities, which means that they are not able to act as project manager but may take part in one or more phases of the process, depending on the type of operation.

In terms of the degree of internationalisation of the offering of corporate and investment banking services, Italian banks operate basically at the domestic level. Although all the banks considered have organisations abroad—varying from highly internationalised positions such as that of UniCredit, which has a network of foreign banks in 22 countries, to Monte dei Paschi di Siena, with just a few liaison offices—all the services offered in this sector overwhelmingly target the domestic market. However, during the last few years three banks, UniCredit, Intesa Sanpaolo, and Mediobanca, have launched actions intended to gain them a larger role on the international markets. In the capital markets, they have increasingly taken part in share- and bond-offering projects. In contrast to their leading role on the domestic market, their lower profile internationally has meant that they have operated by acquiring mandates within offering consortia. The operations concerned have involved offerings by foreign issuers and, in some cases, offerings by domestic issuers on foreign markets, such as the Prada initial public offering. Internationalisation appears to be very important in view of the increasingly globalised, interrelated economic context: since a large proportion of corporate and investment banking services concern operations of extraordinary significance for firms, the aid of an international bank can be highly beneficial. This can apply, for example, to the external expansion of a customer corporation through joint venture or acquisition processes, to capital fund-raising operations in the markets considered most attractive, and to sales—for example, to cover generational handovers.

It appears likely that internationalisation will further extend the split at the heart of the Italian banking system: in general terms, it seems that the market will be divided between a small number of institutions capable of supplying the full array of corporate and investment banking services, responding to the opportunities offered by membership of an international network, and the rest of the market, which will be much more limited and will only be able to supply a small selection of advisory services, typical of the merchant banking sector, operating as originator. Intesa Sanpaolo, UniCredit, and Mediobanca can be expected to draw on the experience already acquired to target the large corporate and mid-corporate clientele, especially customers with high potential for international operations; Monte dei Paschi di Siena, Banco Popolare, and UBI Banca seem destined to operate solely on the domestic market, serving smaller-sized corporate customers whose financial needs are less complex or less linked to internationalisation processes.

Notes

1. A thorough, in-depth analysis of the relationship between small and medium-sized enterprises and the banking system is provided in Caselli (2001). There are many diversities within the category of small and medium-sized enterprises that are worth examining in greater depth. One possible useful

distinction here is the difference between simple and complex enterprises suggested by Zara (2007): the former have traditional financial behaviours, working mainly with banks on a relationship model, while the financial behaviour of the latter is oriented towards a transaction banking model.

2. The 1936 banking law remained substantially unchanged until the mid 1980s, which saw the start of the process of banking system reform, which led, in August 1993, to the introduction of the new banking law, the Consolidated Law on Banking.
3. The information can be obtained from the answers to the following three questions: 1) during the current year, did *the firm want more loans at the prevailing market conditions*? 2) If so, during the year did the firm apply unsuccessfully for more credit? 3) If so, would the firm have agreed to pay a slightly higher loan rate to obtain more loans? Firms that replied yes to all three questions were considered to have suffered strong rationing, while positive replies to the first question were viewed as indicating weak rationing. Firms answering yes to the first two questions are defined as suffering from financial constraint. See UniCredit (2009). tab. 9, p. 126.
4. During 1995–2003 (covered by three surveys), the values averaged around 16.0% for weak rationing, 4.53% for financial constraints, and 2.8% for strong rationing. See Brighi (2009), tab. 2.6, p. 95.
5. Substandard loans are loans to customers suffering from temporary difficulties that are likely to be overcome in a reasonably short time. Restructured loans are loans for which a bank, owing to the deterioration in the debtor's financial condition and operating results, accepts changes to the original terms and conditions of loans that caused a loss. Overdue/overdrawn loans are loans that, at the reference date of the report, have been overdue and overdrawn for more than 90 days, secured and unsecured.
6. The market shares of the banks belonging to the main groups fell from 73 per cent in 1996 to 60 per cent in 2005. See Saccomanni (2006) p. 17. During 1996 and 2005, the small banks' market share rose from 24 to 31 per cent. See Gobbi (2007), p. 33. Overall, during the two years after the summer 2007 financial crisis, the five largest groups' share of the corporate lending market fell by more than five percentage points. See Mieli (2009).
7. Operations of this kind include the acquisition by Banca Popolare di Milano of Banca Akros, by Banco Popolare of Banca Aletti, by Banca Intesa first by Lazard Italia and subsequently, through its merger with Sanpaolo, by Banca IMI and by Capitalia (subsequently incorporated into UniCredit) of Medio Credito Centrale. UniCredit founded UniCredit Banca Mobiliare and then proceeded with further changes to its organisation, while Credem established AbaxBank. Acquisitions of specialist merchant banks include, for example, those of Centrobanca by Banca Popolare di Bergamo (UBI Banca) and of MPS Merchant and Ducato Venture by the Monte dei Paschi di Siena group.
8. At the international level, during the last few years there has been a process of acquisition by the large integrated banking groups, for example: Boston has joined the Crédit Suisse group, Morgan Grenfell and Banker's Trust have been acquired by the Deutsche Bank group, Shroder has been taken over by Citigroup, and more recently Bank of America has acquired Merrill Lynch.

9. The most important foreign players include Rothschild, Morgan Stanley, Deutsche Bank, Goldman Sachs, Lazard, Citi, Credit Suisse, KPMG, BNP Paribas, and Royal Bank of Scotland.
10. This even occurs in the case of groups such as BNP Paribas and Crédit Agricole, which cover the market through their own banking subsidiaries, here Banca Nazionale del Lavoro and CariParma respectively.
11. In the United States, where once there were 17 major investment banks, there now are only 5; as of 2011. Goldman Sachs and Morgan Stanley are the only investment banks to have survived the financial turbulence as independent organisations, and even they have been transformed into bank holding companies, which places them under the surveillance of the Federal Reserve, allowing them to access its system of advances and loans. Bear Stearns was taken over by JPMorgan Chase & Co. at the end of May 2008, while Merrill Lynch was acquired by Bank of America, in effect from the first of January 2009. In September 2008 Lehman Brothers declared itself bankrupt and its European and Asian businesses were taken over by Nomura, and its North American operations by Barclays.
12. Compared to the banks of other countries, which are more dependent on wholesale funding, the Italian banking system enjoys a large supply of retail funds that are relatively immune to market volatility. See Banca d'Italia (2011a).

9
Private Banking and Asset Management in Italy

Valeria Venturelli

9.1 Introduction

This chapter provides an analysis of the asset management industry in Italy from various perspectives. First, I analyse the size and trend of the market for asset management products and services, discussing the main underlying factors. This is followed by a closer investigation of the investment fund sector, one of the asset management industry segments that has experienced the largest drop in the amounts of funds managed during recent years; my aim is to identify the causes of this reduction and possible solutions for overcoming it. The strategic business area of private banking, serving HNWI (high net worth individuals) is also reviewed, to identify elements of similarity or contrast with the asset management industry overall.

In Italy, asset management activities normally are mainly in the hands of the banks, with regard to both production and distribution. At the end of 2010, there were 195 asset management companies[1] operating in Italy, 50 of which belonged to the banking sector, since they were more than 50 per cent owned by banking intermediaries. Banking sector asset management companies handle more than 60 per cent of mutual fund assets and are responsible for about 75 per cent of the distribution of asset management products (PWC-ORFEO 2011); therefore, the Italian banking system plays a fundamental role in the evolution of this sector. Private banking is viewed as a strategic business area of particular interest, due to the fact that this market is still highly fragmented and therefore offers ample growth potential. This is particularly true for Italy, where the expression "spaghetti private banking" has been coined to describe Italian banks' tendency to standardise and homogenise their offerings to HNWI clientele, to the point where for a long time the service actually provided had only a very low degree of personalisation. There are therefore wide margins to manoeuvre with regard to this business, as its value proposition can be upgraded by offering integrated asset management and a truly tailor-made service.

The structure of the chapter is as follows: Section 9.2 provides definitions; this is followed by an analysis of the market concerned (Section 9.3), from the point of view of the trends in demand and supply, for both the mutual investment fund and for HNWI segments. I then discuss the main challenges for the sector with regard to both returns and the regulatory processes currently ongoing (Section 9.4). To conclude, I present a number of considerations concerning possible future scenarios.

9.2 Asset management and private banking definitions

In order to analyse strategic choices with reference to the asset management industry, it is important to define the boundaries of the sector itself. The expression "asset management" usually denotes a business with the following characteristics:[2]

- specialised financial institutions (asset managers) that construct financial portfolios whose primary goal is to exploit the benefits of the diversification process
- the existence of an explicit or implicit financial portfolio management mandate allowing the creation of a direct link between the investment decision made by the asset manager and the investor's situation

This definition also allows classification of the different products/services and intermediaries within the industry.

In the asset management literature, the prevailing tendency is to identify the operators active in the asset management industry with the principal category of institutional investors. However, this may lead to a lack of distinction between the managers and intermediaries that collect funds and the contractual vehicle through which such collection is carried out. In other words, intermediaries active in the asset management industry should not be confused with institutional investors. A realistic representation of the asset management industry allows asset management activities to be analysed and divided along an integrated value chain starting from the moment of production and distribution (Figure 9.1).

Through this representation the following products and participants can be identified:

- Asset managers: operators specialised in the management of funds on behalf of individual (mass, affluent, and high net worth individuals) and institutional investors. The production process can be described as the selection of securities and construction of efficient financial portfolios, followed by other activities linked and functional to the management of investments (settlement, custody, etc.). From an institutional point of view, investment management companies, banks, and insurance companies can all be asset managers.
- Distributors: the intermediaries that distribute asset management products have developed an array of activities related to the evaluation of the customer's financial needs, the finalisation of the contract, and everything linked to client reporting once the relationship has been established. The distribution channels comprise bank branches, insurance agencies, tied agents, insurance brokers, and the various kinds of distance selling techniques. The principal operators active in the distribution stage are banks and insurance companies.
- Institutional investors: once the functions and types of operators active in the production and distribution stage have been defined, institutional investors must be categorised on the basis of the contractual types of funds or portfolio that can be formed using the

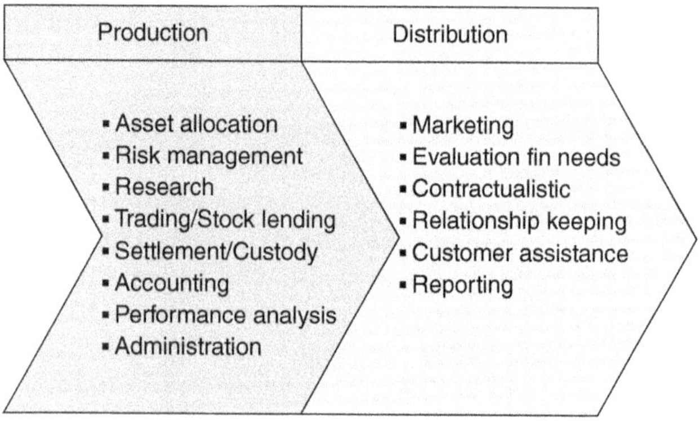

Figure 9.1 The asset management value chains
Source: Adapted from Venturelli (2005).

investment made by the individual investor. Following this line of reasoning, a clear distinction can be made between

1. individual portfolio schemes (discretionary asset management)
2. collective investment schemes (unit trusts, investment funds and pension funds)
3. collective investment schemes that represent a financial liability for the operator (life insurance products).

There is no single definition of private banking: "[The] private bank main rule is that there are no rules..." (Maude 2006). By its very nature, private banking adapts with flexibility to the specific type of customer served and the distinctive features of the financial intermediary offering it (Oriani and Zanaboni 2008). However, on a number of aspects there is a significant convergence of opinion on the part of academics and industry players: private banking involves a focus on a clientele with large amounts of wealth; they are offered exclusive services intended to satisfy their financial and other needs with a high degree of customisation; compared to the bank's other asset management services, private banking services have a number of relational connotations, including confidentiality, customisation of the service, trust, transparency and professionalism (Molyneux and Omarini 2005).

An analysis of the needs of the private clientele reveals the main products that are offered to a HNWI client. The investor's financial requirements, which originate from Maslow's hierarchy of needs (Maslow 1954), include both primary needs (liquidity, protection, welfare) and investment and business needs, through to the redistribution of wealth through charitable giving and the establishment of non-profit foundations and organisations. The transition from needs at the base to those at the top of Maslow's pyramid is proportional to the growth in the investor's wealth; therefore, in the case of private clients, it rises up the scale of needs to reach the most highly evolved requirements.

Figure 9.2 illustrates the correspondence between the offering of financial products and the needs of the demand; the range of products is vast and includes products that can be classified as belonging to the asset management industry (italics) as well as products and services that substitute for them (private equity funds, art and real estate banking, etc.). This explains why asset management products are central but not all-encompassing for private banking clientele, and also explains the high advisory content of the service provided (Di Battista and Venturelli 2004).

Philantropy	No profit activities Charity Alternative assets
Entrepreneurship	Shares and hybrids Mezzanine Corporate financing Private Equity funds
Speculation	*Hedge Funds* Derivative instruments Structured products
Investment	*Investment funds* *Units/Index linked* *Discretiionary asset* *Management* Bonds Deposit accounts
Retirement	*Pension funds*
Protection	Insurance policies
Liquidity	Current accounts Retail financing

Figure 9.2 Needs and product solutions for private customers
Source: Adapted from PWC-ORFEO (2009).

9.3 Asset management

Demand-side dynamics

Assets under management (AUM) in relation to gross domestic product (GDP) can serve as a useful indicator of the relative importance of the industry at the international level. The ratio of total AUM to GDP was 78.5 per cent at the end of 2010 for the Euro Area. This average conceals the wide spectrum that exists across Europe (Table 9.1). The AUM/GDP ratio was well above the area average in some countries: the United Kingdom (171.4 per cent) and France (89.1 per cent). These high ratios give an indication of the relative importance of asset management activities in these countries. Elsewhere in Europe, AUM/GDP ratios were considerably lower, as in Italy (48.2 per cent) in 2010.

Internationally, the Italian situation is atypical because of[3]

- the small size of the institutional investors compared to those elsewhere internationally; managed assets as a proportion of Italian households' total financial wealth are relatively low. While there has been some growth in insurance products (+6.8 per cent between 2000 and 2010), the figure for mutual funds (6.6 per cent) is lower than the value found in the other main countries; that for pension funds (1.8 per cent) is particularly low

Table 9.1 The importance of the asset management industry: per cent composition of household financial assets by instruments

	Italy			France			Germany		
	2000	2010	Var. %	2000	2010	Var. %	2000	2010	Var. %
Investment funds	15.4	6.6	–8.8	11.3	6.6	–4.7	11.6	11.9	0.3
Insurance and pension funds	7.0	13.8	6.8	29.9	36.8	6.9	28.8	33.0	4.2
of which: pension funds	0.6	1.8	1.2	3.1	4.4	1.3	10.5	13.1	2.6
Total	22.4	20.4	–2.0	41.2	43.4	2.2	40.4	44.9	4.5
AUM as a % GDP	55.9	48.2	–7.7	71.8	89.1	17.3	68.9	88.8	19.9
	Euro Area			**United Kingdom**			**United States**		
	2000	2010	Var. %	2000	2010	Var. %	2000	2010	Var. %
Investment funds	11.8	7.6	–4.2	4.9	3.0	–1.9	11.0	12.3	1.3
Insurance and pension funds	24.1	30.2	6.1	52.4	53.9	1.5	28.8	28.5	–0.3
of which: pension funds						0.0	25.2	24.4	–0.8
Total	35.9	37.8	1.9	57.3	56.9	–0.4	39.8	40.8	1.0
as a % of GDP	69.6	78.5	8.9	183.0	171.4	–11.6	130.7	130.5	–0.2

Note: Var % is % Variation.

Source: Processing of Banca d'Italia, Annual Report, several years.

- drastic reduction in the relative weight of mutual investment funds, to an extent not found in the other countries studied. The Italian situation reveals a sharper reduction in the mutual investment fund sector, with the proportion of financial assets directed to these funds continuing to fall even in the most recent period (–8.8 per cent between 2000 and 2010)

One important basis for segmentation in the asset management industry is that between the various types of customers served. One distinction with major operational implications is that between the demand for services from individual investors and what might be defined as second level demand, originating from a clientele of institutions who mandate the intermediary to provide customised management of the assets received from a large number of investors. Institutional clients represent the dominant segment of the European asset management industry. Two key institutional client categories are insurance companies and pension funds, while in Italy the banking foundations are of primary importance. The institutional client market is an international one, in which the main assets managers all compete. The individual client market can be further subdivided on the basis of the volume managed and the investors' degree of financial sophistication (retail and small business clients vs. private banking clients). The retail segment is subject to more geographical restrictions, since products are accessed by means of distribution channels that provide territorial coverage. The Italian clientele is mainly retail (Figure 9.3), although the effects of the financial crisis have led retail clients to flee the market, triggering an increase in the proportion of institutional investors served.

The supply side

With regard to the structure of the supply side (Table 9.2), in 2010 the level of concentration of the Italian investment system, measured in terms of the market share of the 5 largest operators, was 56.5 per cent, higher than in 2005 (55.8 per cent). The market share of foreign groups had risen, indicating the growing internationalisation of the system. In the Italian industry, a polarisation emerged between the three largest groups and the rest of the system. The largest groups are of considerable size and have established a presence on the main European markets (thanks in part to consolidation operations), with a production organisation on an international scale. In spite of this, they are still not large enough to play a role similar to that which they themselves occupy in the banking and insurance markets. At the European

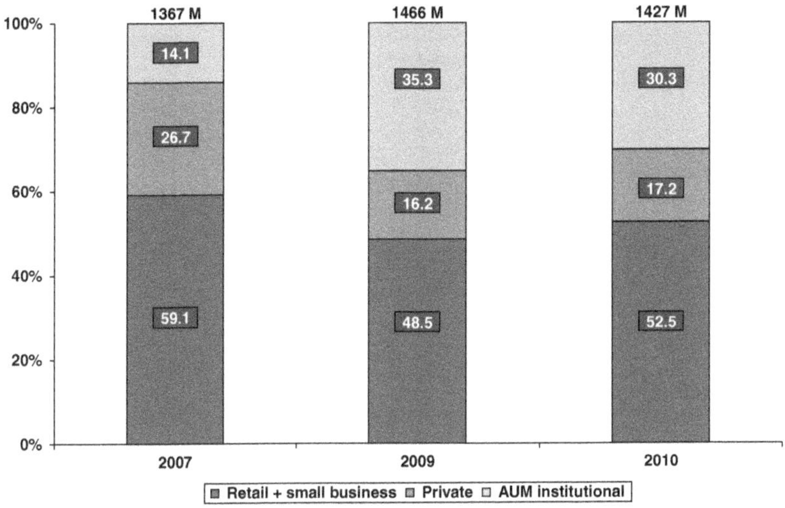

Figure 9.3 Assets under management (AUM) by client segments: per cent and total amount (billions of euros)

Source: processing of PWC-ORFEO (2011).

level, the 30 largest asset management groups include only three Italian intermediaries, compared to eight British, five French, and five German intermediaries. In terms of assets managed, the market shares of the British, French, Swiss, and German operators is around 20 per cent for each national group, compared to 5 for the largest Italian groups (Banca d'Italia 2008b). The rest of the Italian industry consists of an intermediate band of medium-small operators, mainly members of banking groups or bank subsidiaries, and a small number of independent players that have achieved rapid growth but continue to pursue niche strategies and are of only limited size. Therefore, the industry's ownership structure features a prevalence of players belonging to the banking sector, meaning asset management firms that are subsidiaries of domestic groups; however, the market shares of foreign banks and independent operators do appear to be growing.

The banking channel is still by far the predominant channel for the placing of asset management products; this is particularly true in the case of mutual funds. According to some surveys (Banca d'Italia 2008b), the banking channel's share of this market is 83 per cent in Austria, is in excess of 70 per cent in Italy and Spain, and lies between 60 and 70 per cent in Switzerland, Scandinavia, and Germany; however, it is much

Table 9.2 The first 10 operators active in Italy, 2005–10

First 10 operators 2010	AUM 2010	Cumulative market share 2010	First 10 operators 2005	AUM 2005	Cumulative market share 2005
Gruppo Intesa Sanpaolo	218,395.2	21.7%	Sanpaolo – Imi	195,785.7	17.6%
Gruppo Generali	143,143.9	35.9%	Pioneer Investments – Gr. Unicredito It.	160,510.9	32.0%
Pioneer Investments – Gr. UniCredit	129,605.2	48.8%	Gruppo Intesa	118,471.9	42.6%
Gruppo Mediolanum	41,103.4	52.9%	Le Assicurazioni Generali	96,969.5	51.3%
Allianz	36,263.5	56.5%	Banca Monte dei Paschi di Siena	49,478.4	55.8%
Gruppo UBI Banca	33,210.8	59.8%	Fineco – Gruppo Bancario Capitalia	45,922.0	59.9%
Gruppo BNP Paribas	28,025.8	62.5%	Ras	37,217.0	63.2%
Amundi Group	25,055.1	65.0%	Arca	35,825.7	66.4%
Axa	24,945.0	67.5%	Banco Popolare di Verona e Novara	35,104.7	69.6%
Gruppo Bipiemme	23,365.8	69.8%	Banca Nazionale del Lavoro	30,598.5	72.3%

Source: Processing of Assogestioni, Italian Fund Hub, http://www.ifh.assogestioni.it/

lower in France and, above all, in the United Kingdom (36.9 and 14.0 per cent, respectively), numbers that underestimate the real scale of the phenomenon if we consider the fact that networks of financial advisers and other distribution channels may be controlled by the banks themselves.

The figures therefore appear to confirm that European banks identified asset management as one of the areas of business through which they might at least partially recoup the reduction in margins on traditional banking services (Venturelli 2001). They therefore helped to drive the growth in asset management recorded throughout the 1990s, taking advantage of their placing power and the economies of diversification achievable through the integrated offering of a wide range of credit, investment, and insurance products and services. This diversification in the asset management business took the form vertical of integration of the business itself by banking intermediaries with high placing power and large capital resources. Therefore, in Italy the predominant model is one of vertical integration, where production structures are subordinate to distribution (Di Battista and Venturelli 2004).

This specific feature of the market in Italy may partially explain the shrinkage seen in the sector during recent years. Starting soon after 2000, there was a radical change in the background scenario, compared to the previous period.

Since the beginning of this century, the growth of asset management in Italy has been slowed by the gradual reduction in size of the open-ended investment fund sector, with a fall in particular in the number of funds registered in Italy (Table 9.1).

To analyse the causes of this trend, it should first be underlined that households' abandonment of mutual funds reflects their own investment decisions; since the financial bubble burst in 2000, Italian mutual funds have experienced a gradual reduction in the assets invested, with resources switched to the main competitor types of financial products. The reasons for this haemorrhage lie with structural features of the industry itself and with factors linked to the economic situation. During the initial phase, from 2000 to 2007, the switch was from mutual funds (and especially those registered in Italy), to structured products and unit-linked and index-linked life insurance policies. This switch was due to asymmetries in the regulatory framework and distribution policies, with networks pursuing short-term aims by choosing to offer the retail clientele products that generated high upfront commissions and were more opaque and less problematical in terms of after-sales assistance, rather than being due to changes in investors' preferences. In the years since the 2007 financial crisis, mutual investment funds have been replaced by government securities, due to a recomposition in demand arising from a flight to safety on the part of investors. Moreover, the large-scale transfer of assets recorded from products that the banking system distributes to those of which it is itself the issuer has also been the outcome of banks' fund-raising strategies, as banks have attempted to guide clientele towards banks' own products in order to compensate for the credit squeeze on the interbank market and to avoid liquidity problems (Messori 2008; Carosio 2009).

The Italian asset management market therefore has a clearly defined structure. The market is mainly retail, dominated by a non-focused captive asset management firm model. The gradual concentration of asset management business in the hands of the asset management firms, which have acquired the form of specialist production units within groups, has been accompanied by the widespread adoption of a business model based on close vertical integration between production and distribution, with the large banking and insurance distribution networks playing a central role (Beltratti 2008). For non-focused asset managers, the opportunity to benefit from the captive networks' placing power has been their main competitive advantage; in exchange, the asset managers rebate almost all their management commissions to the distributor (sometimes also in the form of dividends).[4] Therefore, the sales network is paid not by the clientele but by the product production unit; from this point of view, investors do not pay explicitly for the advisory service received.

The challenges

The challenges facing the sector relate to asset management margins and to the consequences of a number of major regulatory measures.

With regard to returns in the asset management industry, from the 2010 McKinsey survey we discover that during 2007–10, operating profits (bps-basis points) as a proportion of assets under management) in the western European asset management industry fell from 16.6 in 2007 to 12.5 percent in 2010. While costs increased slightly (+1 per cent), earnings fell by 6 per cent. At the European level, the drop in margins is mainly explained by the shift towards less-expensive asset classes (bonds/money markets, etc.) and repricing (reduction in management commissions in favour of incentive commissions).

As far as the domestic situation is concerned, Italian asset management firms are part of a strong pan-European polarisation; in terms of asset mix, Italian investors are traditionally "bond people," used to a low return. Proving this, the equity and alternative component of Italian retail investors' assets amounts to only 14 per cent of the total, compared to 25 per cent for Europe as a whole. In terms of client mix, the percentage of institutional clientele is low compared to the international norm; with regard to the channel mix, in Europe 75 per cent of retail assets are distributed through proprietary networks or related intermediaries, while in Italy this percentage soars to 93 per cent. This initial finding reveals that the Italian asset management industry could experience an even sharper reduction in margins than its European counterparts.

The main regulatory measures that will affect the asset management sector at the Italian and European level include the European Undertaking for Collective Investment in Transferable Securities IV (UCITS IV) and Markets in Financial Instruments Directive (MiFID), not forgetting the effects arising from the capital adequacy and deleveraging provisions of Basel III.

The declared aim of the innovations brought in by the UCITS IV directive is to improve the efficiency of the asset management industry, partly to enable it to deal with a particularly competitive context resulting from the development of other types of financial products. The directive includes measures to encourage the internationalisation of the industry. Significant from this point of view is the fact that asset managers will in effect be granted a European passport, offering them greater flexibility, since there will now be fewer restrictions on where they can locate their businesses, and there will be regulations intended to reduce the costs and times involved in cross-border distribution.

To achieve this, the directive provides measures for the appropriate division of jurisdiction between supervisory authorities and ensures that a UCITS authorised in its member state of origin has the right of access to the market of another member state, by means of a much simpler, quicker notification procedure. The directive also introduces solutions to encourage funds' growth in size, with the aim of achieving significant cost savings through the opportunity for economies of scale. Further innovations under the directive include common regulations governing mergers between UCITS and a measure allowing the creation of master-feeder structures, in which the UCITS referred to as the feeder invests all or almost all (at least 85 per cent) of its assets in another UCITS, known as the master. Last but not least, UCITS IV requires investors to be provided with a document known as the Key Information Document (KID), containing a brief, easily comprehensible description of the UCITS' main characteristics (e.g., investment aims and policy, costs and charges, etc.) to enable investors to asses whether or not the security in question meets their needs.

Amongst the various innovations made by the MiFID, it is important to consider the effects of the directive on product placing procedures. The regulations covering advisory services, reintroduced by the MiFID as a new investment service, and the rules concerning inducements, appear to be particularly significant in this regard. Both regulations aim to ensure that the costs incurred by the clientele are specifically stated. The rules governing inducements allow production and distribution costs, when permitted, to be specified and thus indicated separately, while the new regulations on financial advisory services allow them to be charged for at a stated rate.

Turning to the impact of Basel III on the asset management sector, consideration must be given to the capital adequacy levels set, which will tend to force retail banks to dispose of their main "non-core" assets.

The three new regulatory measures thus seem to point the way to the future developments of the industry.

The sector's new structure will be shaped by two trends, the full effects of which will gradually make themselves felt: internationalisation and business specialisation. In terms of specialisation, the market will be polarised to a greater extent between the large groups, with more opportunities to pursue economies of scale and scope, and small specialist operators. Product specialisation will also influence the management strategies adopted, with some operators specialising in passive management products (exchange-traded funds or ETFs) and others implementing an active management strategy (α builders, hedge funds, private equity), which will lead to greater competition in price (passive management) and performance (active management) in the wholesale market. Active management products will continue to justify high levels of commissions through excellence in management, which is a scarce resource; passive products will be offered at lower and lower prices, thanks to the efficiency in production processes made possible by rising volumes. With regard to internationalisation, market players agree that the definitive implementation of UCITS IV will trigger a reinforcement of the process of globalisation within the industry, and at the same time will cause a gradual increase in the importance of foreign intermediaries. Last but not least, the industry's new structure will receive an indirect boost from the impacts of the new Basel III capital adequacy regulations on the banking sector. Many operators claim that the greater, tighter capital constraints imposed by these regulations might lead some Italian banking groups to sell their asset management companies, in order to rationalise their business and dispose of assets not considered as strategic. If, under these circumstances, some Italian banks sell off their production units, international banking/financial firms might be plausible counterparties.

The regulations will also affect distribution. Sales networks will play a role of absolute importance in the new competitive environment and will be increasingly specialised by customer segment, with reinforcement of the open architecture model, which might lead to greater competition in distribution. However, open architecture in the distribution sector will not be sufficient on its own to generate loyalty amongst the clientele; as the overlaps between the various offering catalogues increase, advisory expertise will come to the fore and may become a factor of competitive advantage in the placing of investment products. With more complex product offerings, the ability to select and offer clients the securities best suited to their investment objectives, income, and wealth will gain in importance.

To conclude, both economic and structural considerations urge caution as to whether and to what extent investors will return to mutual investment funds in the future. In the short term, there are several factors that may obstruct a recovery in the industry, mainly linked to the risk-aversion of retail clientele and institutional investors; the high degree of market volatility, which adds to the sense of insecurity; and the banking industry's need to solve its liquidity problems and achieve greater stability in its fund-raising. In spite of these possible obstacles, the "debt crisis" may prove to be the turning point in private risk allocation, with the potential for a switch away from the traditional conservative asset allocation. Otherwise, in the medium to long term, the return to mutual investment funds depends on the finding of solutions, through self-regulation or secondary regulatory measures, to the problems that led to the collapse: the lack of a level playing field between mutual funds and other alternative products, and the critical factors in the market structures.

Although the competitive disadvantages compared to other securities are being reduced by increases in the transparency of the alternative financial products and the recent revision of the Italian system for the taxation of mutual funds,[5] the removal of the critical market structural factors must be viewed in the light of the forces acting on both the Italian and the European systems of asset management firms. The various regulatory measures (MiFID, Basel III, UCITS IV, etc.) will tend split the sector off from the banking industry, both on the production side – the need for retail banks to dispose of non-core assets as a result of Basel III – and on the distribution side, architectures that, if not open, are at least MiFID-compliant. The development of new sales models (advisory services) and an increase in international competition (in both production and distribution) will encourage formation of joint ventures, some merely commercial and some farther reaching.

9.4 Private banking

Demand-side dynamics

For obvious reasons of confidentiality, it is difficult to provide a detailed map of private banking services. There are no statistics concerning the number of HNWIs in the various countries or the size of their wealth, and certainly no historic series for analysis of the past and possible future behaviour of the clientele (Maude 2006).

Globally, it is estimated that there are 10.9 million HNWIs, equally spread over the macro-areas of the globe (about 30 per cent in Asia-Pacific, Europe, and North America). In 2010 HNWIs' financial wealth reached US$42.7 trillion, surpassing the 2007 pre-crisis peak (Merrill Lynch – Capgemini 2011). The global HNWI population nevertheless remains highly concentrated. The United States, Japan, and Germany still accounted for 53.0 per cent of the world's HNWI population at the end of 2010, down only slightly from 53.5 in 2009 (Table 9.3). In 2010, India became the twelfth-largest home to HNWIs, due to a considerable rebound; in fact, the global HNWI recovery was generally stronger in emerging and developing nations than in mature ones. Beyond that, the HNWI ranks were spread across the globe in much the same proportions in 2010 as they had been in 2009.

For Italy (Table 9.4), about 611,400 HNWIs comprised the potential private banking market in 2010, with assets of over €500,000 under the Italian Private Banking Association (AIPB) definition. Under the international definition, where the wealth threshold adopted to identify private banking clientele is at least €1 million, about 195 thousand HNWI households comprise the potential market. The discrepancy between the AIPB data (Table 9.4) and Merrill Lynch-Capgemini data (Table 9.3) concerning the number of private households with wealth of over €1 million reflects the difficulty in estimating the size of the potential market.

Table 9.3 High net-worth individuals (HNWIs), population by country (in thousands), end of 2010

Country	Number of HNWIs (in thousands)	Ratio of total worldwide population	Cumulative percentage
United States	3,104	28.5	28.5
Japan	1,739	16.0	44.5
Germany	924	8.5	**53.0**
China	535	4.9	57.9
United Kingdom	454	4.2	62.1
France	396	3.6	65.7
Canada	282	2.6	68.3
Switzerland	243	2.2	70.6
Australia	193	1.8	72.3
Italy	170	1.6	73.9
Brazil	155	1.4	75.3
India	153	1.4	76.7
Other countries	2,533	23.3	100.0
Total	10,881		

Source: Processing of Merrill Lynch – Capgemini (2011).

Table 9.4 The Italian private banking market: the potential market of households

	Number of families (thousands)		Wealth/household (€ bln)	
	2010	2009	2010	2009
> €1 million	196.0	191.5	598	574
€500,000 to 1million	415.5	399.1	299	293
Total	611.4	590.6	896	868

Source: Processing of AIPB (2010).

During the last few years, the growth of private wealth has been mainly fuelled by the entrance of new households within the perimeters of the private banking sector. The performance of invested financial wealth as a result of the market effect has increased the total, but to a lesser extent than the new entrants have done (AIPB 2010).

The percentage of HNWIs' wealth managed by private banking organisations has grown constantly since 2007. The ratio of private banking clients served by dedicated financial structures increased from 41.9 per cent in 2007 to 47.0 per cent in 2010 (AIPB 2010). Under the definition used here, operators with dedicated structures may be domestic or international independent private banks, individual Italian or foreign banks or divisions of banking groups, specialised asset management firms, or securities firms/banks with their own networks of financial advisers. HNWIs served by commercial banks, individual Italian or foreign retail banks, or retail divisions of banking groups, or banks with networks of financial advisers and securities firms, are not considered as served by dedicated organisations. The percentage of HNWIs' wealth managed by private banking organisations is a physiological ceiling; as we will see in greater detail below, during the last few years it has remained basically unchanged, in spite of the multiplication of the numbers of foreign players and family offices. The general opinion is that a certain proportion of Italian HNWIs are reluctant to abandon their established bank branches to move to private banking divisions, or make use family offices as sources of advice while remaining faithful to their usual banks.

In terms of geographical spread, 70 per cent of private wealth in Italy is concentrated in five regions: first and foremost, Lombardy with € 248.4 billion, or 30 per cent of the total, followed by Emilia Romagna, Veneto, Piedmont, and Lazio. Of the provinces, Milan is by far the province with the greatest private wealth, and is also the one with the highest average wealth per HNWI family, with about € 2 million per household. The wealthiest province in the south of the country is Naples (42nd position) with an average of €1.3 million per household. Smaller provinces, such as Modena, Parma, and Mantua, contain households with higher average wealth levels (AIPB 2009).

When it comes to style of investment, Italian private banking clients, like the retail clientele, choose a lower rate of exposure to risk than the European average (AIPB 2010). Compared to their European counterparts, Italian private banking clients prefer to invest a larger proportion of their portfolios in investment products, leaving only 11.8 per cent in deposit accounts, compared to the European average of 24 per cent. They also structure their portfolios to ensure a constant flow of income by investing in fixed-rate securities. The percentage of treasury securities and bonds in the portfolios of Italian private banking households is more than twice the European figure. Last but not least, Italians place less of their wealth in the hands of asset managers, with a figure 4 percentage points below that for European portfolios in 2010.

The Italian clientele's level of multibanking is stable but is higher than abroad; in fact, the figures for multibanking abroad show that 79 per cent of European private-wealth clients use fewer than two private banks and only 3 per cent use more than four private banks. In Italy 8 per cent of private clients use more than four private bank counterparts (IBM Consulting Services 2005).

The supply side

There are considerable differences between the main players operating in the sector with regard to the type of clientele served, the offering range, distribution policies, positioning along the value chain, geographical coverage and, of course, size of business.

In general, in line with the scenario internationally, the Italian market is dominated by specialist operators and dedicated private banking models, often within medium/large universal banks.

In 2010, there were 237 players operating on this market in Italy (Table 9.5). The main market share was managed by the 51 Italian banks with specialist private banking divisions. UniCredit PB and Intesa Sanpaolo PB are the main players, holding more than 48 per cent of the assets under management between them. The next largest share, 17.7 per cent of assets, was in the hands of the 33 foreign firms serving the Italian market. Of these, 12 were Swiss (UBS Italia, Crédit Suisse Italy, Pictet & Cie Europe, Banca Albertini Syz, Banca Arner, Gestion de Patrimonies,

Table 9.5 Market players and market shares in Italy for private-wealth clients

	Number of players		Market share (%)
Kind of player	**2010**	**2009**	**2010**
Italian universal banks	51	50	56.8
Foreign investment banks	34	35	17.7
Italian specialised banks	10	10	9.1
Networks of financial advisers with private banking organisations	3	4	7.2
Family offices	117	105	5.5
Investment firm/financial boutique	22	22	3.7
Total	237	226	100.0

Source: Processing of Il Sole 24 Ore – Dossier Reti e Private Banking – 25 June 2011.

Vontobel, Banca del Ceresio, B. Morval, J. Baer, Finpromotion, and Banca del Sempione); 5 were American (Morgan Stanley, JP Morgan, Goldman Sachs, Merrill Lynch Wealth Management, and Advanced Capital Securities); 3 were French (BNP Paribas, Crédit Agricole, and LCF Rothschild); 3 were British (Schroders, Barclays and Europe Arab Bank); 3 were Austrian (Alpen Bank, Hypo Tirol Bank, and Raiffeisen Salzburg); 2 were from Luxembourg (COFI and Farad International); and 2 were German (Deutsche Bank and Allianz Group), with just 1 player each for the Netherlands (Bank Insinger De Beaufort), the Principality of Monaco (Compagnie de Gestione Privée Monegasque), and Spain (Banco Santander). The degree of concentration was also high amongst foreign players: UBS Italia, BNL-BNP Paribas, and Crédit Suisse Italy alone held 52.6 per cent of the private banking market handled by foreign investment banks and held 9.3 per cent of the private banking market served in Italy. The 10 Italian banks specialising solely in private banking were in third place in terms of market share, while investment boutiques, asset management firms, and securities firms accounted for 3.7 per cent of the market. In Italy there are currently three networks of financial advisers in operation (Banca Fideuram, Azimut, and Euromobiliare), while the number of family offices rose from 9 in 2003 to 117 at the end of 2010.

Each of the two models, the private banking division of a universal bank or a specialist bank, enjoys specific competitive advantages. A universal bank may be more efficient in the delivery of services to the private banking market, because it is able to spread the costs (regulatory, information technology, and human resources) involved in the maintenance of offices in the major financial centres over a larger number of product lines. Moreover, simultaneous presence in private banking and in the other strategic business areas (retail, investment banking, corporate finance, and asset management) can generate beneficial synergies between the various business units with regard to both production and distribution.

However, specialist operators also have a series of strong points. They are able to monitor the development of new products and the quality with which these services are delivered to clients more closely, and they may become independent multibrand brokers, assessing, selecting, and combining the products and services of others. In addition, their exclusive focus on private banking enables them to build up and foster a clearer identity for their brands, ensuring that they are recognised by the potential clientele as signifying a higher quality, more exclusive offering (Oriani and Zanaboni 2008).

The challenges

Margins in the private banking sector dropped by more than 30 per cent between 2007 and 2010; average unit margins on portfolios fell from 0.35 per cent in 2007 to 0.24 per cent in 2010. This trend of decreasing margins reflects the clientele's repositioning of their portfolios towards products with lower risk levels; the change in the customer's asset mix triggers a reduction in returns for the intermediary. Moreover, the regulations on inducements and the related elimination of rebates by the asset management service, and the reduction in the size of asset management product portfolios had a significant impact on the size and structure of earnings. In addition, the increased competitive pressure, combined with the cost rigidity typical of this business, explains why returns fell in spite of a recovery in the amount of assets managed and the number of private banking clients.

Margins in the private banking business are unlikely to be recouped through a reduction in costs; several surveys conclude that this business has a high incidence of fixed costs, which cannot be reduced in the short term. Furthermore, private banking is a business with a high human-capital intensity, since the relationship manager accounts for about 60 per cent of personnel costs; it is also a business with diseconomies of scale. As Table 9.6 reveals, a reduction of the ratio of clients to relationship manager is cost-effective; the most efficient intermediaries, meaning those with the lowest cost-income ratio, are the ones who have been most successful in increasing the number of clients that each customer relationship manager handles.

Table 9.6 Average number of clients per CRM (customer relationship manager) (million)

Wealth threshold	All participants	Average number of clients of the 10% of participants with the lowest cost/income ratio
> €50 million	18	2
€20million to €50 million	41	5
€1 million to €20 million	83	42
€500,000 to €1 million	149	90
€100,000 to €500,000	273	137

Source: Processing of PWC (2005).

To return margins to their pre-crisis levels, action must be taken on the earnings side. The introduction of a pay-to-use advisory service that extends the range of services offered, combined with the positive effect of a recovery in the performance of the financial markets, should succeed in increasing margins and satisfying clients' needs. The regulatory changes introduced by the MiFID and the structural consequences of the financial crisis are changing the competitive paradigm in private banking, forcing – but also creating the opportunities for – the system to rethink its business models and offering. The focus is shifting from the management of financial assets to the management of differentiated requirements; since the crisis, many clients have terminated their total mandates but still wish to receive advice on how to invest. In concrete terms, this means greater demand for a pay-to-use advisory service. During the last few years, the Italian banking sector has been travelling along the path marked out by the MiFID to establish an advisory service for clients. After an initial phase of adaptation to the regulations, at present the players in the system are reinforcing and enriching their service with features and contents for which the clientele is willing to pay a premium price. This involves changes to the organisational structure, with major investments in information technology.

The drivers of success probably lie in the following paradigms: a client-centred business model; advisory services and professional expertise; reputation and brand. Service strategies will tend to be redrawn by reviewing clientele segmentation criteria and providing an offering differentiated by segment; the aim is to rebuild and consolidate relationships of trust. This re-establishment of trust will be facilitated if the intermediary has acquired a broad, independent product offering, and if it builds up a truly customised relationship with the client, capable of aligning products and services with the latter's preferences and objectives.

Further innovations are to be expected from the review of the MiFID (MiFID2), in the light of recent events in the United Kingdom, where the Financial Services Authority (FSA) has introduced a ban, to come into force before the end of 2012, on the rebate of commissions from investment funds and insurance products to financial advisers, with the aim of ensuring that investment recommendations are not influenced by the margins on the various products. This will modify the way in which earnings are generated. From a model of product-based earnings calculated as a commission on the security sold, which includes the advisory service, there will have to be a transition to a model based on explicit payment for the advisory service, with a fee payable that is unrelated to any product commission. In the most highly developed markets, this change is already under way. In response to strong regulatory pressure, in the United States about 25 per cent of financial advisers work on a fee-only basis, with no income from commissions.

The new earnings model will also affect production, since the value chain will have to be refocused to concentrate on asset allocation and best provider selection processes, with the cost of the product as the discriminating factor, a situation in which exchange-traded funds/ index-linked products are often the best solution for the client, and direct asset management services are only provided by organisations with the proven, sustainable ability to produce α returns. Once again, these changes can already be observed in the leading markets; in Switzerland top players such as Julius Baer have shown no hesitation in redefining their business model, shutting down their asset management operations. Italy is certain to be affected by these trends, and a number of Italian banks will be forced to separate production from distribution by introducing a clear division between wealth management and asset management.

Notes

1. Limited liability companies permitted to provide both collective and individual asset management services. They are authorised to establish mutual investment funds, to manage their own mutual funds and those of other institutions and the assets of open-ended investment companies, and to offer asset management services to individuals.
2. On this topic see Onado (1997); Walter (1999); Davis and Steil (2001); Franks and Mayer (2001); Brighi et al. (2004); Venturelli (2005).

3. For further details see Chapter 3.
4. According to Barucci (2007) and CRA International (2006), rebates account for about 70% of the TER (Total expenses ratio) granted to the distribution channels by Italian asset management firms (2006 figures), one of the highest figures in Europe.
5. Until July 2011, Italian mutual funds were taxed on gains accrued, not on gains realised.

10
Italian Banks between Scylla and Charybdis?

Stefano Cosma and Elisabetta Gualandri

10.1 Introduction

At the beginning of the great financial crisis, Italian banks were just emerging from a process of consolidation, and were enjoying gains in efficiency, positive performance, low risk levels, and adequate capitalisation. Several factors helped them to escape the subprime phase of the crisis comparatively unscathed, in particular their conservative attitude to financial innovation, their maintenance of a traditional business model, their strong local roots, and their well-balanced funding gap. In fact, no Italian banks had to be rescued or failed, and the extent of government intervention with public facilities (through the so-called Tremonti bonds in 2008–09) was the lowest of any Organisation for Economic Co-operation and Development (OECD) country: 0.3 per cent of GDP, against an average of 30 per cent for European Union states.

However, the situation in the second phase of the crisis has been dramatically different, due to two main factors. The first is that Italy's poor economic growth, a problem dating from the late 1990s, has deteriorated into a recession that is causing serious difficulties both for businesses, leading to stagnating investments and an increase in bad loans for banks, and for households, with a slump in consumer spending. It should be remembered that services to enterprises and households make up the core business of Italian banks. In view of this traditional business model, the outlook for bank profitability is decidedly negative. The second factor is the Italian sovereign debt crisis. Italian banks' situation became more critical as this crisis worsened in the summer of 2011 since, as in the other affected countries, their creditworthiness was associated to that of the country itself, increasing the market's perception of their risk level. The contagious effect of the doubts surrounding Italian sovereign debt has made it more difficult for the banks to access the wholesale financial markets and thus sources of funding; moreover their capital adequacy was placed under stress.

It is not easy to predict possible future scenarios for Italian banks. To do this, we must first of all acquire some idea of the prospects for the economic and financial context within which they operate. As a second step, Italian banks' financial stability must be assessed, both in relation to the market turmoil triggered by the crisis and with regard to the regulatory changes now under way in the areas of liquidity and capital adequacy. The final step is to assess the implications of these factors for the banks' microeconomic equilibrium.

10.2 The economic and financial scenario

At the time of writing in Spring 2012, the financial crisis centred on the EU peripheral states has not yet been resolved and forecasters are predicting a period of recession, varying in depth in the different EU states, but certainly serious for Italy (Visco 2012)[1].

In our opinion, given this situation, a number of measures are essential to improve the safety and soundness of European banks in general, and thus also those within the Italian system. First and foremost, the European Union must speed up the major reform of its governance now under discussion, ensuring its swift completion to achieve both deficit reduction and growth. The cutting of the government deficit and especially of the public debt is necessary to improve the stability of financial markets, but it will not be enough unless combined with measures intended to ensure the growth of the economy. The EU is currently working on major changes to its economic governance, based on the so-called fiscal compact, involving a requirement for balanced government budgets with automatic corrections and semiautomatic sanctions when this aim is not achieved. However, decisive action to encourage growth in the EU is still lacking, although several countries are being seriously affected by the impact on consumer spending of the austerity measures already introduced.

Moreover, swift action is needed to reinforce Europe's capacity for action to reduce the sovereign debt risk affecting a number of member states, by rendering the European Financial Stability Facility (EFSF) fully operational (Visco 2012). Saving sovereign states from the risk of default is fundamental in preventing possible contagion of the banking system, against which all the bank recapitalisation measures already adopted would be to absolutely no avail.

Another major step required to ensure a safe exit from the crisis is the completion of the international financial reforms now planned, intended to respond to the regulatory failures revealed by the crisis and to ensure safe and sound banking and financial systems. This must be done by continuing the work of Basel III, with its measures to reinforce capital adequacy and introduce global liquidity standards. The need is also obvious for greater uniformity in supervisory approaches – but this must emphatically not be achieved at the expense of laxer controls. The greater resilience of the banks of countries such as Italy during the first phase of the crisis was partly due to more intrusive supervision, while the light-touch strategy proved completely inadequate in countries such as the United Kingdom.

In this context, as far as Italian banks are concerned, the two specific aspects to be considered are the sovereign debt risk and the country's economic growth, for which the indicators are currently far from encouraging. Since the end of 2011, economic policy has been firmly directed towards measures that aim to ensure the sustainability of the public debt, in order to ward off the danger of financial instability and allow the debt itself to be refinanced more easily. Thanks in part to this policy, since January 2012 the Italian BTP– German bund spread has fallen steadily, to levels more sustainable for the cost of servicing Italy's public debt. Major measures and reforms to encourage growth are currently in the pipeline. Only the solution of these two aspects can reverse the trend and trigger an upward spiral, crucial for the recovery of Italy's economy and the future of its banks.

10.3 The financial stability of Italian banks

The key issues for assessing Italian banks' financial stability are funding, liquidity and refinancing risk, and capital adequacy.

The main effects of the second phase of the crisis for European banks included liquidity risk and refinancing risk. Light started to be visible at the end of the tunnel with the two 3-year Long-Term Refinancing Operations (LTROs) at 1 per cent launched by the European Central Bank (21 December 2011 and 29 February 2012); combined with the earlier unconventional measures, they have made a vital contribution to reducing stresses on the interbank market, which it is hoped will have positive effects on the availability of credit within the economy.

In mid-2011, when the stresses on the financial markets became systemic further to the announcement that the private sector was to face losses in the strategy for dealing with the Greek crisis, European banks in general began to suffer an ever-increasing liquidity squeeze and more and more difficulties in obtaining funding. The situation for Italian banks became more critical as the sovereign debt crisis worsened. As a consequence, from July 2011 onward they faced increasing problems in obtaining finance on the international wholesale funding markets, which had seized up. From summer 2011, they had growing recourse to Eurosystem refinancing to offset these difficulties.

As the end of 2011 approached, concern mounted regarding the liquidity situation forecast for 2012, because it was clear that European banks would need to tap the wholesale bond markets for considerable amounts. In the case of the 32 biggest Italian banking groups subject to weekly liquidity monitoring by the Bank of Italy, the amount of securities maturing by the end of 2012 totalled €88 billion, 3.3 per cent of their total liabilities and about a quarter of the total outstanding, in line with the situation of the main groups across Europe. Throughout the period in question, the liquidity position of Italian banks was constantly closely monitored by the Bank of Italy (Banca d'Italia, 2011b).

The stresses throughout Europe were eventually relieved by the two LTROs launched by the European Central Bank (ECB), for a gross total of €1,020 billion. The Italian banking system received about a quarter of the funds granted on both occasions, to a large extent against collateral consisting of government guarantees costing 0.7 per cent. The first LTRO overwhelmingly attracted the large banks; the second time around, more applications were received from small and medium-sized institutions, proving that in this phase the crisis also hit the smaller banks.

The banks have used this source of refinancing to make advance repayments of expensive previous bond issues, to form liquidity reserves to repay bonds expiring in the near future, and to return to the government security market as investors. For the time being, policies directly aiding the economy have not become apparent. It may take time for the full supportive impact on banks' lending to households and firms to emerge.

Since the second LTRO, the liquidity situation of Italian banks has therefore eased, and their reserves are now more than sufficient to refinance the bonds due for expiry during 2012. In the medium term, it remains to be seen how long they will have to wait for a real recovery of the international wholesale market and the bond market.

The other main issue in financial stability is banks' capital adequacy. As a consequence of the crisis, Basel III has raised both the quantity and the quality of capital banks that are required to allocate to cover their risks and it has also introduced a leverage ratio. Italian banks are faced with the need to bring their capital structures into line with the new rules at a time of low profitability, when the markets are still far from stable. There is the risk of a decrease in the financing of the economy.

The capital position of Italian banks was more than adequate at the beginning of the crisis. During its first phase, the Bank of Italy encouraged them to increase the amount and quality of their capital, moving in the direction required by Basel III. The Bank of Italy's regular monitoring of a large sample of banks confirmed that their capital ratios were improving and they were gradually smoothly moving into line with Basel III, scheduled for full implementation by 2019.

The sovereign debt crisis made recapitalisation operations more urgent for many banks and also drastically increased the amounts involved. The European Banking Authority (EBA) demand for an additional temporary capital buffer in December 2011 has proved particularly expensive for Italian banks. The EBA measure has affected the five largest banking groups: UniCredit, Intesa Sanpaolo, Banca Monte dei Paschi di Siena, Banco Popolare, and Unione di Banche Italiane. Apart from Intesa, for which no further increase is required, it has been calculated that the other four groups will have to find additional capital of €15,366 million if they are to achieve the 9 per cent target[2]. UniCredit has covered these new needs by means of a capital increase in February 2012. This operation has provided about half the total recapitalisation required by the Italian banking system. UniCredit is subject to additional capital requirements due to its status as an SIFI (systemically important financial institution). Implementation of this regulation will begin in 2012 and full implementation is due by 2019.

Apart from recourse to the market, the recapitalisation options available are caps on dividends and staff bonuses, the buyback of poor quality capital instruments, and the restructuring of existing hybrid instruments. The Bank of Italy is responsible for approving the recapitalisation plans requested by the EBA, to be introduced by June 2012. The aim is to avoid deleveraging strategies, which might tighten the credit squeeze on the economy even further (Saccomanni 2012).

The expectation is that the new additional requirements will be lightened thanks to the improvement on the Italian sovereign debt market since the beginning of 2012. In fact, the Bank of Italy has confirmed that it will follow the EBA's recommendation with the flexibility required by the changing market conditions (Saccomanni 2012).

The further capital requirements set by Basel III and the EBA put question marks over the role of the historic shareholders, since they open out opportunities to prospective new shareholders, expected to lead to changes in banks' ownership structures. The support of the banking foundations was vital during the first phase of the crisis, but the relative size of their holdings is currently being reduced. In the event that the thresholds set by the Banking Law are exceeded, potential new shareholders must be assessed by the Bank of Italy on a case by case basis, using the criterion of safe and sound management.

10.4 Effect on traditional intermediation model of Italian banks: The microeconomic equilibrium

The economic and financial situation of the European Union, and especially its peripheral states such as Italy, is deteriorating and in some respects it is now worse than in the first phase of the crisis.

In Italy, the economic downturn is due mainly to the sharp drop in consumer spending and internal demand, which is undermining the stability of the large number of businesses that only serve the domestic market. This is being reflected in the generalised impoverishment and weakening of the Italian retail banks' main customers: firms and households.

Firms, already scarred by the earlier crisis, are being faced with a fresh deterioration of the economy. In response to this recessionary trend, their financial needs are rising, as a result of the increase in working capital generated by longer customer payment times, the drop in the quality of their commercial portfolios, and the drop in sales, which reduce their capacity for self-financing, and also as a result of the need to make vital investments in innovation and, above all, internationalisation.

Italian households, the rock on which the banking system's resistance to the 2008 crisis was founded, are now the main target of the government's budget-balancing austerity measures. The economic crisis, the trend in the labour market, and the turmoil in the financial markets have reduced households' disposable income and their wealth, causing them to make major changes in their financial behaviour and especially, from the banks' point of view, reducing their propensity to save and thus contribute to the Italian financial system's traditional source of liquidity.

Real disposable income has been falling continually since 2008, and financial wealth has plummeted by almost 25 per cent compared to 2006 (Prometeia 2012). These trends show no sign of improving in the short term because of the weight of taxation, the deindexing of pensions, the public-sector pay freeze, and the cuts in health and welfare services introduced as part of the government's deficit-reduction measures.

Retail banking is the traditional credit intermediation model under which funding is received from households in the form of deposits and used to finance lending to households and small and medium-sized enterprises (SMEs), especially by branches. It is founded on a broad customer portfolio and normally on lasting, long-term relationships with customers. The large number of customers tends to stabilise the banking business's volumes and margins, by providing naturally diversified, granular loan and deposit portfolios. Within a bank's operations, retail banking brings stability to profit margins, since it tends to compensate the trend in income from services (non-interest income and fees) against the trend in the net interest margin.

The crisis has cast doubt on the sustainability of this traditional banking model, based on funding from retail deposits and lending to households and businesses and with less dependence on wholesale funding and a low funding gap. The gradual, unrelenting deterioration in the economic and financial conditions of households and firms, on which Italian banks' credit model is based, and the structural changes in their financial behaviours, means that banks must rethink the fundamental assumptions that underlie their business, especially in terms of the pricing of loans and stabilisation of retail funding.

Their higher loan exposure to corporate customers and the high proportion of their earnings derived from retail and corporate clientele are amongst the reasons why the second phase of the crisis hit Italian banks so much harder than the first, as the worsening of firms' financial situations, the increase in bad debts, and the slump in household incomes and consumption all came into play.

On the assets side, during the last six months of 2011 banks were forced to revise their lending policies in terms of both volume and prices, conducting a thorough review of their relations with firms and households in order to deal with the changes in liquidity and risk conditions and the new microeconomic equilibriums.

During 2008–11, the annual growth in lending to the private sector of the economy averaged 3.3 per cent in Italy, compared to 2.8 for the Euro Area as a whole. The Italian banking system showed an impressive ability to deliver credit, but it must be borne in mind that the Italian business system is bank based and, as such, is more dependent on credit for the structural development and coverage of its financial needs.

On the credit side, the crisis reached its zenith during November–December 2011, when there was a sharp reduction in lending figures (–0.8 per cent in December) with a steep rise in interest rates (Banca d'Italia 2012), which in fact reflected a credit squeeze on firms, especially the smallest among them, and households.

For large and medium-sized firms, lending slowed but did maintain minimal growth, while for very small and small businesses the growth rate was slightly negative (Gobbi 2012).

In contrast to events in 2009, the credit squeeze involved not only the largest banks but the whole of the industry, including the smallest institutions, which in this case did not act as a financial buffer for Italian businesses. It is also important to note that the Italian banking system did not cut the availability of credit across the board but made selective reductions in a real flight to quality, which repositioned the loans portfolio towards the highest quality borrowers (Gobbi 2012).

The credit squeeze, the tougher economic conditions and the more restrictive selection criteria, combined with the worsening of the economic situation, generated a significant rise in new impaired loans during the last quarter of 2011, especially to SMEs and households (Saccomanni 2012).

The ECB refinancing measures, that we have already, described effectively relaxed the financial and liquidity stresses that hit Italian banks at the end of 2011, significantly reducing the refinancing risk involved in the recourse to the market necessary to refinance the bank bonds coming up for repayment.

The availability of credit to firms and households should be improved by both banks' greater liquidity and by the reduction in the cost of borrowing arising from the decrease in their funding costs. At the time of writing, signs of recovery are appearing in the credit market, especially on the supply side, which during the last few months of 2011 was responsible for a slowdown in lending and a credit squeeze for Italian businesses and households.

The second phase of the crisis had a significant impact on both wholesale and retail funding. The inflow of funds in the domestic market fell considerably, with a significant increase in the relative cost, while it became virtually impossible to obtain funds in the international markets. Even small and mutual banks recorded negative positions on the interbank market. The ECB refinancing operations have reduced stress levels in the short term, but at present two problems remain unresolved: the evolution of funding over the long term, with the associated question of banks' financial equilibrium; and the credit intermediation model, which requires rapid review of pricing strategies to ensure that lending is economically sustainable.

The restrictive effects on volume and the growth in lending to firms and families are only the first consequence of the crisis; Italian banks still need to bring the pricing of credit, traditionally based mainly on interbank and/or ECB refinancing rates, into line with their actual funding costs, increasingly dependent on the trend in sovereign debt risk levels and the yields of government securities. It was the latter that proved tempting to investors during 2011 and, together with the reform of the taxation on investment earnings, reduced the relative appeal not only of bank bonds and longer-term deposits but also of current account deposits, the short-term component of retail funding. In this scenario, the solution may lie in term deposits, which provide households with greater security and higher returns but involve a lower interest rate risk for banks, since their duration is shorter than that of conventional bonds.

Notes

1. The sovereign debt crisis has worsened again around the middle of 2012 before subsiding in August. The epicentre was in Spain, with serious risk of contagion for Italy. The events of summer 2012 has further underlined the need for measures on European governance and instruments to deal with the crisis.
2. To meet the EBA requirement (Core Tier 1 ratio of 9 per cent), in June 2012 BMPS has applied to the government for a further facility of €2 billion, giving a total amount of €3.9 billion.

References

ABI-PROMETEIA (2006) *Finanza e sviluppo delle PMI in Europa: ruolo delle banche e dell'intervento pubblico*, Roma: Bancaria Editrice.

ACRI – Associazione di fondazioni e di casse di risparmio spa (2011) *Sedicesimo rapporto sulle Fondazioni di origine bancaria*, Roma.

AIPB (2010) *Stima del mercato potenziale. Private 2010*, Milano.

AIPB (2009) *Il mercato potenziale private in Italia 2009*, Milano.

Albareto, G, M. Benvenuti, S. Mocetti, M. Pagnini, and P. Rossi (2008) 'L'organizzazione dell'attività creditizia e l'utilizzo di tecniche di scoring nel sistema bancario italiano: risultati di un'indagine campionaria', Banca d'Italia, *Questioni di economia e finanza*, N. 12.

Alessandrini P., and A. Zazzaro (2007) 'Quale finanza per il Mezzogiorno: le vie da seguire', *QA – Rivista dell'Associazione Manlio Rossi-Doria*, 1: 135–53.

Allen, F., and D. Gale (1995) 'A Welfare Comparison of Intermediaries and Financial Markets in Germany and the US', *European Economic Review*, 39: 179–209.

Amatori, F., M. Bugamelli, and A. Colli (2011) 'Italian Firms in History: Size, Technology and Entrepreneurship', Banca d'Italia, *Quaderni di Storia Economica*, N. 13.

Asset Management Expert Group (2004) *Financial Services Action Plan: Progress and Prospects*, Final Report, May.

Assofin, CRIF, Prometeia *Osservatorio sul credito al dettaglio*, various years.

Autorità garante della concorrenza e del mercato (2008) *La corporate governance di banche e compagnie di assicurazioni*, Indagine Conoscitiva, N. 36.

Assogestioni *Italian Fund Hub*, http://www.ifh.assogestioni.it/

Banca d'Italia (2008a) *Economic Bulletin*, N. 50, October .

Banca d'Italia (2008b) *Rapporto del Gruppo di lavoro sui fondi comuni italiani. Fondi comuni italiani: Situazione attuale e possibili linee di intervento*, Luglio.

Banca d'Italia (2009a) *Annual Report 2008*, Rome, 29 May 2009.

Banca d'Italia (2009b) *Economic Bulletin*, N. 51, January.

Banca d'Italia (2010a) *Annual Report 2009*, Rome, 31 May 2010.

Banca d'Italia (2010b) *Financial Stability Report*, N. 1, November 2010.

Banca d'Italia (2010c) 'Household Wealth in Italy', Supplementi del bollettino statistico

Banca d'Italia (2011a) *Annual Report 2010*, Rome, 31 May 2011.

Banca d'Italia (2011b) *Financial Stability Report*, N. 2, November 2011.

Banca d'Italia (2011c) Supplementi al Bollettino Statistico, *'Indicatori monetari e finanziari, Conti finanziari'*, Nuova serie, Anno XXI – 8 Novembre 2011.

Banca d'Italia *Annual Report*, various issues.

Banca d'Italia *Economic Bulletin*, various issues.

Banca d'Italia *Bollettino statistico*, various issues.

Banca d'Italia 'Moneta e Banca' (2012) *Supplementi al Bollettino Statistico*, N. 13.

Banca d'Italia 'Online Statistical Database' (www.bancaditalia.it).

Banca d'Italia 'Banking Group Register and Supervisory Lists'.

Bank for International Settlements (2011a) *81th Annual Report*, 1 April 2010–31 March 2011, Basel, 26 June.

Bank for International Settlements (2011b) 'The impact of sovereign credit risk on bank funding conditions, Report submitted by a Study Group established by the Committee on the Global Financial System', CGFS Papers, N. 43, July 2011.

Barucci, E. (2007) 'Raccolta e performance dei fondi comuni di investimento in Italia', Assogestioni Working Paper, 2007/1.

Basel Committte on Banking Supervision (2010), Basel III: *'A global regulatory framework for more resilient banks and banking systems'* December 2010 (rev June 2011).

Belli, E., and F. Giordano (2007) 'Governance, mercati e struttura finanziaria delle imprese', in S. Monferrà (ed.) *Il rapporto banca-impresa in Italia*, Roma: Bancaria Editrice.

Beltratti, A. (2008) 'Gestione finanziaria e consulenza: mercato e integrazione verticale', Assogestioni Working Paper, 2008/3.

Bentivogli, C., E. Cocozza, A. Foglia, and S. Iannotti (2007) 'The bank-firm relationship after Basel II: a survey on Italian firms', Banca d'Italia, *Questioni di economia e finanza*, N. 6.

Beretta E., and S. Del Prete (2007) 'Aggregazioni bancarie e specializzazione nel credito alle PMI: peculiarità per are geografica', *Banca d'Italia, Temi di discussione*, N. 644, Roma.

Berger, A. N., and G. F. Udell (1995) 'Relationship Lending and Lines of Credit in Small Firm Finance', *The Journal of Business*, 68, 3: 351–81.

Birindelli, G., and M. Modina (a cura di) (2010) *Imprese, banche e finanza. Le evidenze di un'analisi territoriale alla luce della crisi finanziaria*, Milano: Franco Angeli.

Bisoni, C., and A. Landi (eds) (1999) *Il finanziamento dello sviluppo delle piccole e medie imprese*, Roma: Bancaria Editrice.

Bonaccorsi di Patti, E., G. Eramo, and G. Gobbi (2005) 'Piccole e grandi banche nel mercato del credito in Italia', *Banca Impresa Società*, 24, 1: 3–34.

Bonaccorsi di Patti E., and G. Gobbi (2007) 'Winners or Losers? The Effects of Bank Consolidation on Corporate Borrowers', *Journal of Finance*, 62: 669–95.

Bongini P., and G. Ferri (2005) *Il sistema bancario meridionale. Crisi, ristrutturazione, politiche*, Bari: Laterza.

Brandolini, A., and M. Bugamelli (eds) (2009) 'Rapporto sulle tendenze nel sistema produttivo italiano', Banca d'Italia, *Questioni di Economia e Finanza*, N. 45.

Brigham, E. F., and M. C. Ehrhardt (2011) *Financial Management: Theory and Practice*, 13th edition, Cincinnati, Ohio, United States: South Western Educational Publishing.

Brighi, P. (2009) *Credito e finanza d'impresa. Aspetti teorici ed evidenze empiriche*, Bologna: Bononia University Press.

Brighi, P., L. Landi, and G. Lusignani (2004) 'L'evoluzione del risparmio gestito nei principali sistemi finanziari', in M. Onado (ed.) *Il risparmio gestito. Strategie, organizzazione e performance in N governance and organization in the support of bank-firm relationship*, Bancaria, N.11, pp. 38–54.

Bruno, G., and R. De Bonis (2009) 'Do Financial Systems Converge? New Evidence from Household Financial Assets in OECD Countries', OECD Statistical Working Paper Series, February.

Capizzi, V. (ed.) (2007) *L'investment banking in Italia*, Roma: Bancaria Editrice.

Carosio, G. (2009) 'Fondi comuni e crisi dei mercati', Intervento del Vice Direttore Generale della Banca d'Italia, Assemblea annuale Assogestioni, Milano, 18 Marzo 2009.

Caruso, A., and F. Palmucci (2008) 'Scelte di finanziamento della crescita: un'indagine sulle Pmi italiane', *Banca Impresa e Società*, 28, 3: 453–76.

Caselli, S. (2001) *Corporate banking per le piccolo e medie imprese: il cambiamento delle strategie e dei processi gestionali della banca per lo sviluppo del rapporto con le PMI*, Roma: Bancaria Editrice.

Caselli, S. (2003) *PMI e sistema finanziario. Comportamento delle imprese e strategie delle banche*, Milano: Egea.

Caselli, S., and S. Gatti (2005) *'Structured Finance: Techniques, Products and Market'*. Berlin: Springler Verlag.

Cenni, S. (2006) 'La domanda di servizi di corporate banking e la finanza delle imprese', in R. Corigliano (ed.) *Corporate banking, credito e finanza delle imprese*, Roma: Bancaria Editrice.

Cerasi, V., and L. Crosato (2009) 'Dimensione e concentrazione dei gruppi bancari italiani nell'ultimo decennio', *Economia e Politica Industriale*, 3: 21–39.

Cesarini, F. (2003) 'Il rapporto banca-impresa tra relationship banking e ricorso al mercato finanziario', *Bancaria*, 12: 2–8.

Ciocca, P. (1991) *Banca Finanza Mercato*, Torino: Einaudi.

Clark, T., A. Dick, B. Hirtle, K. J. Stiroh, and R. Williams (2007) 'The Role of Retail Banking in the U.S. Banking Industry: Risk, Return, and Industry', *FRBNY Economic Policy Review*, 13, 3: 39–56.

Corigliano, R. (ed.) (2006) *Corporate banking, credito e finanza delle imprese*. Roma: Bancaria Editrice.

Cosma, S. (2002) *Il rapporto banca-impresa: le variabili relazionali e comportamentali nella valutazione del rischio di credito*, Torino: G. Giappichelli Editore.

Cosma, S., and U. Filotto (2011) *Il manuale del credito al consumo*, Milano: Egea.

Cosma S. (2009) *Integrazione e competizione fra banche e società specializzate nel credito al consumo*, XIV Rapporto sul sistema finanziario italiano, Fondazione Rosselli, Edibank

Cosma, S., A. Landi, A. Martinez, A. Rigon, and P. Vezzani (2003) 'The Organisational Model of Large Italian Banks in the SME Business Area', Conference *Clusters, Industrial Districts and Firms: the Challenge of Globalization*, Modena, 12–13 settembre 2003.

CRA International (2006) *Potential cost savings in a fully integrated European investment fund market*. Brussels: European Commission.

Davis, E. P., and B. Steil (2001) *Institutional Investors*, Cambridge, MA USA: MIT Press.

De Angeli, S. (2010) 'La via italiana al credito popolare: alcune considerazioni', *Banche e Banchieri*, 4, 277–85.

De Angeli, S., M. Oriani, and F. Poli (2007) *Le relazioni fra banche e piccole imprese*, Milano: Università Cattolica del Sacro Cuore.

De Bonis, R., and M. Stacchini (2009) 'What determines the size of bank loans in industrialized countries? The role of government debt', Banca d'Italia, Temi di discussione, N. 707, marzo.

De Laurentis, G., and S. Caselli (2004) *Miti e verità di Basilea 2. Guida alle decisioni*, Milano: Egea.

Del Giovane, P., G. Eramo, and A. Nobili (2010) 'Disentangling Demand and Supply in Credit Developments: a Survey-Based Analysis for Italy', Banca d'Italia, Temi di Discussione, N. 764.

De Mitri, S., G. Gobbi, and E. Sette (2010) 'Relationship lending in a financial turmoil', Banca d'Italia, Temi di discussione, N. 772.

De Socio, A. (2010) 'The economic and financial situation of Italian non financial corporations: an international comparison', Banca d'Italia, Questioni di economia e finanza, N. 66.

DeYoung, R., and T. Rice (2004) 'How Do Banks Make Money? A Variety of Business Strategies', *Federal Reserve Bank of Chicago Economic Perspectives*,28: 52–68.

Decreto legislativo 385/1993 'Testo Unico Bancario'.

Di Battista, M. L., and V. Venturelli (2004) 'Le strategie di diversificazione dei grandi gruppi bancari europei nell'asset management e nel private banking', in M. Onado (ed.) *Il risparmio gestito. Strategie, organizzazione e performance in Italia e in Europa*, Roma: Bancaria Editrice.

Directive 2009/65/EC of the European Parliament and of the Council of 13 July 2009 on the Coordination of Laws, Regulations and Administrative Provisions Relating to Undertakings for Collective Investment in Transferable Securities (UCITS).

Directive 2004/39/EC of the European Parliament and of the Council of 21 April 2004 on Markets in Financial Instruments Amending Council Directives 85/611/EEC and 93/6/EEC and Directive 2000/12/EC of the European Parliament and of the Council and Repealing Council Directive 93/22/EEC.

Draghi, M. (2009a) 'Intervento del Governatore della Banca d'Italia', Convegno AIAF – ASSIOM – ATIC Forex, Milano, 21 febbraio 2009.

Draghi, M. (2009b) 'Intervento del Governatore della Banca d'Italia', Associazione Bancaria Italiana, Assemblea Ordinaria, Roma, 8 luglio 2009.

Draghi, M. (2009c) 'Intervento del Governatore della Banca d'Italia', ACRI, Associazione di Fondazioni e di Casse di Risparmio Spa, Giornata Mondiale del Risparmio del 2009, Roma, 29 ottobre 2009.

Draghi, M. (2010a) 'Intervento del Governatore della Banca d'Italia', Convegno AIAF – ASSIOM – ATIC Forex Milano, 13 febbraio 2010.

Draghi, M. (2010b) 'Intervento del Governatore della Banca d'Italia', Associazione Bancaria Italiana, Assemblea Ordinaria, Roma, 15 luglio 2010.

Draghi, M. (2010c) 'Intervento del Governatore della Banca d'Italia', ACRI, Associazione di Fondazioni e di Casse di Risparmio Spa, Giornata Mondiale del Risparmio del 2010, Roma, 28 ottobre 2010.

Draghi, M. (2011a) 'Intervento del Governatore della Banca d'Italia', Convegno AIAF – ASSIOM – ATIC Forex Milano, 26 febbraio 2011.

Draghi, M. (2011b) 'Intervento del Governatore della Banca d'Italia', Associazione Bancaria Italiana, Assemblea Ordinaria, Roma, 13 luglio 2011.

Draghi, M. (2011c) 'Intervento del Governatore della Banca d'Italia', ACRI, Associazione di Fondazioni e di Casse di Risparmio Spa, Giornata Mondiale del Risparmio del 2011, Roma, 26 ottobre 2011.

European Credit Research Institute ECRI (2011) Lending to Households in Europe-Statistical Package.

European Central Bank ECB *Economic Bulletin Statistics*, various issues.

European Central Bank ECB (1999) *Money and Banking Statistics Sector Manual. Guidance for the Statistical Classification of Customers*, 2nd Edition, November.

European Central Bank. *ECB Report on EU Banking structure*, various issues and years.

European system of Central Banks, (ESCB), *Bank Lending Survey*, various years)

European Banking Authority EBA (2011) *Recommendation and final results of bank recapitalisation plan as part of co-ordinated measures to restore confidence in the banking sector*, London, 8 December 2011.

European Commission (2010) 'An EU Framework for Crisis Management in the Financial Sector', COM (2010) 579 final, Brussels, 20 October 2010.

European Commission (2011) 'State aid: Overview of pending decisions and ongoing, in-depth investigations in the context of the financial crisis', MEMO/11/858, Situation as of 1 December 2011, Brussels, 1st December.

Eurostat (2011) *Key figures on European business*, Publications Office of the European Union, Luxembourg: Eurostat.

Financial Stability Board FSB (2011) 'Peer Review of Italy', Review Report, 27 January.

Fleuriet, M. (2008) *Investment Banking Explained*, New York: McGraw-Hill.

Focarelli, D., F. Panetta, and C. Salleo (2002) 'Why do banks merge?', *Journal of Money Credit and Banking*, 34, 4: 1047–66.

Franks, J., and C. Mayer (2001) 'Risks and Regulation in European Asset Management: Is There a Role for Capital Requirements?' European Asset Management Association, January.

Gobbi, G. (2007) 'Tendenze evolutive del rapporto banca-impresa in Italia', in S. Monferrà (ed.) *Il rapporto banca-impresa in Italia*, Roma: Bancaria Editrice.

Gobbi, G. (2012) 'L'offerta di credito durante la crisi' in Workshop 'Domanda e offerta di credito in Italia durante la crisi finanziaria' Parma, 8 Marzo 2012.

<check in google>Gualandri, E. (2008) 'Crisi finanziania: qualilezioni per le autorita di vigilanza,' *Bancario*, 10: 3–15.

<check in google>Gualandri, E., A. Landi, and V. Venturelli (2009) 'Financial crisis and new dimensions of liquidity risk: rethinking prudential repulation and supervision', *Journal of Money Investment and Banking*, 8: 25–42.

Guelpa F., and V. Tirri (2004) 'Market Structure and Relationship Lending: Reflects on the Likelihood of Credit Tightening in the Italian Banking Industry', Banca Intesa, Collana Ricerche, N. 2.

Iannotta, G. (2010) *'Investment Banking. A Guide to Underwriting and Advisory Services'*, Springer-Verlag GmbH.

IBM Consulting Services (2005) *'European Wealth and Private Banking Industry Survey'*, London: IBM.

Il Sole 24 Ore (2011) *Dossier Reti e Private Banking*, 25 June 2011.

International Monetary Fund IMF (2006) 'Italy: Financial System Stability Assessment', IMF Country Report No. 06/112, March.

International Montary Fund (IMF) *World Economic Outlook Database*, various issues.

Istat (2011) *Struttura e dimensione delle imprese anno 2009*, Roma: Istat.

Kuhn, R. L. (1990) *Investment Banking. The Art and Science of High-Stakes Dealmaking*. New York: Harper & Row.

Landi, A., and V. Venturelli (2004) 'Struttura e tendenze del sistema bancario e finanziario dell'area euro e prospettive per le banche italiane', in Prometeia Previsione dei bilanci bancari, Rapporto semestrale, N. 29, aprile.

Landi, A., and V. Venturelli (2005) 'Evoluzione e convergenza dei sistemi finanziari europei', in Prometeia Previsione dei bilanci bancari, Rapporto semestrale, N. 31, aprile.

Lanoo, K., and M. Levin (2003) *Pan-European Asset Management. Achievement and Regulatory Impediments*, CEPS Task Force Report, N. 44, April.
Liaw, T. K. (2011) *The Business of Investment Banking. A Comprehensive Overview*, Hoboken, New Jersey: Wiley & Sons Ltd., Inc.
Maslow, A. (1954) *Motivation and Personality*, New York NY, USA: Harper & Row, Publishers, Inc.
Mattesini, F., and M. Messori (2004) *L'evoluzione del sistema bancario meridionale: problemi aperti e possibili soluzioni*, Bologna: Il Mulino.
Maude, D. (2006) *Global Private Banking and Wealth Management: The New Realities*, Chichester, West Sussex: Wiley Finance.
McKinsey (2010) Will the goose keep laying golden eggs? Milano, Italy, June. http://www.mckinsey.com
Mediobanca, R&S (2011a) *Dati cumulativi delle principali banche internazionali e piani di stabilizzazione finanziaria*, giugno, Milano, Italy.
Mediobanca, R&S (2011b) *Piani di stabilizzazione finanziaria – Interventi pubblici a favore delle banche e degli istituti finanziari in Europa e negli Stati Uniti*, Aggiornamento al novembre 2011, Milano, Italy.
Mediobanca, R&S (2011c) *IMF World Economic Outlook Data Base*, September.
Merrill Lynch and Capgemini (2011) 'World Wealth Report', http://www.ml.com/media/114235.pdf.
Messori, M. (2008) 'I problemi del settore italiano del risparmio gestito', Assogestioni working paper, N. 4, 2008, Luglio.
Mieli, S. (2009) 'Fare credito in tempi di crisi', intervento al Convegno Associazione Bancaria Italiana 'Accesso al credito e garanzie per le imprese: garantire lo sviluppo, crescere nella stabilità', Roma, 15 dicembre 2009.
Molyneux, P., and A. Omarini (2005) *Private Banking in Europe – Getting Clients & Keeping Them!*, mimeo.
Mottura, P. (2011) *Banche. Strategie, organizzazioni e concentrazioni*, Milano: Egea.
Mottura, P., and Paci S., (2009) 'Evoluzione dei modelli della banca e dell'assicurazione', in In P. Mottura, and S. Paci, *Banca. Economia e gestione*. Milano: Egea.
Mussari, G. (2010) 'Basilea III e l'impatto sui finanziamenti bancari alle imprese italiane', *Bancaria*, N. 10, 2–8.
Onado, M. (1997) 'Il risparmio gestito in Italia', Consob, Quaderni di Finanza, N. 21.
Oriani, M., and B. Zanaboni (eds) (2008) *Conoscere il private banking*. Roma: Bancaria Editrice.
Padoa-Schioppa, T. (1995) 'Global Banking in Italia', Banca d'Italia, Bollettino Economico, N. 24.
Panetta, F. (2003) 'Evoluzione del sistema bancario e finanziamento dell'economia nel Mezzogiorno', in F. Panetta (ed.) *Il sistema bancario italiano negli anni novanta*. Bologna: Il Mulino.
Panetta F., and F. M. Signoretti (2010) 'Domanda e offerta di credito in Italia durante la crisi finanziaria', Banca d'Italia, Questioni di Economia e Finanza, N. 63.
Pelliccioni, G., and G. Torluccio (2007) 'Il rapporto banca-impresa: le determinanti del multiaffidamento in Italia', in S. Monferrà (ed.) *Il rapporto banca-impresa in Italia*. Roma: Bancaria Editrice.

Petersen, M. A., and R. G. Rajan (1994) 'The Benefit of Lending Relationships: Evidence from Small Business Data', *Journal of Finance* 49, 1: 3–37.

Petrovic, A., and R. Tutsch (2009) 'National Rescue Response to the Current Financial Crisis', European Central Bank, Legal Working Paper Series, No. 8, July.

Prometeia. *Analisi dei Bilanci Bancari*, Rapporto, vari anni, Bologna.

Prometeia (2012) Rapporto di previsione, Bologna.

PWC (2005) 'Global Private Banking/Wealth Management survey', http://www.pwc.com.

PWC, ORFEO – Orfeo Osservatorio dei Risparmi delle Famiglie (2009) 'La filiera del Risparmio Gestito, prime evidenze dall'Osservatorio Permanente', Parma.

PWC, ORFEO – Orfeo Osservatorio dei Risparmi delle Famiglie (2011) 'La filiera del Risparmio Gestito, prime evidenze dall'Osservatorio Permanente', Milano.

Rajan, R.. and L. Zingales (2003) 'Banks and Markets: The Changing Character of European Finance', European Central Bank, 2nd Annual Conference, Frankfurt.

Rinaldi, R. (2009) 'Indagine Conoscitiva sul Credito al Consumo', Camera dei Deputati, 11 novembre.

Rossi, P. (2008) 'L'offerta di mutui alle famiglie: caratteristiche, evoluzione e differenze territoriali. I risultati di un'indagine campionaria', Banca d'Italia, *Questioni di Economia e Finanza*, Occasional paper, N. 13, giugno.

Rossi, P., and A. M. Tarantola (1998) 'Intermediari finanziari e sistema delle imprese: profili istituzionali ed evoluzione recente', *Rivista internazionale di scienze sociali*, 106, 2: 215–39.

Ruozi, R., and C. Zara (2001) 'Il rapporto banca-PMI: caratteristiche strutturali e tendenze evolutive', *Bancaria*, 10: 2–16.

Saccomanni, F. (2006) 'Il ruolo delle banche italiane per lo sviluppo del Sistema Paese', Banca d'Italia, *Bollettino Economico*, N. 47.

Saccomanni, F. (2012) 'Indagine conoscitiva sui rapporti tra banche e imprese. Questioni relative alla patrimonializzazione delle banche', Testimonianza del Direttore Generale della Banca d'Italia, Commissione 6 del Senato della Repubblica (Finanze e tesoro), Roma, 31 gennaio 2011.

Sapienza, P. (2002) 'The Effects of Banking Mergers on Loan Contracts', *Journal of Finance*, 57, 1: 329–67.

Scardovi, C. (2009) 'Hybris dell'investment banking e nemesi dei mercati: nuovi modelli di business in un mondo incerto e rischioso', *Bancaria*, 2: 46–54.

Schwert, G. William (2011) 'Stock Volatility During the Recent Financial Crisis', NBER Working Paper N. 16976, April.

Stiroh, K. J. (2004) 'Diversification in Banking: Is Noninterest Income the Answer?' *Journal of Money, Credit, and Banking*, 36, 5: 853–82.

Tarantola, A. M. (2007) 'Banche e imprese: opportunità e sfide alla luce di Basilea II', intervento al Convegno 'Banca e Impresa. Nuovi scenari, nuove prospettive', Fondazione 'CESIFIN-Alberto Predierì, Firenze, 10 dicembre.

Tarantola, A. M. (2008) 'Strategie delle banche per il territorio nel mercato globale', intervento alla XLI Giornata del Credito, ABI, Roma, 3 aprile.

Tarantola, A. M. (2009) 'Le banche popolari nel confronto competitivo: vocazione territoriale e profili di governance', Intervento al Convegno dell'Associazione Nazionale delle Banche Popolari, Taormina, 27 febbraio.

Tarantola. A. M. (2011) 'Il Credito Cooperativo del domani: sviluppo, efficienza e solidarietà', Intervento al XIV Congresso Nazionale del Credito Cooperativo, Roma, 9 dicembre.

Testo unico delle leggi in materia bancaria e creditizia, Decreto legislativo 1 settembre 1993, n. 353; versione aggiornata al decreto legislativo 30 dicembre 2010, n.239; gennaio 2011.

Unicredit (2009) *Rapporto Unicredit sulle piccole imprese,* Milano: Unicredit, VI edizione 2009–2010.

Vaciago, G., and G. Zadra (2009) 'La reazione delle banche alla crisi e le strategie per il futuro', Associazione per lo Sviluppo degli Studi di Banca e Borsa, Quaderno 248.

Venturelli, V. (2001) 'Le strategie di diversificazione delle banche europee. Determinanti ed effetti in termini di efficienza e di profittabilità', *Banche e Banchieri,* N. 4, luglio-agosto, pp. 322–38.

Venturelli, V. (2005) 'Profili regolamentari e procedurali nel comparto dell'Asset Management', in G. N. Mazzocco (ed.) *Asset Management: prospettive di convergenza tra banche e assicurazioni. Profili regolamentari e gestionali,* Torino: G. Giappichelli Editore.

Visco, I. (2012) 'Intervento del Governatore della Banca d'Italia', Convegno AIAF – ASSIOM – ATIC Forex Parma, Milano, 18 febbraio 2012.

Walter, I. (1999) 'The Global Asset Management Industry: Competitive Structure and Performance', *Financial Markets, Institutions and Instruments,* 8, 1: 1–78.

Wu, Z., P. L. Hedges, and S. Zhang (2007) 'Effects of Concentrated Ownership and Owner Management on Small Business Debt Financing', *Journal of Small Business Management,* 45, 4: 422–37.

Zara, C. (2007) 'Complessità d'impresa e comportamenti finanziari nel rapporto tra banche e PMI. Evidenze dal mercato italiano', in S. Monferrà (ed.) *Il rapporto banca-impresa in Italia,* Roma: Bancaria Editrice.

Index

α returns, 190

active management
  products, 182
  strategy, 182
advisory services, 113, 154, 163–4, 167, 181, 183, 189
Allianz, 178, 187
Amato law, 61, 65, 113
American, *see* United States (US)
Amundi, 178
Arca, 178
areas of business, 161, 163–4
asset management industry, 8, 11, 41, 115, 157, 160, 170–6, 179–82
  area of business/division, 105–9, 132, 157, 178
  companies/firms/groups, 52, 170, 177, 180, 183, 185, 187
  households' services, 43, 114
  products and services, 8, 110, 162–4, 170–4, 177–9, 188, 190
  value-chain, 172
asset managers, 171–2, 180–1, 186
asset mix, 180, 188
Austria, 17, 25, 61, 82, 84–7, 177
Austrian banks, 88, 187
AXA, 178

bad debts, 13, 124, 126, 129, 148, 198
bad loans, 60, 192
Banca d'Italia, *see* Bank of Italy
Banca Monte dei Paschi di Siena, 19, 23, 29, 58, 63, 68, 107, 160, 161, 162, 165–7, 178, 196
Banca Nazionale del Lavoro (BNL), 115, 169, 178
Banca Popolare di Milano, (BPM), 19, 23, 115, 168
Banche del Monte, *see* banks
banche di credito cooperative, *see* banks, mutual banks
banche popolari, *see* banks, cooperative banks
Banco Bilbao Vizcaya Argentaria (BBVA), 60, 68–71
Banco Popolare, 19, 23, 29, 58, 68, 70, 107, 109, 160–2, 165–8, 178, 196
Banco Santander, *see* Santander
bank bonds, 29, 39, 41, 43, 45, 116, 135, 137, 199, 200
bank capitalisation, 47, 66, 81, 82, 83, 91, 117, 150, 192
bank consolidation, 3, 5, 10, 29, 34, 49, 50–3, 55–60, 64, 65, 192
bank despecialisation, 149
Bank for International Settlements (BIS), 23
bank governance, *see under* governance
Bank of Italy, 10, 12, 13, 15, 16, 18, 19, 27–32, 64, 141, 144, 152, 195–7
bank ownership, 3, 4, 5, 10, 15, 49, 50, 53, 55, 56–8, 60–2, 65–7, 90, 97, 98, 102, 150, 156, 177, 197
bank performance, 4, 5, 6, 10, 13, 60, 67–8, 71–4, 76, 77, 82–3, 85, 88–94, 192
bank privatisation, 3, 55, 56, 65
bank restructuring, 10, 49, 52, 99, 156, 164
bank undercapitalisation, 141, 151
bank-firm relationship, 7, 146, 149, 151, 153, 155–6
  transaction based, 144
  relationship based, 141
banking circuits, 41, 50
banking foundations, 4, 53, 56, 57, 60–3, 65–6, 176, 197
banking groups, 3–6, 11–15, 22, 31, 47, 56–60, 62–5, 67–9, 71–4, 78, 80–1, 98–9, 104–10, 113, 115, 119, 131, 133–5, 159–60, 168, 177, 182, 185, 195–6
  divisionalised, 106, 161
  multifunctional, 98, 160

banking intermediation ratio, 44
banking models
  commercial banking model, 65
  divisional banking model, 6, 98, 99, 101–3, 105–8, 110, 151, 161
  federal banking model, 103–7, 108–9, 114, 161
  group model, *see* banking groups
  universal banking model, 5, 6, 47, 97, 99, 101–2, 106, 115
  see also business and organisational models
banks
  commercial, 2, 50, 52, 59, 73, 76, 88–93, 116, 117, 158–60, 164, 185
  cooperative, 50–2, 62–4, 66, 72, 73, 88–92, 111, 115
  mutual, 4, 50, 52, 56, 57, 62–5, 66, 98, 101, 104, 105, 110, 111–14, 149, 199
  publicly owned, 3, 50, 56, 61, 65
  savings, 50, 56, 61, 64, 65
  specialised, 64, 89, 92, 187
  universal, 50, 52, 149, 158, 165, 186, 187
Barclays, 60, 68, 69, 70, 71, 169, 187
Basel Accord, 32, 48
  I, 12
  II, 7, 30, 117, 150–3
  III, 7, 14, 15, 32, 180–3, 194, 196, 197
Basel Committee, 15
Belgian banks, 23, 24, 88
Belgium, 16, 17, 25, 27, 61, 83, 84, 85, 86, 87
betas, 5, 85, 87, 88, 92, 94, 95
BNP Paribas, 60, 68, 69, 70, 71, 115, 169, 178, 187
Brazil, 184
British banks/intermediaries/ operators, *see under* United Kingdom (UK)
business and organisational models, 4, 6, 12, 14, 32, 43, 68, 97, 98, 100, 105, 130, 160, 180, 189, 192
  investment banking business *see under* corporate and investment banking
  traditional business model, 3, 192
  wholesale/broker-dealer business model, 160
  see also banking models
Canada, 184
Canadian banks, 23
capital adequacy, 13, 14, 15, 20, 29, 31, 54, 80, 117, 180, 181, 182, 193, 194, 196
  Accord, *see* Basel Accord
  assessment process, *see* Internal Capital Adequacy Assessment Process (ICAAP)
capital markets, 27, 55, 66, 108, 157, 158, 160, 163, 167
capital requirements, 24, 28, 117, 196, 197
  see also regulatory capital
Capital Requirements Directive (CRD), 32
Capitalia, 58, 168, 178
captive asset management, 179
Casse di Risparmio, 61
  see also banks
chief bank, *see* main bank
China, 184
client manager, 151, 165
Commerzbank, 60, 68, 70
Commissione di Vigilanza sui Fondi Pensione (COVIP), 29
Commissione Nazionale per le Società e la Borsa (CONSOB), 30
commissions, 71, 74–6, 182, 190
  incentive, 180
  management, 180
  net, 71, 76, 77
  upfront, 179
Committee of European Banking Supervisors (CEBS), 14
competition, 10, 45, 50, 52, 55, 58, 64, 105, 106, 111, 124, 127, 132–3, 137, 149, 160, 182–3
compound annual growth rate (CAGR), 84, 88–90, 93–4, 122
conflicts of interest, 111
Consolidated Law on Banking, 66, 148, 150, 168
consolidation, *see* bank consolidation
consortium, 98, 101, 111–12, 114, 167
Core capital, 13, 15, 80
Core Tier 1, 13, 24, 26

corporate and investment banking (CIB)
business area, 162–3
definition, 152
Italian market, 156
market segmentation, 163–4
services demand, 157–8
services supply, 158–9
corporate finance, 164, 188
services, 113, 157, 163
strategies, 159
cost-income ratio, 77–8, 188–9
cost savings, 49, 181
credit
availability, 146
circuits, 59
constraints, 144
growth, 7, 146
rationing, 7, 59, 117, 140
risk, *see under* risks
squeeze, 78, 128, 148, 179, 196, 199
Crédit Agricole, 60, 68, 70, 115, 169, 187
credit cards, 116, 131–2
credit scoring, 128, 130
Credit Swisse, 60
Credito Valtellinese, 19, 23, 115
creditworthiness, 123, 124, 127, 130, 141, 143, 144, 150, 151, 152, 156, 192
customer segment, 98, 101, 106, 108–11, 182
Cyprus, 25

Danske Bank, 60
Denmark, 17, 25, 61
deposit funded model, 6, 117, 138
depositor protection scheme, 18, 19, 22
depreciations, 72
deregulation, 5, 55, 97, 99
despecialisation, *see* bank despecialisation
Deutsche Bank, 60, 68, 69, 70, 71, 115, 168, 169, 187
Dexia, 60
distribution networks, 42, 49, 51, 53, 108, 114, 142, 162, 180
distributors, 104, 172, 180
diversification, 5, 6, 55, 60, 73, 97–9, 103, 105, 110, 157, 171, 178

Economic and Financial Affairs Council of the EU (ECOFIN), 26
economic growth, 12, 13, 34, 53, 72, 73, 192, 194
efficiency, 4, 5, 10, 12, 49, 55, 57, 65, 67, 76–7, 97, 102–4, 109, 114, 149, 153, 181, 182, 192
Euro Area, 2, 18, 20, 23, 25, 27, 32, 35–49, 51, 118–24, 129, 135–6, 138, 139, 141, 174, 175, 198
Euro Zone, *see* Euro Area
European
Central and Easter Countries, 78
countries, 3, 5, 10, 11, 13, 14, 26, 35, 43, 44, 45, 83, 123
currency, 83
governance, *see under* governance
passport, 181
European Banking Authority (EBA), 15, 23, 24, 25, 26, 27, 29, 31, 196, 197
European Central Bank (ECB), 3, 13, 17, 28, 35, 37, 38, 40, 42–9, 51–2, 54, 193, 195, 199–200
European Commission (EC), 13, 16, 29, 65
European Financial Stability Facility (EFSF), 193
European interbank offered rates (EURIBOR), 129
European Monetary Union (EMU), 9, 32, 83, 85, 87, 88, 92
European Union (EU), 9, 11–14, 19, 22, 23, 26, 28, 158, 192, 193
core countries/states, 83, 85
directives, 1, 30–1, 65
peripheral countries/states, 9, 15, 23, 83, 85, 87, 193, 197
exchange traded fund (ETF), 182, 190

facilities, 165
see also public facilities
family offices, 185, 187
federal model, *see under* banking models
Federcasse, 111, 112

fee-only basis, 190
financial advisers, 107, 109, 130, 178, 185, 187, 190
financial costs, 141, 159
financial fragility, 141
financial innovation, 3, 12, 53, 192
financial instability, 12, 194
financial intensity, 35, 38–9
financial intermediation ratio (FIR), 35–6, 38–9
Financial Sector Assessment Program (FSAP), 10
Financial Services Authority (FSA), 190
Financial Stability Board, 11
Financial Stability Committee, 30
financial structure
  firms, 7, 35, 57, 79, 141, 154–5
  households, 35
Fineco, 178
foundations, *see* banking foundations
France, 3, 13, 16–17, 25–7, 35–8, 40–9, 51–2, 61, 82, 84–7, 157, 174, 175, 178, 184
French banks/intermediaries, 24, 49, 88, 177, 187
French firms, 44
funding, 24, 26, 27, 39, 45, 113, 116, 118, 137–9, 155, 159, 160–1, 164, 166, 169, 193–5, 198, 200
  capacity, 131
  cost, 27, 74–5, 128, 199, 200
  gap, 7, 117, 138, 192, 198
  interbank, 49
  model, 135
  retail, 3, 6, 7, 12, 34, 53, 117, 134–5, 138–9, 198, 200
  wholesale, 7, 24, 117, 138, 198

Generali, 178
Germany, 3, 13, 16, 17, 25–7, 35–40, 42, 44–52, 61, 83, 84–8, 157, 175, 177, 184
German
  banks/intermediaries, 23, 24, 47, 50, 87, 177, 187
  bund, 194
  government securities, 118
global liquidity standards, 15, 31, 194
governance
  bank, 3, 4, 55, 56, 62, 64, 65, 99, 101, 103, 149
  banks' internal corporate, 32
  European, 25, 26, 32, 193
  provisions, 10
  SMEs, 7, 141, 156, 158
governments, 1, 44
  capital injections, 14
  facilities, *see* Italian government; public facilities
Great Britain, 13, 17
Greece, 2, 9, 15, 17, 23, 25, 26, 27, 61, 83, 84, 85, 86, 87
Greek
  crisis, 23, 32, 195
  banks, 88

high net worth individuals (HNWIs), 170, 171, 173, 183–6
Hong Kong and Shanghai Banking Corporation (HSBC), 60, 68, 69, 70–1
households, 63, 64, 108, 116
  behaviour, 41, 123, 126, 129, 130, 131–2
  financial asset, 28, 39, 43, 174
  loans, 39, 118–19, 124–6, 128, 198
  savings, 118, 137–8
  wealth, 137, 185, 197
Hungary, 25

impaired loans, 78–80, 129, 148, 199
index linked, 174, 179, 190
India, 184
inducements, 181, 188
inefficiency, 144
information, 45, 101, 105, 130, 134, 144, 148, 150–4, 156, 158, 168
  asymmetries, 150, 151
  costs, 143, 152
  economic and financial, 153
  qualitative, 151–3, 156
  soft, 150–2
information technology (IT), 55, 152, 187, 198
ING, 60
institutional investors, 4, 28, 34, 41, 56, 66, 106, 138, 171, 172, 176, 183

insurance companies, 29, 41, 44, 60, 172, 176
interbank deposit market, 11, 18, 31
Internal Capital Adequacy Assessment Process (ICAAP), 31
internal ratings, 152
International Accounting Standards (IAS), 82
International Financial Reporting Standards (IFRS), 82
International Monetary Fund (IMF), 10
internationalisation, 35, 68, 113, 160, 166, 167, 176, 181, 182, 197
Intesa Sanpaolo, 28, 29, 58–60, 63, 68–9, 96, 106–8, 159–61, 165, 167–8, 178, 186, 196
investment banking, *see* corporate and investment banking
investment funds, 73, 173–6, 179, 183, 190
investment management companies, 172
investment vehicles, 12
Ireland, 9, 15–17, 23, 25–7, 61, 83, 84–8
Irish banks, 5, 88
Island, 17
Istituto Centrale delle Casse Rurali ed Artigiane (ICCREA), 111–14
  BCC Credito Consumo spa, 114
  Iccrea BancaImpresa, 113
Istituto per la vigilanza sulle assicurazioni private e di interesse collettivo (ISVAP), 29, 30
Italian budget, 197
Italian deficit, 193, 198
Italian government, 2, 10–11, 13, 15–16, 18–20, 27, 47, 60, 124, 125, 129
  bail-outs, 88
  borrowing, 39
  guarantees, 195
  intervention, 192
Italian government bonds/security, 2, 11, 27, 39, 41, 43, 45, 47, 54, 118, 119, 137, 179, 195, 200
Italian markets, 11, 108
Italian public facilities, 2, 13, 16–17, 192

Japan, 25, 27, 184

key information document (KID), 181
Kredietbank ABB Insurance CERA Bank (KBC), 69–71

labour market, 138, 197
Lehman Brothers, 9, 11, 12, 15, 19, 128, 131, 135, 169
level of financialisation, 6, 117, 119
level of indebtedness, 54, 141
liberalisation
  branch, 146
  flows of capital, 38
light touch supervision, *see under* supervision
limited companies, 56, 61, 63
liquidity, 7, 13, 15–16, 18, 20, 28, 65, 79, 90, 91, 117, 119, 138, 148, 173–4, 183, 193, 195, 198–9
  Basel liquidity standards, *see* global liquidity standards
  crisis, 18, 160
  management, 64
  position, 31, 118, 195
  provisions, 15, 18
  ratios, 12–13
  reserves, 195
  risk, *see under* risks
  risk management, 31
  squeeze, 131, 195
  structures, 31
listed Italian banks, 4, 82, 85
Lloyds Banking Group, 60, 68, 70
loan to value (LTV), 124, 127
loans
  bad, *see* bad loans
  portfolio, 6, 11, 47, 117–19, 126, 198, 199
  pricing, 129, 130, 156, 198, 200
  quality, 11, 14, 79, 146, 148
  non purpose, 131, 132
  special purpose, 132
  personal, 116, 131–2, 134
Long-Term Capital Management (LTCM), 67
long term refinancing operations (LTROs), 28, 194–5
Luxembourg, 17, 25, 61, 187

main bank, 7, 57, 81, 102, 144, 146, 154
Malta, 25
mark-down, 74, 75
mark-up, 74, 75
markets
  banking, 5, 43, 47, 58, 64, 97, 98, 109
  bond, 13, 14, 30, 44, 180, 195
  consumer credit, 118, 124, 126, 130–5
  corporate bond, 11
  equity, 11, 27, 41, 43, 44, 68, 82, 88, 94, 95, 96, 141, 154–6, 157
  financial markets, 9, 10, 19–22, 24–7, 30, 33, 34, 41, 53, 56, 62, 71, 76, 87, 94, 149, 159, 160, 165, 167, 170, 171, 179, 181, 190, 193, 196, 199
  interbank deposit, 12, 18, 27, 31, 49, 179, 194, 199; *see also* interbank deposit market
  performance, 68, 89, 189
  property, 119, 123, 137
  returns, 84
  security, *see* markets, bond
  stock, *see* markets, equity
  value, 4, 41, 71, 88, 93, 117
  wholesale, 78, 182, 193, 195
  wholesale funding, 24, 81, 138, 195
Markets in Financial Instruments Directive (MiFID), 180, 181, 183, 189, 190
Maslow's hierarchy and pyramid, 173
master-feeder structure, 181
Mediobanca, 159, 160, 161, 162, 164, 165, 167
Mediolanum, 178
Memorandum of Understanding (MoU), 30
merchant banking, 108, 157, 162–4, 167
merger & acquisition (M&A) operations, 3, 6, 10, 47, 56, 57–9, 65, 71, 82, 90, 99, 106, 108, 109, 151, 163, 166, 168, 181
Ministero dell'Economia e delle Finanze/Ministry of Economy and Finance (MEF), 18, 20, 21, 22, 29, 30
monetary financial institutions (MFIs), 27, 35, 36, 38, 43–4, 45, 119
Monte Paschi di Siena, *see* Banca Monte dei Paschi di Siena
moratoria/Measures to support mortgage borrowers – ABI Agreement, 129
Morgan Stanley Capital International (MSCI) EMU Price Index, 87, 88, 92
Mortgages, 12, 126, 128
  fixed interest rate, 129
  home purchase loans, 126
  loans, 117, 124, 127
  market, 126–8, 130
  subprime loans, *see* subprime, mortgage loans
  variable interest rate, 129
multibanking, 7, 141, 143, 144, 146, 149, 153, 186
mutual investment funds, *see* investment funds

national discretion (principle), 1, 12, 30
Netherlands, 17, 25, 27, 187
New Basel Accord, *see* Basel Accord
New-MIC, 18, 21, 31
non-performing loans, 11, 79, 124
Nordea, 60
Norway, 25

open architecture model, 182
operational costs, 10
Organisation for Economic Co-operation and Development (OECD), 8, 27, 192
organisational models, *see* business and organisational models
originate-to-distribute model (OTD), 1
override mechanism, 153
ownership, *see* bank ownership

passive management, 182
pecking order theory, 158
pension funds, 28, 29, 37, 38, 41, 44, 45, 173, 174, 175, 176
performance, *see* bank performance

Pillar 2, 30, 32
Pioneer, 178
Poland, 25
portfolio management mandate, 171
Portugal, 9, 15, 17, 23, 25–7, 61, 84–8
Portuguese banks, 88
price-to-book value (PBV), 90, 91
private banking, 8, 56, 88, 99, 100, 105, 107–10, 162, 170–1, 173, 176, 177, 183, 187–8
  clients, 109–10, 184, 185, 186, 188
  market, 8, 109, 184, 185, 187
  organisation, 185
  services, 183
  supply, 186
privatisation, *see* bank privatisation
production process, 6, 99, 100, 133, 156, 172, 182
profitability, 4, 5, 13, 14, 24, 67, 71, 76, 93–4, 117, 132, 144, 192, 196
  analysis, 72
project finance, 157, 164
public aid, *see* public facilities
public debt, 2, 11, 24, 25, 27, 28, 33, 193, 194
  /GDP ratio, 24, 27, 39
public deficit, 25, 26, 193
  /GDP ratio, 26, 27
public facilities, 2, 4, 13, 15–17, 65, 192
public interventions, *see* public facilities
publicly owned banks, *see under* banks

Rabo bank, 60
RAS, 178
real estate banking, 173
rebate, 180, 188, 190, 191
recapitalisation, 4, 14, 15, 16, 18, 19, 21, 22, 23, 27, 28, 29, 31, 33, 65, 194, 196
  EBA Recapitalisation exercise/plan, 24, 25, 26
regulation, 1, 12, 16, 31, 54, 103, 115, 153, 155, 181, 182, 188, 189, 196
  capital, 81
  light touch, *see under* supervision
  self-, 183
regulatory approach, 12, 103, 159
regulatory capital, 18, 20, 22, 29, 80, 117
regulatory changes, 7, 131, 189, 193
regulatory costs, 187
regulatory failures, 194
regulatory framework, 3, 12, 15, 55, 61, 78, 97, 117, 158, 179
regulatory measures, 180, 182, 183
regulatory pressure, 190
regulatory processes, 8, 171
regulatory requirements, 130
regulatory standards, 10
reputation/al, 104, 132, 137, 189
rescue measures/operations/packages, 2, 11, 15–16, 18, 57, 192
  see also public facilities
restructuring, *see* bank restructuring
retail banking, 6, 99, 116–17, 161–2, 198
return on equity (ROE), 14, 72, 73, 93, 94
risk capital, 155, 158, 159
risk management, 4, 31, 32, 67, 79, 97, 101, 103, 113, 114, 128, 140, 143, 150, 157, 163–4, 170, 172
risks, 93, 94, 102, 119, 124, 127, 128, 129, 140, 141, 146, 150, 152, 154, 164, 186, 188, 192, 193, 196, 198
  aversion, 183
  concentration, 143
  counterparty, 138
  credit, 31, 78, 117, 140, 143, 144, 151, 153
  funding, 194
  interest rate, 118, 127, 129, 200
  liquidity, 31, 81, 160, 161, 194
  refinancing, 194, 199
  sovereign, 118, 194, 200; *see also* sovereign debt
  systematic, 4, 5, 85, 87, 88, 92, 93
  systemic, 10, 12, 24, 26
Royal Bank of Scotland (RBS), 60, 68, 69, 70, 71, 169

Santander, 60, 68, 69, 70, 187
Save Italy decree, 28
savings banks, *see under* banks
Scandinavia, 177

securitisation, 7, 12, 79, 113, 117, 130, 131, 134, 164, 166
shareholders, 53–66, 89, 111, 143, 155, 197
  major, 4, 56, 62
  minority, 92
shares, 21, 22, 40, 42, 46, 47, 48, 63, 82, 87, 90, 91, 93, 120, 139, 174
  beta, *see* betas
  common, 89, 91, 92, 93
  ordinary, 60
  price, 4, 85, 88, 89
  saving, 88, 91, 93
  turnover, 88, 89
Slovenia, 25
small and medium-sized enterprises (SMEs), 6, 7, 11, 18, 19, 59, 62, 113–14, 116–18, 140, 141, 144, 150–2, 154, 156, 158, 162, 165, 198–9
Société Générale, 60, 68–70
sovereign debt, 1, 2, 85, 118, 119, 148, 193
  contagion, 33
  crisis, 9, 14–16, 23–4, 26, 31–2, 141, 192, 195, 196, 200
  market, 11, 196
  risk, 2, 54, 193, 194
sovereign funds, 4, 66
spaghetti private banking, 170
Spain, 3, 9, 15, 17, 23–7, 35–51, 61, 71, 83, 84–7, 177, 187
Spanish banks, 49, 69, 70, 87, 88
special purpose vehicles (SPVs), 164
specialisation, 3, 10, 53, 55, 78, 98, 100, 103, 104, 105, 114, 133, 149, 182
specialised financial institutions, 103, 114, 132, 133, 134, 171
specialised intermediaries, *see* specialised financial institutions
standard deviation (SD) of monthly returns, 85, 86, 88, 89
state aid, 16
stock market return, 84
stocks
  common, 88
  non-voting, 88, 89
  see also shares
strategies, 1, 8, 43, 51, 76, 99, 105, 110, 113, 126, 127, 128, 130, 138, 149, 151, 158, 182, 189, 196
  acquisition, 104
  financial, 35, 163
  financing, 41, 43
  fund-raising, 179
  growth, 133, 156
  niche, 167
  pricing, 200
stress tests, 12, 24, 30, 31
structured
  finance, 108, 163, 164, 166
  investment vehicles, 12
  product, 174, 179
subprime
  crisis, 1, 2, 23, 89, 192
  mortgage loans, 9, 11, 119
supervision, 1, 29, 194
  light touch, 1, 12, 30, 194
  off-site, 30
  on-site, 30
  prudential, 30
supervisory activities, 30, 32
supervisory approach, 12, 54, 194
supervisory architecture, 29
supervisory authorities, 1, 14, 15, 26, 32, 57, 66, 115, 181
supervisory framework, 10, 12, 78
supervisory function, 12
supervisory operations, 30
supervisory policy, 30, 149
Supervisory Review and Evaluation Process (SREP), 30, 32
systematic risk, *see under* risks
systemic, 30, 195
  crises, 52
  risk, *see under* risks
systemically important financial institutions (SIFI), 15
Sweden, 25
Switzerland, 17, 61, 177, 184, 190
Swiss banks, 23, 177, 186

technical reserves, 40, 41, 42
Testo unico bancario, 65, 66
  see also Consolidated Law on Banking
Tier 1, 14, 15, 18, 22, 23, 81, 95

Tier 1 ratio, 80, 81
Tremonti bonds facilities, 13, 16, 18, 19, 22, 23, 148, 192

undercapitalisation, *see* bank undercapitalisation
Undertakings for Collective Investment in Transferable Securities IV (UCITS), 180, 181–3
UniCredit, 28, 29, 58, 59, 60, 63, 68, 69, 96, 106–8, 148, 159, 160, 161, 164, 165, 166, 167, 168, 178, 186, 196
Unione Banche Svizzere (UBS), 60, 186, 187
Unione di Banche Italiane (UBI banca), 29, 58, 68, 69, 70, 71, 107, 109, 160, 161, 162, 165, 166, 167, 168, 178
unit linked, 179
United Kingdom (UK), 3, 16, 25, 26, 27, 35–42, 44–53, 70, 83–6, 119, 157, 174, 175, 178, 184, 190, 194
  banks/intermediaries/operators, 157, 177, 187
  households, 123
  investment bank model, 160, 162
United States (US), 1, 3, 13, 16–17, 26–7, 53, 95, 123, 157, 169, 175, 184, 190
  banks, 23, 60, 157, 187
  households, 123
  investment bank model, 160, 162

value chain, 172, 186, 190
vertical integration, 179, 180

wholesale funding, *see under* funding
write-downs, 11, 41, 68, 72, 73, 78, 119